Environment, Ideology and Policy

ENVIRONMENT IDEOLOGY and POLICY

Francis Sandbach

ALLANHELD, OSMUN Publishers
Montclair

ALLANHELD, OSMUN & CO. PUBLISHERS, INC
Published in the United States of America in 1980
by Allanheld, Osmun & Co. Publishers, Inc.
19 Brunswick Road,
Montclair, New Jersey 07042

Library of Congress Cataloging in Publication Data

Sandbach, Francis
  Environment, ideology & policy.

  Bibliography: p.
  Includes index
  1. Environmental policy.   I. Title.

  HC79.E5S257   363.7   80−65192
  ISBN 0−916672−53−0

Printed in Great Britain

Contents

Figures

Tables

Preface

In the 1960s and 1970s there has been unprecedented international concern about environmental issues, notably land planning, resource scarcity, technological choice, and pollution control. This concern has generated an extensive literature, both technical and polemical, not all of which is readily accessible to the non-specialist. Despite this wealth of information, there have been few attempts to delineate the various 'schools of thought' which often influence environmental policy, and to compare and assess them in relation to environmental issues. Such is the aim of this book.

Many of the views expressed in the environmental debate appear, at least superficially, to be based firmly on scientific evidence but a closer inspection shows them to be steeped in ideology. The discussion that follows attempts to assess and explain these often controversial statements and also to account for the widespread acceptance of some of them despite the lack of conclusive evidence to support them. The questions posed can be reduced to this: can environmental problems be adequately understood without reference to the social, economic and political organization of the societies from which they arise?

Chapter 1 describes the rise of the environmental movement as one of the major social phenomena of the 1960s and 1970s. A variety of explanations of the rise and fall of social movements have popular currency in the academic community. In the second part of the chapter two conceptual frameworks are put forward for comparison: a functionalist and pluralist viewpoint on the one hand, and a Marxist and materialist analysis on the other. The differences between scientific and ideological explanations of environmental issues are explored in this comparison.

The second part of the book examines techniques of resolving the environmental problems associated with pollution and planning, with scarcity, need and distribution. Chapter 2 discusses the limitations and ideology of neo-classical economies in relation to the economic analysis of various pollution control strategies and cost–benefit analysis. Both theory and practice, it is argued, tend to reinforce the economic and social order of capitalist societies. In Chapter 3 behaviourist and holistic approaches to environmental evaluation are reviewed. The first, it is claimed, often leads to an acceptance of socially determined perceptions and attitudes towards the environment as if these provided an objective picture of conditions in the environment. Holistic assessments, involving environmental impact assessment, while they have the appearance of objectivity, tend also to reinforce dominant economic and social interests. In Chapter 4 the behaviourist perspective is explored further in association with the plural-ist account of pressure group behaviour. Do neo-classical economic models of pollution control and environmental evaluation lead to efficient and fair decision-making? Can a behaviourist or pluralist interpretation of the ways planning and pollution control are influenced by pressure groups be considered scientific? Is planning the outcome of a plurality of interests in perfect competition? Or does a Marxist account, which emphasizes the importance of the objective interest of capital, offer a more scientific explanation?

The third part of the book looks at scarcity and need with relation to the technological base of production. Are environmental and social problems determined by an independent development of technology or are tech-nologies and their associated problems a product of economic supply and demand factors? Is the choice of development path a free choice, in the sense of being an unconstrained political decision which is a response to a plurality of interests? Alternatively, what influences do the social rela-tions of production and economic organization have on the development of technology? These questions are examined, firstly in Chapter 5 which deals with the development of technology under capitalism; secondly in Chapter 6 which suggests some different paths of development, including outlines of ecologically sound and more benevolent alternative tech-nologies; and thirdly in Chapter 7 which deals with the development of technology in China.

The final section of the book, Chapter 8, considers various possible directions for the future. The question of whether or not there will be a shortage of resources and a degree of pollution which seriously constrains economic growth is approached from various conceptual standpoints, including neo-Malthusian, economic and technological determinist and Marxist ones. In Chapter 8 these standpoints are tested for their ideologi-cal and scientific content. However, what actually happens will depend to a considerable extent on the way society responds to the present economic problems, issues and contradictions. While it is possible to argue optimis-tically about the future supply of resources it is not possible to predict with the same certainty whether the problems of safely supplying those resources will act as a catalyst towards different forms of social organization.

While this book is largely concerned with science and ideology in environmental studies, much of the argument is relevant to other areas of practical and theoretical importance in the social sciences. In addition, the questions of the validity of welfare economics, pluralism, conflict theory, political economy and so on that are raised in connection with environmental problems are encountered in all other forms of social inquiry.

Acknowledgements

In preparing this book I have been helped by numerous people, especially the students and staff at the University of Kent. The actual process of writing has been closely tied to teaching, working and learning within the university. I owe an enormous debt to a large number of people, but I should particularly like to thank Philip Lowe of University College, London, and David Reason of the University of Kent, who commented upon the draft manuscript. I have been fortunate indeed in having a father who has helped me to express myself more clearly and who has also been a lively critic. My wife and family have provided stimulating distractions without which writing would have been a more onerous occupation.

Much of the material included in Chapter 1 was previously published in my paper 'A further look at the environment as a political issue', which was published in the *International Journal of Environmental Studies* (1978, 12, 99–110), and is here reproduced by kind permission of the editor, Dr. J. Rose, and the publishers, Gordon and Breach Science Publishers Ltd., London. Much of the material in Chapter 8 was published in my paper 'The rise and fall of the limits to growth debate', which appeared in the *Social Studies of Science* (1978, 8, 495–520), and is reproduced here by kind permission of the editors and of the publishers, SAGE Publications, London and Beverly Hills.

For permission to reproduce figures and tables, the author and publishers are grateful to the following: Agency for International Development, US and Dana Dalrymple (tables 5.2, 5.3); George Allen and Unwin (tables 1.3, 2.1, 2.5, 2.6; figure 2.3); American Economic Association and William D. Nordhaus (tables 8.2, 8.3); Anthony Barker and the Civic Trust (figure 1.4); California Governor's Office, Office of Planning and Research and California Legislature, Assembly, Committee on Local Government (table 3.3); Elsevier North Holland, Inc., New York (figure 1.1); Gordon and Breach Science Publishers (table 5.1); The Controller of Her Majesty's Stationery Office (tables 2.2, 2.3, 2.4, 3.1); Kenneth E.

Hornbach (figure 1.2); *The Journal of Legal Studies* (table 8.1); Manchester University Press and the United Kingdom Energy Authority (table 2.8); Methuen and Co. (tables 2.9, 2.10); Robert Cameron Mitchell and *Resources for the Future* (figures 1.3, 5.1); *New Scientist*, London, the weekly review of science and technology (table 5.4); The Organization for Economic Cooperation and Development, Paris (table 2.7); Oxford University Press and Howard Pack (figure 6.1); *Peking Review*, China (table 7.2); Pergamon Press (table 7.1); Amos Rapoport and Paul Oliver (figures 3.1, 3.2); The Regional Studies Association (figures 3.3, 3.4); Saxon House and Timothy O'Riordan (table 3.4); *Undercurrents* (table 6.1); UNESCO (table 6.2).

1 The Environmental Movement

Without doubt historians of the future will regard the late 1960s and early 1970s as a period when most industrially developed countries became deeply concerned about environmental problems. Already numerous studies have described this increase in public concern, which has been variously called 'the ecology movement', 'the new conservation movement' or just 'the environmental movement'. More recent studies have shown that certain aspects of this movement have begun to wane. It is probably safe to concur with J. S. Bowman who, writing in 1975, said: 'Few would disagree that we are witnessing a gradual decline of intense interest in the environment' (1975:93).

The rise and fall of the environment as a political issue may be charted by examining a variety of indicators and sources, for example: news media and literature; public opinion and social survey data; environmental pressure group involvement; the introduction of new political institutions and environmental legislation; and finally the history of environmentalism itself. The collection of evidence about changes in the intensity or the objects of public concern is fraught with methodological problems, and interpretation of the results has given rise to much controversy. The type of analysis, its presentation, and its interpretation have given rise to numerous descriptive and explanatory accounts. These accounts are considerably influenced by differences in social science theory and explanation. On one hand, there are the dominant schools of thought which are usually unsystematic abstractions of economic and social behaviour, and are unrelated to the basic form of economic organization. On the other hand, there are the Marxist and materialist explanations which see production, distribution, exchange and consumption as parts of one whole; environmental and other social problems and policies cannot be divorced from the contradictions arising from the underlying relations of production. The differences between these types of explanation will be a major theme throughout the book. An introduction to the variety of interpretations and models will be provided at the end of this chapter.

Indicators of the environment as a public issue

CONTENT ANALYSIS OF NEWSPAPERS AND PERIODICALS

Virtually no research has been done in this field in the UK, apart from a poorly constructed analysis of the amount of space devoted to environmental concerns in *The Times* between 1953 and 1973 (Brookes *et al.,* 1976). Justification for choosing *The Times* was based upon its reputation, especially among the directors of Britain's top five hundred companies. It is, however, questionable whether or not content analysis of *The Times* provides an adequate indicator of popular concern. It is worth noting that in 1977 sales of *The Times* amounted to only 307,000 per day, compared with 3,864,000 for the *Daily Mirror*, 3,777,000 for the *Sun*, 2,580,000 for the *Daily Express*, 1,170,000 for the *Daily Mail*, and 1,301,000 for the *Daily Telegraph* (*The Times Higher Education Supplement*, 24 June 1977). Furthermore, content analysis of *The Times* is bound to reflect the political and ideological interests of the paper and its readers. Content analysis of a less conservative paper might have given rise to somewhat different results. A better justification for using *The Times* would have been to make a sample survey of the indexes. A rough and ready survey of the number of articles on different subjects for each three-monthly period could then have been used to suggest critical periods for more thorough analysis.

The Times study was designed to test the subjective view commonly held that the environment suddenly emerged as a political issue. A thirteen-category coding frame was used to determine the 'environmental' or 'non-environmental' nature of the news at four-year intervals over the twenty-year period from 1953 to 1973. The results were presented in terms of newspaper area devoted to environmental issues in comparison with the total area of the newspaper devoted to the news which was called the 'news hole' (this excluded horse-racing form, television listings, comic strips and other non-news items). The study demonstrated an increased interest by the news media in environmental problems towards the end of the 1960s and early 1970s, as expected, but was insufficiently detailed to test the hypothesis; the data failed to show whether there had been a dramatic increase during any critical period of time, whether a saturation point was reached, and whether there had subsequently been any decline in interest. The authors could only suggest that an 'explosive' view of the growth of environmental coverage should be qualified due to the consistent level of interest during the 1950s and 1960s. Even a less rigorous analysis of *The Times* indexes would have indicated that some increase in 'pollution' and 'conservation' coverage took place in 1969, that there was much greater coverage of these issues in 1972 than in 1973, and that between 1973 and 1975 there has been a slight but not so dramatic decline in news coverage. Consequently, a more dramatic rise in public concern about the environment could be confined to a limited period from 1969 to 1972. Indeed, two of the research team involved in this study have expressed this view without the empirical support that could have been offered by the content analysis of *The Times*:

In Britain the take-off point for the environmental issue was probably the late 1960s and reached a peak in 1972 when the United Nations Conference on the Environment captured public and press attention. There may have been a slackening of media interest since then, although the level at which it has settled is much greater than before (Brookes and Richardson, 1975:328).

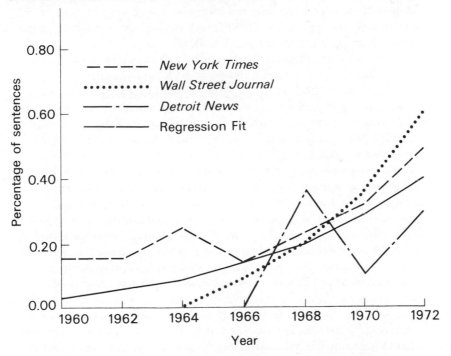

Figure 1.1   Percentage of sentences in editorials emphasizing environment category by alternate years.

(Source: De Weese III, *Public Opinion Quarterly*, 40, 1976:99)

The authors of *The Times* study also argued that a gradual rise in environmental concern could be compared with a more meteoric rise of environmental concern in the United States. They based this claim on an American study by J. C. Moloney and L. Stovonsky (1971) which asserted that editors of newspapers had moved from a position of indifference to one of hysteria. However, content analysis of editorials in three American newspapers (*New York Times, Wall Street Journal, Detroit News*) (see figure 1.1) has shown that, although there was an exponential rise in emphasis upon environmental categories, there was no clear 'take-off' in any one year (De Weese III, 1976).

An analysis of three major news magazines (*Times, Newsweek,* and *US News and World Report*), while showing a dramatic rise in environmental coverage between 1968 and 1969 (see figure 1.2), also showed a build-up of interest during the mid-1960s (Hornback, 1974:228; Munton and Brady, 1970; Funkhouser, 1973). The survey demonstrated that during the 1960s environment and pollution ranked eighth among fourteen major issues in terms of number of articles published. Between 1969 and 1970 there was a very marked increase in such articles, and in 1970 environment and pollution (41 articles) ranked third behind campus unrest (52 articles) and Vietnam (44 articles).

Studies in other countries have similarly demonstrated a build-up of mass media interest during the mid- to late 1960s. For example, M. Reich and E. G. Huddle (1973:39) have reported that in Japan the percentage of articles relating exclusively to environmental problems, based upon samples of articles taken from the February and August newspapers of 1960, 1965 and 1971, rose from 0.4 per cent in 1960 to 0.7 per cent in 1965, and to 2.8 per cent in 1971.

The development of an environmental focus to literature was reflected in the increasing number of specialist journals concerned with environmental issues. The *International Journal of Environmental Studies*, which made its first appearance in 1970, is a particularly apposite example. Of fifteen journals categorized by the *Environmental Periodicals Bibliography* (1976) as 'broad interest and public concern journals' only two had been formed before 1967 and eleven began publication in the four years from 1967 to 1970. The new environmental literature had a receptive audience as environmental education programmes were set up in the field of higher education. Environmental research and education were also encouraged by the foundation of specialist institutions such as the influential Institution of Environmental Sciences (UK), which was founded in 1968/69. A 1973 directory listed some 1,068 education programmes in 740 colleges and universities in seventy countries (Quigg, 1974). Students in these institutions were no doubt reading some of the three hundred-plus books on environment, ecology and pollution that had been published in the United States alone in 1972 (Sinclair, 1973).

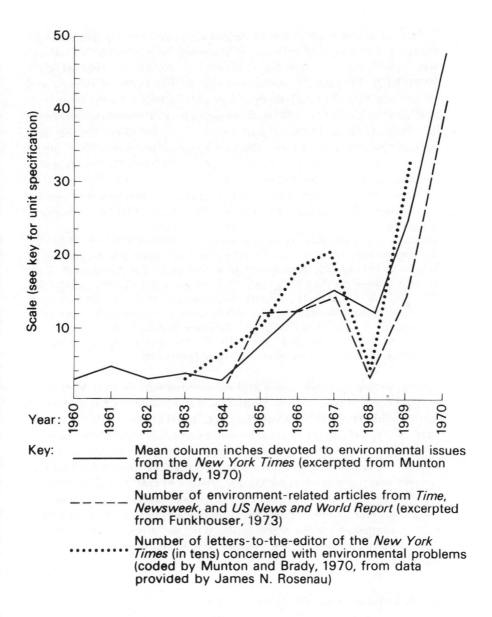

Key:

—————— Mean column inches devoted to environmental issues from the *New York Times* (excerpted from Munton and Brady, 1970)

– – – – – Number of environment-related articles from *Time, Newsweek,* and *US News and World Report* (excerpted from Funkhouser, 1973)

••••••••• Number of letters-to-the-editor of the *New York Times* (in tens) concerned with environmental problems (coded by Munton and Brady, 1970, from data provided by James N. Rosenau)

Figure 1.2   Development of environmental interest by selected indicators of the printed media content over time

(*Note:* These figures have not been corrected for the increase in overall column inches of newspapers during the 1960s)
(*Source:* Hornback, 1974:228)

Sales of environmental literature had also risen rapidly. For example, the sales of the journal *Environment* increased from 2,000 in 1967 (when it was called *Science and the Citizen*) to 30,000 in 1973 (Nelkin, 1977(a):82). However, *Environment* (November 1973:24) noticed with some alarm that all of the half-dozen magazines begun during or after the publicity for Earth Day 1970 had now collapsed. Popular environmental magazines continued to feel the squeeze from falling sales after this date. For example, the distributors' sales of the popular magazine *The Ecologist* fell from 7,000 in 1973 to 3,000 in 1977. During 1973 the magazine disappeared from all but the biggest bookstalls. D. L. Sills' study on the environmental movement and its critics has also shown how the news and magazine headlines reflected a change in the fortunes of the environmental movement:

'Environmentalists at Bay' was the title of a *Wall Street Journal* editorial on January 3, 1974 (p. 10); 'Environmentalists foresee 1974 as Toughest of Recent Years' headlined the *New York Times* on February 3, 1974 (p. 38); on March 1, 1974, John R. Quarles, Jr., Deputy Administrator of the US Environmental Protection Agency, thought it appropriate to address the conservation foundation on the topic 'The Land Use Challenge – Re-energizing the Environmental Movement'; and the March 30, 1974 issue of *The Economist*, in its 'American Survey', found that 'the environment is short of friends' (p. 45) (1975:7).

This survey of news media and environmental literature suggests a gradual rise in interest during the mid- and late 1960s; the period 1969–72 marked a high point in literature coverage; and that interest began to wane from 1973 to 1977. A comparison between American and British concern is not yet feasible, mainly due to the weakness of empirical studies of British sources. A tempting hypothesis would be that the growth of American concern was more gradual during the 1960s and that public opinion rose more sharply in Britain during 1969–72 as environmental concern rapidly became an international affair. This is essentially the opposite hypothesis to that suggested by the authors who analysed news coverage by *The Times*, but a lot more evidence would be required to prove the point one way or the other.

PUBLIC OPINION AND SOCIAL SURVEY DATA

H. Erskine's (1972) review of public opinion polls between 1965 and 1971 illustrated a similar rise in public concern about the environment. In 1965 only three or four people out of ten questioned said they were willing to spend any money to help control air and water pollution, but five years later the number had risen to well over 50 per cent. Comparison of Harris surveys, for instance, indicated that the numbers reported 'willing to pay

$15 a year more in taxes to finance a federal programme to control air pollution' had between 1967 and 1971 risen from 44 per cent to 59 per cent. In another type of survey some 70 per cent felt there was a 'lot of air pollution around here' in 1970, compared with some 56 per cent three years previously. Such surveys have, however, been severely criticized during recent years for their reliance on specific proposals which were not compared with competing social objectives. Responses to surveys have also been shown to vary significantly according to slight differences in the wording of the questions (Dillman and Christenson, 1974).

The Most Important Problem (MIP) type of format in Gallup Surveys first included a general 'pollution–ecology' code in January 1970. Here respondents were asked to name the most important problem facing the nation from a short list of social and economic problems. However, the codes used for comparison have been highly variable over short periods of time and have usually been orientated towards issues. Moreover, comparison between various studies shows a great deal of variation in results, which considerably weakens the use of such opinion surveys (Hornback, 1974:227).

In 1971, a Harris survey (Erskine, 1972:125) indicated that of sixteen social problems, control of air and water pollution were considered by 41 per cent to be among the two or three top problems facing the American people. This percentage was surpassed only by concern for the state of the economy (63 per cent) and was greater than the percentage for the war in Vietnam, crime, student unrest, education, and racial problems. Clearly, results from comparisons between priorities depend upon whether one is concerned with the most important problem or whether one aggregates the first, second, third . . . most important problems together. A survey by N. Wiedenmeyer (1976) of polls between 1968 and 1975 indicates that there were never more than 6 per cent of people questioned in the USA, Great Britain and Germany who felt that pollution issues were the most important problem. Only in the Netherlands was the percentage greater with 16 per cent in December 1971 and 19 per cent in September 1972 stating that pollution, rather than nine other economic and social problems, was the most urgent problem or task to be solved by the government. In all the countries surveyed, 1972 marked the high point of concern (see also Bowman, 1977). However, another study by R. E. Dunlap and K. D. Van Liere (1977) of Harris MIP surveys indicated a waning of public concern from 1970 to 1971 (see figure 1.3).

Decline in environmental concern since 1972 is also indicated by a *New Society* National Survey into British attitudes to money and wealth (Forester, 1977). This showed that those rating the beautification of cities and the countryside as either first, second or third in importance among eight objectives had fallen from 23 per cent in 1973 to 13 per cent in 1977.

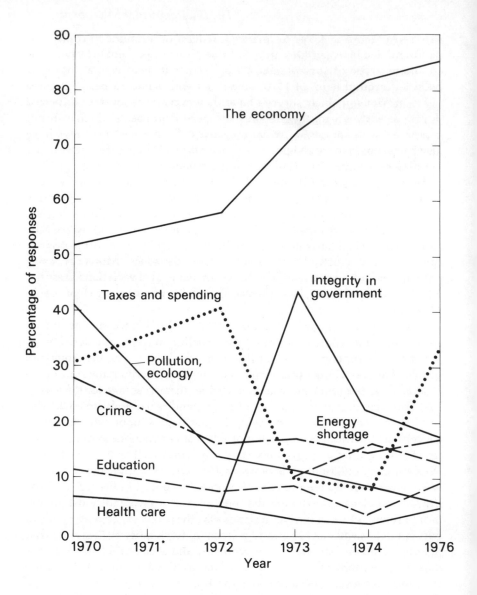

Figure 1.3 Biggest problems facing people

Harris Survey question: 'What are the two or three biggest problems facing people like yourself which you would like to see the next President (Congress) do something about? Any others?' (Problems, omitted are welfare reform, older people, foreign policy, racial discrimination, and housing.) *No data were available for 1971.

(*Source:* Mitchell and Davies, 1978)

In 1973 3 per cent had ranked the beautification of cities and countryside as first priority compared with 2 per cent in 1977. A similar study in 1974 gave a 3 per cent first ranking (Abrams, 1977). Given the methodological problems and the consequent hazards of interpretation, this type of data gives a very limited view of changes over a period of time. Consequently it provides only a weak quantitative confirmation of the view that the environment rose in importance as a public issue, and then began to decline in importance after 1972.

Other reviews of social surveys have tried to show not only longitudinal differences in public attitude, but also correlations with various social factors. Responses to individual environmental issues have been shown to be correlated with an overall 'environmental concern' solicited by more general questions (Springer and Constantini, 1974). Similar rather unremarkable surveys have shown that:

1 Americans in 1972 earning more than $10,000 per annum were likely to show greater concern for the environment than those earning less than $5,000 (McEvoy III, 1972);
2 between 1958 and 1970 support for the environmental movement was drawn increasingly from broader bases of the social structure (Buttel and Flinn, 1974);
3 those with nine or more years of education were more likely to be concerned about air and water pollution than those with eight years or less (Buttel and Flinn, 1974).

However, as with the longitudinal studies, there has been little consensus among research workers, and other studies give only very tenuous support to the view that environmental concern is class-related, or that it is correlated with age, or indeed with political commitment (Springer and Constantini, 1974; Abrams, 1977). During the extensive public debate on nuclear power during early 1977, an Opinion Research Centre survey on attitudes towards nuclear power indicated that more of the working class were concerned about the safety of nuclear power stations than were the upper-middle classes (White, 1977). However, most studies have shown that the organized environmentalists are dominated by the upper-middle classes (see Buttel and Flinn, 1976).

It is very doubtful whether any of the social survey results provide a good guide to political commitment. Indeed it has become much more widely accepted that social survey evidence is unreliable at indicating deeply-held views or commitment to environmental improvement (see O'Riordan, 1976(a)). Ironically this is illustrated by the poor correlation between responses to those types of questions aimed at eliciting concern for environmental problems and those aimed at ascertaining commitment to a variety of reform measures (Martinson and Wilkening, 1975). At best, public opinion survey data reveal only very general attitudes based on hypothetical questions with no direct political, social or economic consequences, and more often than not these attitudes are based upon very sketchy exposure to the issues raised by the problems in question. In this respect, it is interesting to note that in a survey of attitudes towards the safety of nuclear power only 5 per cent said they trusted the opinions of newspapers and television, 4 per cent trusted the government, but 69 per cent said they would trust scientists and some 17 per cent said they would trust the manufacturers (White, 1977). In this case, it is hard to believe that reported attitudes towards environmental safety could have been based upon adequate information, and it certainly would not have reflected the commitment and strength of the pro- and anti-nuclear power lobbies.

PRESSURE GROUP MEMBERSHIP

Besides the signs already mentioned, the growth of environmental societies and their memberships indicate clearly that there was a very significant rise in public interest during the 1960s and early 1970s. In A. Barker's (1976) survey of 605 local amenity societies in existence during 1974, only 15 per cent had been founded before 1958. In the next four years, 1958–61, 10 per cent of the societies were founded, between 1962 and 1965 a further 18 per cent, followed by 20 per cent between 1966 and 1969, and finally 37 per cent between 1970 and 1974 (see figure 1.4).

The number of societies registering with the Civic Trust has also increased dramatically and there are few signs that this is beginning to level off. There were 1,130 registered societies in May 1974, 1,250 in 1976, 1,303 in May 1977, and 1,313 in September 1978. Some of this increase is accounted for by local federations which have been growing steadily in number. Unlike public opinion surveys and media coverage there is less support for the view that interest in the environment has been declining. This doubt is confirmed by the growth of membership figures for the major national societies. The fastest growing societies since 1972 have all been involved in active conservation rather than environmental politics. The National Trust, the Society for the Promotion of Nature Conservation, and the Royal Society for the Protection of Birds have led the growth league, while the Friends of the Earth and the Council for the Protection of Rural England have only made slight gains in memberships, and the Conservation Society's membership has actually declined from its peak in 1973 (see table 1.1).

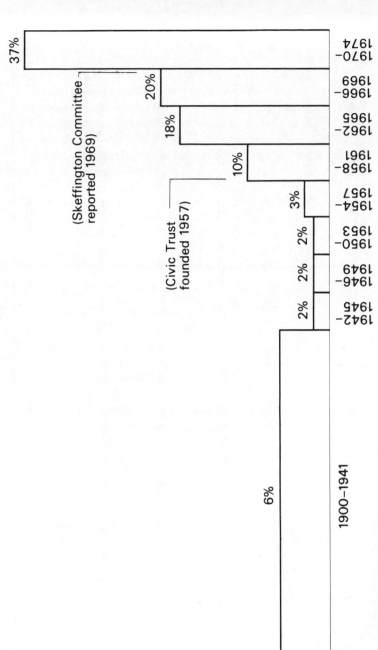

Figure 1.4 Founding dates of 605 amenity societies

(*Source:* Barker, 1976:22)

Table 1.1 *Growth of membership of various leading UK environmental societies*

	1966	1967	1968	1969	1970	1971	1972	1973	1974	1975	1976	1977
Conservation Society	200	380	800	1,200	2,800	5,700	8,320	8,734	7,400	6,915	6,474	
Ramblers Assoc.		14,000					26,000					30,000
Friends of the Earth									5,000	5,000	5,000	6,000
The Soil Assoc. Home Membership at 31 Dec.				3,232	3,637	3,806	3,729	3,795	3,558	3,623	3,779	3,974 at 31 May
National Trust	164,527			176,970	226,200	278,300	346,000	428,384	463,556	539,285	548,657	
Society for the Promotion of Nature Conservation			35,000	42,500	55,500	63,500	75,000	84,500	97,000	100,000	109,000	
The Royal Soc. for the Protection of Birds	31,738	35,917	41,260	52,911	65,577	81,223	108,268	138,467	165,716	180,725	204,416	244,841 (June)
The Council for the Protection of Rural England		15,000			20,695				27,100			28,446

(*Source:* Sandbach, 1978(a):103)

Interpretation of membership figures must be very cautious: no doubt some people join societies like the Royal Society for the Protection of Birds because they want to receive their excellent mail order catalogues. Nevertheless the figures do suggest a shift away from active politics, especially of the more radical kind involving population stabilization, which was one of the major goals of the Conservation Society. Conservation and the protection of local amenities through the development of civic societies receive, however, more support than ever before. Of the local societies, the Friends of the Lake District had the largest membership figure of 6,670 in 1976 and has had probably the best reputation for setting up campaigns to fight afforestation, reservoirs, motorways and electricity developments. The total membership of the local amenity movement is estimated to be about 300,000 with eight or nine persons in every thousand belonging to an amenity society. This may be compared with the twelve per thousand who belong to the Labour party (*Civic Trust News*, July/August 1977).

In the United States the extent of citizen participation is even greater. The National Centre for Voluntary Action has estimated that there are 40,000 environmental/conservation voluntary organizations. These may represent 20 million citizen environmentalists. Some 5.5 million people are estimated to belong to or contribute to the nineteen so-called primary environmental organizations (Fanning, 1975:213). The three largest American environmental organizations are the National Wildlife Federation, the National Audubon Society and the Sierra Club. These organizations, and many others, had their origins in the nineteenth-century conservation movement when wilderness preservation became an important issue. In the 1950s and 1960s there were new conservation battles, for example, those involving the redwoods in California and the Grand Canyon, to name just two that caused a good deal of conflict. However, new issues such as nuclear fallout, pesticides, and pollution began to be taken up by these older groups, especially by some new activist groups such as the Environmental Defence Fund, the National Resources Defence Council, Zero Population Growth, Friends of the Earth, and Environmental Action.

Membership of the large national organizations – the Sierra Club, the National Audubon Society and the Wilderness Society – doubled or trebled in the years 1965–69 (McEvoy III, 1972). The number of full-time staff employed by these organizations also increased from the early 1950s. R. C. Mitchell and J. C. Davies, III describe the staff employment trend of the Sierra Club, and the Friends of the Earth:

It wasn't until 1952 that David Brower was hired by the Sierra Club as its first full-time executive director. A decade later the first Sierra Club Washington office was established with one staffer. The major growth in the Club's Washington office occurred after 1972 when its staff expanded from two to its present seven to eight. Nationally the Sierra Club has a total of eighty-five full-time staff including support personnel. Friends of the Earth, with a far smaller membership, expanded its staff (including support personnel) from seventeen in 1972 to thirty-seven in 1977 (1978:16–17).

Many other national groups have had similar trends. In 1975 the Wilderness Society had forty staff members who were financed by a $1 million budget. This represented a fourfold increase over its budget of 1970. In these five years its membership had risen from 60,000 to 90,000 (Magida, 1976:63). Membership of other major environmental societies has shown little sign of levelling off (see table 1.2). Even during a ninety-day period from November 1973 to January 1974, when the energy crisis following the action of OPEC was at its worst, membership of the National Audubon Society had the greatest increase in its history (Quigg, 1974). The newer organizations involved in litigation have also continued to grow. The Environmental Defence Fund Inc., founded in 1967, had only 11,608 members in 1970 but by 1976 it had 40,000 members. Its budget of $1.3 million had grown about five times during this period. The Natural Resources Defence Council Inc. has also grown rapidly. It was found in December 1969 with a staff of ten and a $124,000 budget. In 1975 it had sixty lawyers, scientists and supporting staff and its budget was over $1.6 million (Magida, 1976).

On the other hand, membership of Zero Population Growth (ZPG) has declined throughout the 1970s. ZPG began in 1968 and rapidly grew to over 30,000 members, but has since declined to under 8,000. According to Richard Hughes, Business Manager of ZPG, the decline was primarily caused by 'a public conception that because the US fertility rate declined to almost what we recommended, zero growth has been achieved' (letter to author, 18 August 1977). The Friends of the Earth was founded in 1969 and within about two years its membership had grown to about 23,000. Since then there has been little change with fluctuations of three to four thousand either way (T. Turner, Administrative Director of FOE, to author, 27 July 1977).

Bowman (1975) has argued that after 1972 anti-establishment pressure groups were unable to gain access to political machinery, and the lack of official recognition resulted in their having much less success than the old pressure groups which were not so radical in their politics. J. Harry (1974) has also pointed out that the student environmentalist organizations appeared in 1970, with the rise of concern culminating in Earth Day, but in 1974 most of them had gone out of existence. Environmental Action Inc. was founded on Earth Day and gained an instant membership of 100,000, but by 1975 its membership had shrunk to 15,000 (Magida, 1976).

Table 1.2   Growth of membership of various leading US environmental organizations

	1966	1967	1968	1969	1970	1971	1972	1973	1974	1975	1976	1977
Sierra Club[a]	44,584	54,867	67,570	84,402	114,336	131,630	136,127	139,064	144,263	153,004	163,661	178,402
National Audubon Society[b]	43,940	53,715	66,026	78,061	104,676	138,638	164,444	201,712	237,203	257,043	269,470	286,540
Zero Population Growth[c]								18,665	12,235	10,103	9,672	8,285
Environmental Defence Fund[d]						25,000			38,545	39,570	44,473	45,699
Environmental Action[e]					44,000	3,000	3,500	4,000	6,000	9,000	18,000	20,000

[a] As of December each year for 1966–70. October for years 1971–76, and 1977.
[b] As of 30 June each year. The membership figures includes family membership. When family memberships are counted as two individuals, the Society showed a total membership on 30 June 1977 of 373,092 whereas the actual number of memberships recorded amounted to 286,540.
[c] As of March each year. Zero Population Growth began in 1968 and rapidly grew to over 30,000 members.
[d] As of December each year with the exception of 1977 which is the July figure. The Environment Defence Fund began its membership recruitment programme in early 1970. It achieved rapid growth for about 18 months, with an active membership of over 25,000 by the end of 1971. After that the growth rate began to slow down.
[e] In 1970 membership was free. In 1976 there was a deliberate attempt to increase membership.

(*Source*: Sandbach, 1978(a):103)

A. Schnaiberg (1975) suggests that as with other aspects of the environmental movement there are clear indications that the radical environmentalism of ecology and transcendentalism has faded away and instead policy proposals are coming from moderate reformist groups. These groups are concerned with plans to overcome scarcity of energy and materials rather than dramatic changes in policy based on environmentalist beliefs. Nevertheless, it is true to say that the older environmental groups were transformed during the late 1960s and early 1970s. Indeed the gap between old and new groups narrowed considerably as the old became more radical and the new more conservative. The tactics of the Friends of the Earth and the Council for the Protection of Rural England in Britain, for example, were at one time poles apart. The Friends of the Earth quickly made their name for campaigns involving direct action – placing non-returnable bottles in large quantities on the doorsteps of the Schweppes headquarters, demonstrations in favour of waste-paper recycling, and so on. Their effectiveness depended upon mass participation. The Council for the Protection of Rural England, on the other hand, campaigned quietly through traditional political channels, depending in the main upon the work of its executive officers.

Today the Friends of the Earth have adopted a more 'respectable' image, often working in close contact with the Council for the Protection of Rural England on energy, transport and other issues. While mass campaigns are still regarded as important, the Friends of the Earth have recognized the need to adopt the lobbying tactics of older environmental pressure groups. The Council for the Protection of Rural England also changed from a strictly preservationist lobby (it was originally called the Council for the Preservation of Rural England) to one which has adopted many of the conservationist and environmentalist principles that were popularized during the 1960s and 1970s.

Analysis of environmental pressure groups in America and Britain has shown that their memberships are predominantly upper-middle class. One study by Allison (1975) of two British amenity societies showed that 85 per cent of the Conservation Society officers were doctors, professors, had civil awards or had titles. The other society, the Council for the Protection of Rural England, had a similarly high proportion of high-status executive members (see table 1.3).

Despite the obvious class bias of the active membership of the environmental movement, there has been some doubt whether or not political cleavages exist. Several studies have claimed a lack of correspondence between party identification or ideology and environmental attitude (Buttel and Flinn, 1974 and 1976; Munton and Brady, 1970; Dillman and Christenson, 1972; Springer and Constantini, 1974). However, there is considerable evidence from America that Democratic Party élites tend to

Table 1.3 *Membership of the Council for the Protection of Rural England*

	Executive Committee of the CPRE and full-time administrators[1]		Chairman and Secretaries of County branches of the CPRE[2]	
	N	%	N	%
In the House of Lords	6	17	7	9
Justice of the Peace or with Civil honour	11	30	13	16
With relevant technical qualifications	8	22	13	16
With other academic qualifications	6	17	8	10
Of military rank	3	8	25	31
Males with none of the above	9	25	21	26
Females with none of the above	1	3	10	12½

[1] 31 members of the Executive Committee and 5 full-time administrators.
[2] 80 in all.
N represents the number holding the distinction or qualification.
(*Source:* Allison, 1975:118)

vote in favour of environmental legislation much more often than their Republican counterparts (see Dunlap, 1973). In Britain, an analysis of the Friends of the Lake District campaign against the A66 road proposals showed that thirty-one Conservative Members of Parliament were contacted as opposed to nine Labour members (McCarthy, 1976). On the other hand, S. Brookes and J. Richardson argue that 'one of the key characteristics of the environmental issue is its straddling of conventional political cleavages' (1975:324). They support this claim by pointing to a number of permanent all-party committees such as the Conservation Group (Historic Buildings), the Ecology Group, the Anti-Pollution Group, the Inland Waterways Group, and the Committee for the Conservation of Species and Habitats.

NEW POLITICAL INSTITUTIONS AND ENVIRONMENTAL LEGISLATION

The rise in public concern for the environment, increased coverage by the news media and growing pressure group involvement were also accompanied by the creation of new government institutions and legislation. In Britain this involved the setting up of a central scientific unit on pollution, a standing Royal Commission on Environmental Pollution, working parties on refuse disposal, the creation of the Department of the Environment (DOE) and general legislation such as the Control of Pollution Act

1974. There was overwhelming support from all the major British political parties in creating comprehensive environmental legislation during 1973–74 when control of pollution Bills were introduced both by the Conservative party and later by the Labour party after a change of government. The Control of Pollution Act finally came onto the statute books in the summer of 1974, but since then its implementation has been considerably curtailed by cuts in public expenditure. Part II of the Act dealing with water pollution still remained virtually unimplemented in 1978 despite river pollution survey results that showed a slight deterioration of rivers in England and Wales between 1972 and 1975 (Sandbach, 1977(a)). The fact that orders for effluent treatment plants have declined rapidly since 1973 also suggests that water pollution will become more severe in future (MacRae, 1977).

The diminishing political commitment to environmental protection in the face of economic difficulties has been demonstrated by a trend in recent legislation to curtail a right to inquiry. Take, for example, the Opencast Coal Act 1975, the Community Land Act 1976 and the Offshore Petroleum (Scotland) Act 1975. The latter Act facilitates government acquisitions of land for North Sea oil development by limiting public inquiries and Parliamentary inquiry procedure when energy policy could be jeopardized by time-consuming attention to environmental and local interests (Council on Tribunals, *Annual Report* 1974–75; Flood and Grove-White, 1976). On the other hand, where public opposition has been strongest and planning has been concerned with long-term policy, as in the case of nuclear power and motorway planning in Britain, there has been a tendency to strengthen the role of public inquiries.

In the United States rather similar changes in political commitment have taken place although general environmental legislation came earlier with the passage of the National Environmental Policy Act (NEPA) in 1969. This Act committed the federal government:

to use all practicable means consistent with other essential considerations of National Policy to ensure that each generation of Americans will have a safe, healthful, productive, and aesthetically and culturally pleasing environment (Kelley, Stunkel and Wescott, 1975; 118).

To ensure compliance with these principles all federal agencies were required to prepare an 'environmental impact statement' (EIS) when policies involved significant environmental consequences. By 30 June 1974 over 8,700 statements had been submitted and the submission rate had risen to some two hundred a month in 1976 (Nelkin, 1977(a)). The EIS has to document the probable effects of the proposed action on the environment and put forward any alternatives. The statement also has to specify any unavoidable and irreversible repercussions over short- and long-term periods. The EIS procedure, together with the more open administration in America, has been a huge stimulus to environmental legal action as well as the the employment of professional ecologists. T. O'Riordan (1976(b)) notes that in the three years after the passage of NEPA, there were over two hundred judicial decisions which clarified the question of standing or the right of a plaintiff to have his case heard in the courts. The courts also established a number of other principles favouring environmental protection (see Chapter 3).

NEPA brought into being the Council on Environmental Quality (CEQ) to advise the President on the state of the environment through the annual presentation to Congress of Environmental Quality Reports. The CEQ is a Cabinet-level body of three members and, like Britain's Royal Commission on Environmental Pollution, it was to make recommendations for policy review and legislation. NEPA was followed by significant pollution control legislation, notably the Clean Air Act 1970 and the Federal Water Pollution Control Act 1972. Offenders are liable to extensive fines of up to $25,000 per day and one-year jail sentences. The British Control of Pollution Act 1974, by comparison, raised penalties on summary conviction to a maximum of £400 or £50 a day for each further day on which the offence continues. However, on conviction or indictment either a fine or imprisonment of up to two years or both are now possible.

In December 1970, Congress established the Environmental Protection Agency which brought together under one large umbrella many of the agencies responsible for regulating pollution. These included the Federal Water Quality Administration which had previously been in the Department of the Interior, the National Air Pollution Control Administration, the Bureau of Water Hygiene and the Solid Waste Management programme which had been part of the Department of Health, Education and Welfare. The Environmental Protection Agency has the duty of co-ordinating federal environmental programmes, monitoring pollution, enforcing the laws, and reviewing environmental impact statements.

Similar changes can be noted in other countries. A 1976 United Nations Environment Programme (UNEP) survey report established the fact that seventy countries had created central organizations like the Department of the Environment or the Environmental Protection Agency, and that only twenty-eight countries, nearly all of which were less developed, had failed to establish such organizations (Document: The State of the Environment in 1976). Several countries with a federal government structure have adopted EIS procedures, notably Australia and Canada. In Europe France, Germany and Ireland have adopted a limited version of the scheme, and Denmark, the Netherlands and the UK, among others, have been actively assessing its value (Elkington, 1977). However, despite the similarities between comparative development of political institutions and procedures, the degree of public involvement varies considerably from the relatively closed and consensus-orientated decision-making systems of, say, the USSR and Japan to that of the relatively open and conflict-orientated policy-making system in the United States. Britain lies somewhere in the middle, with fairly open access in the environmental planning sphere but with much secrecy in the pollution sphere. The exclusive policy-making process in Japan has severely inhibited an effective contribution from the environmental lobby (Kelley, D. R. *et al.*, 1975). The same applies to pollution control in Britain where the development of active pollution control pressure groups has been inhibited but the growth of general amenity groups has been encouraged.

In the United States, as in Britain, implementation of environmental legislation has been thwarted. As early as 1972, there were signs that many federal agencies were avoiding the EIS requirements on the grounds that the information was confidential. By adding small amounts of confidential data to the general information, federal agencies could avoid the Freedom of Information Act. Alternatively, information was often delayed so as to appear late in the policy-making process (O'Riordan, 1976(b)). The EIS system also received insufficient financial support. The Council on Environmental Quality, which was responsible for reviewing the EIS, employed only thirty professionals, of whom only about six worked regularly on impact statements (Nelkin, 1977(a)). After the oil crisis in 1973 NEPA was threatened by exemptions in new legislation, for example, to enable the speedy construction of the Alaskan pipeline (Fanning, 1975). In 1974, President Ford vetoed the first strip-mining Bill which had reached the White House in the thirty-four years since Congress had been involved on the grounds that the Bill would result in unemployment for 35,000 people and would worsen the energy situation. A similar Bill was vetoed in 1975, the same year that the Ford Administration accelerated its leasing programme of offshore tracts for oil and gas drilling despite strong opposition from environmentalist groups (Magida, 1976). Proposals for further pollution control legislation have also failed to materialize. C. W. Heckroth noted that during 1976 Congress:

failed on the air law even though it discussed it all year; proposed water-law amendment stagnated in conference when Congress adjourned in October. Despite extended debate, House and Senate Conferences were unable to reach agreement (1976:26).

In October 1977 lobbyists for the electrical utilities were successful in delaying the 'best available technology' requirements of the Clean Air Act 1970.

ENVIRONMENTALISM

The environmental movement of the last decade is not entirely new. In earlier periods of history there have been spasmodic but notable reactions against the environmental consequences of urban and technological change, especially during the upheavals in the nineteenth century as many of the now advanced countries made their first uneasy steps towards industrialization. In Britain there were movements concerned with public health involving Chadwick, Simon and others imbued with the utilitarian spirit of reform. In America the utilitarian movement was expressed in the National Park Service, the Forest Service and the Soil Conservation Service. There were also the romantics who were critical of what they saw as a philistine obsession with 'machinery'. Matthew Arnold condemned the materialist society in *Culture and Anarchy* (first published 1869) and William Morris, in 1891, visualized a London whose population and industry had largely dispersed, leaving the city in a clean, healthy and natural state. Goethe, Blake and Wordsworth were all concerned about the destructive nature of post-Newtonian science (see Roszak, 1972) and Henry Thoreau advocated a 'back-to-nature' existence in the mid-nineteenth century. Environmental Utopianism were prescribed and practised by Robert Owen and his followers (see Noyes, 1966) while Prince Peter Kropotkin argued in favour of an anarchist solution involving small-scale production and a communitarian existence. Preservation groups such as the Commons, Open Spaces and Footpaths Society (founded in 1865) and the National Trust (founded in 1895) in Britain, and the Sierra Club (founded in 1892) in America were formed to safeguard rural areas and urban common land. There was the Pinchot-Muir era or the 'First Conservation Movement' between 1895 and the First World War which went so far as to involve President Roosevelt (see Nash, 1967; Hays, 1959). George Perkins Marsh (1864) drew attention to the industrial threat to ecological systems, and Alfred Wallace (1903) became alarmed by the environmental consequences of imperialism.

In the 1960s many of these different types of reactions were united under the banner of environmentalism. This term has been interpreted in various ways: a social movement, a set of ideas based upon ecology, a 'back-to-nature' philosophy, or just a greater interest in environmental affairs. The quality of life in a local context is a single unifying factor and is seen to be no less important than the 'survival of mankind' issue in a global context. There was also a close tie between environmentalism and the anti-science movement of the 1960s, both being connected with holistic and anti-mechanistic tendencies (see Cotgrove, 1975).

S. Cotgrove (1976) has made a useful distinction between two main types of environmentalism – a traditional and a liberal type. However, I prefer to make a slightly different distinction. My first category is an ecological or scientific brand of environmentalism. This type sees the importance of sustaining a viable physical and biological environment as the first priority, and any technological or economic changes are to be determined by this principle. It attempts to influence policy by presenting a valid, scientifically argued case based upon ecology and systems analysis. The second type of environmentalism is less concerned with environmental systems, but more with whether or not science and technology are compatible with humanistic principles. Unlike the more widespread ecologically based environmentalism, the latter standpoint has been more influenced by the New Left, anarchism and the counter-culture. The anti-establishment character of this type of environmentalism is reflected in the adoption of the title *Radical Technology* (rather than *Alternative Technology*) by the *Undercurrents* fraternity in 1975–76 when the 'technological fix' aspects (solar power, wind power, alternative housing, and so on) started to become part of establishment policy (Harper *et al.*, 1976). To illustrate the distinction one may refer to *A Blueprint for Survival*, produced by the editors of the journal *The Ecologist* in 1972. Although it makes use of ideas developed within both types of environmentalism, it falls much more clearly into the first category. The emphasis upon traditional hierarchy and authority and its essentially conservative character is closely associated with the dominant theme of analysis which explains environmental and social problems in terms of natural laws and physical factors such as the size of communities. This distinction between the two forms of environmentalism will become clearer on further analysis.

Ecological/scientific environmentalism
The conservation idea of ecological management was expressed as early as 1864 by Marsh in *Man and Nature*. Roosevelt and Pinchot, among many other influential spokesmen, made conservation a popular idea in America by the turn of the century. Conservation was not therefore a new idea, but it did receive a new boost in the 1960s. Conservation expressed the priority of sustainable environmental exploitation, consequently it came into conflict with policies based upon short-term economic criteria. This different approach to environment policy is illustrated in the development of energy analysis and accounting. For example, in *Fuel's Paradise* Peter Chapman argues for changes in policy relating to production, distribution, consumption and disposal not in economic terms but in terms of the energy demands made by different processes. In the tradition of Rachel Carson's book about society deluged by pesticides (see *Silent Spring*, 1962), Chapman describes the Utopian Isle of Erg whose housekeeping is carried out in kwat units rather than monetary currency. As in

other environmental literature, the emphasis is upon creating a sustainable social order that relies particularly on renewable resources. Kaycal, the Minister for Industry on the Isle of Erg, speaks for the environmentalist when he says: 'At the moment our population density is only a quarter of a typical European country. This makes it easy for us to grow more than enough food without resorting to intensive methods of agriculture' (1975:19). Emphasis is also placed upon individual self-sufficiency:

If we had bought all our food in a government shop it would have cost between 600 and 700 kwats, and if the fuel bills had been anything like those we had in London we would have needed 1,600 kwats to pay them. With electricity costing 4 kwats a unit and coal 400 kwats a hundredweight it is not surprising that all the Erg houses have windmills connected to electricity generators, solar roofs for water heating and wood-fired cookers (1975:15).

Guidelines for environmental policy were, according to modern environmentalists, synonymous with ecological concepts. These could be expressed simply in layman's language, as Barry Commoner's (1972) widely quoted four principles of ecology testify: every separate entity is connected to all the rest; everything has to go somewhere; you cannot get something for nothing from it; and nature knows best. *The Ecologist's A Blueprint for Survival* (1972) lays emphasis on these principles, and especially emphasizes the importance of returning to 'natural' mechanisms. Its recommendations include: 'natural' control of pests (that is, biological control through judicious crop rotations, and so on) as opposed to the use of artificial pesticides; the use of organic manure instead of inorganic fertilizers; the use of ecologically sound alternative technologies; the decentralization of the economy to make reasonably self-sufficient communities possible; and a reduction of the British population to a level sustainable by indigenous renewable resources. A similar statement of ecological principles as a guide to policy has been expressed rather polemically by Max Nicholson (ex-director of the Nature Conservancy in Britain):

The ecologists and their fellow travellers bid fair in history to relegate Karl Marx to the status of a small-time bungling amateur at the task of triggering world revolution. It is time that we learnt more about the ecology of ecologists and about the laws of ecological succession which their social impacts involve (1976:463).

The implications of the interconnectedness of nature were brilliantly illustrated in Rachel Carson's *Silent Spring* (1962). The seemingly minute levels of persistent pesticides, released for medical and agricultural control of pests, could be concentrated in food chains and hence become a serious environmental problem. The discovery of pesticide residues in penguins living thousands of miles from the source of pollution brought home the importance of ecology. Fragmented scientific disciplines came under attack for adopting a blinkered outlook and failing to understand the complex relationships between all parts of the natural world. Barry Commoner expressed this concern in *Science and Survival*: 'The separation of laws of nature is a human conceit; nature itself is an integrated whole' (1966:25). With the development of a holistic ecology, there was an attempt to incorporate other sciences, rather than to see ecology slowly eroded by a reductionist biology. This 'holistic' or 'systems' approach to science became a major theme in the popular environmentalist literature. H. M. Enzensberger's analysis of ecology brought out the same point:

One of the best known ecological handbooks – *Population, Resources, Environment* by Paul and Anne Ehrlich – deploys evidence from the following branches of science either implicitly or explicitly: statistics, systems theory, cybernetics, games theory and prediction theory; thermodynamics, biochemistry, biology, oceanography, mineralogy, meteorology, genetics; physiology, medicine, epidemiology, toxicology; argricultural science, urban studies, demography; technologies of all kinds; theories of society, sociology and economics (the latter admittedly in a most elementary form). The list is not complete. It is hard to describe the methodological confusion that results from the attempt at a synthesis of this sort (1974:4).

Similar attempts at multi-disciplinary synthesis are typical of other environmentalist literature. *The Limits to Growth* study produced by the Club of Rome (Meadows *et al.*, 1972) being perhaps the best known. *The Limits to Growth* took a systems dynamics approach to produce an overall view of interactions between population, capital, resources, pollution and agriculture, with different disciplines making their own subordinate contributions to various parts of the total interactive model. Ecology and systems dynamics were both concerned with negative and positive feedback loops in the natural world: what was appropriate to ecology was also considered to be appropriate to the study of society at a global level. The influence of systems thinking is illustrated in the following excerpts from E. Goldsmith's essay on 'De-industrializing society' (a five-year postscript to *A Blueprint for Survival*):

The most basic principle of the behaviour of the biosphere is that it is goal-directed, as can be shown to be the case with all the behavioural systems which comprise it. The goal is stability . . . It can be shown that primitive societies were geared to precisely this goal. The main preoccupation of their members was to observe their traditional customs, and to hand them down as intact as possible to their children. It is only a very abstract society such as ours that is geared to systematic change in a given direction, and one that can survive for but a limited period of time.

.... the problems facing the world today can only be solved by restoring the functioning of these natural systems which once satisfied our needs (1977:131 and 134).

The anti-scientific slant of this kind of environmentalism was confined to anti-reductionism. What was needed was greater authority for ecology. The status of science itself was not questioned, indeed greater attention to the right kind of scientific analysis was desperately needed. J. McHale is typical in making this claim in an attempt to legitimate environmentalist thinking:

As a 'value-affirming and goal-setting' agency, its [science's] status is now equal and in many areas, greater than the older social institutions (for example, church, government, family, education), upon which this function traditionally developed (1971:25–26).

It is perhaps not surprising that many professional ecologists had in the first place welcomed the rising tide of enthusiasm for ecology, which included the massive and costly support by the International Biology Programme (IBP); between 1970 and 1974, the IBP spent $39 million on funding large-scale computer modelling of individual ecosystems. The failure of this programme to lead to any substantial theoretical break-through and the demarcation problem that arose between what was considered professional ecology and 'pop' or charlatan ecology made it less acceptable for well-known scientists to engage in popularist writings, as had been the case in the late 1960s (Nelkin, 1977(a)).

The critics of environmentalism have pointed out the authoritarian and technocratic nature of the claims of many of its adherents who wish to hand over the responsibility of policy-making to the computer modellers and systems analysts (see Simmons, 1973). Ecological environmentalism offers a model of society which would help to reinforce the existing social order (see Lowe and Worboys, 1978). It depicts a systems analyst's view of man's relation to nature which ignores the importance of class relations and economic organization. *The Ecologist*'s emphasis upon ecological stability led to the belief that growth was undesirable because it was a prime cause of social instability. Physical limits to growth resulted from the incapacity to absorb changes (see Chapter 8). Much of the environmentalist literature focused upon the complex cumulative impact of technological development. In a rapidly changing world it seemed almost impossible to avoid unintended consequences (see Farvar and Milton, 1972).

Policy recommendations to limit population, houses, cars, and so on, according to ecological calculations aimed at elucidating the carrying capacity, imply that political consensus may be achieved through a comprehensive, objective and value-free scientific analysis. It is this view that seems distasteful to the many, whether they be on the left or right of the political spectrum, who still cherish the ideals of liberty. The rulers of the new Utopia, with its orderly harmonious world, would not be Plato's philosopher kings, nor Skinner's behaviourists, but ecologists aware of the interconnectedness of natural and social systems.

Anti-establishment environmentalism

In contrast to environmentalism with an ecological emphasis, the anti-establishment movement's principal concern has been with man's alienation from society and from nature. Unlike earlier Marxists, the New Left and anarchists both saw the problem of alienation and social control as a product of science and technology. L. Winner (1977) examined the obsession in modern times with the ideas and images of what he calls 'technics-out-of-control'. There are many people throughout history who have been critical of technological society. Robert Owen, Charles Fourier, Mikhail Bakunin, Prince Peter Kropotkin, William Morris, John Ruskin, and Lewis Mumford were just a few who contributed to the debate. Critiques of science and technology became extremely popular in the late 1960s. The views of Jacques Ellul, Hannah Arendt, Jurgen Habermas and Herbert Marcuse were widely influential, especially in America. Ellul (1964) stressed the view that the dynamics of a destructive technological society were to be located in the inexorable march of technique. Arendt (1958) similarly questioned whether or not we were still masters of our machines, or whether machines had developed their own momentum and begun to rule and destroy the world. Habermas (1971) was concerned with the influence of science of politics. Marcuse (1964) saw science and technology as forces of social control.

Within this framework, popular ecology, systems analysis, cybernetics, decision theory, technology assessment and cost-benefit analysis could be seen as agents of social control rather than liberation. Technical rationality and pseudo-scientific thinking had increasingly penetrated policy-making and hence political rationality (see Chapters 2 and 5). The Alternative Technology movement's diagnosis of society's ills was closely dependent upon this type of analysis. It sought to lay down criteria necessary to ensure social control over technological development. Alternative technologies would be designed so as to minimize social misuse of technology, to require few specialist skills, as well as to be non-polluting and use only renewable resources such as wind and solar power (see Chapter 6).

In the environmental field the concern about scientific and technical rationality became linked with explanations of environmental abuse. Post-Newtonian science and technology, which became increasingly interdependent in the nineteenth century and after, were the principal culprits. Theodore Roszak (1968 and 1972), among others, argued that the Baconian scientific programme had emphasized an experimental world without purpose and without animism – views that had previously been held first by the Aristotelians and later by the Renaissance alchemists and hermeticists. Instead of seeing the world of nature as alive and sentient the new metaphysics had become mechanistic in character. The point some environmentalists want to make is that objectivity and rationality impose a distance between the scientist and the subject of investigation. This, together with a depersonalized scientific jargon, allows the legitimate abuse of nature or society under the pretext of furthering knowledge, of achieving technological progress, or of contributing to economic growth. Other writers, sparked off by a much quoted article by Lynn White (1967), joined in the debate by arguing that the Western Judaeo–Christian tradition was thoroughly anthropocentric and through its rejection of paganism emphasized the spiritless state of the natural world (see Barbour, 1973; Nasr, 1968; Yi-Fu Tuan, 1970, Black, 1970, Glacken, 1970, Passmore, 1974; Leiss, 1974).

Environmentalists saw the lack of ethical inhibitions in societies influenced by Christianity and modern science in stark contrast to the respect for the environment shown by other societies. For example, the Hopi Indians live in close touch with the environment. Their view of the universe envisages a harmonious and interdependent relationship between nature, gods, plants, animals and men. According to A. Rapoport, their mutual welfare depends upon a reciprocal system of obligations and ceremonials:

For example, a hunted animal is propitiated, one apologizes to it, explaining that it is being killed only because of great need – one never kills more than is needed and every part of the animal must be used; similarly, only the number of plants needed is picked; the first plant of the type sought is never picked: an offering is placed before it and others sought (1969(a):70).

The environmentalist answer to environmental destruction is a spiritual revival that treats nature with respect. In America the transcendental influence on the environmental movement has been particularly strong, as illustrated in Henry Thoreau's Utopia of Walden and in the writings of recent environmentalists such as Rachel Carson and David Brower (see Fleming, 1972).

The yearning for a mystical reunion with nature reached its zenith at the height of the hippie movement in 1968/69. The environmentalist rhetoric was well expressed in Charles Reich's book *The Greening of America* (1971): 'The new consciousness is sweeping the high schools, it is seen in the smiles on the street. It has begun to transform and humanize the landscape. When, in the fall of 1969, the courtyard of Yale Law School, the Gothic citadel of the élite, became for a few weeks the site of a commune, with tents, sleeping bags, and the outdoor cooking, who could any longer doubt the cleaning wind was coming?' (see Seddon, 1972:432). At this time romantic idealism emphasized the importance of an alternative environmental ethic. Roszak (1968 and 1972), who was a main prophet of the counter-culture, spoke of the sounder environmental ethics of animistic cultures.

However, the argument that the solution to environmental problems lies in the adoption of new non-alienative technology and in a transcendental ethic has not been without its critics. Some economists have pointed out the economic inefficiency of many of the proposed alternative technologies. Others have argued that technological development is more closely related to the ownership of the means of production than had been assumed by the 'technics-out-of-control' school of thought. Without changes in the economic bases of society alternative technology would remain Utopian (see Chapters 5–7).

Passmore (1974), among others, found Lynn White's thesis far from satisfactory on the ground that Western traditions are much more complex and diversified than White supposes. Moreover, Passmore rejects the idea that mystical contemplation will solve environmental problems. Instead his recipe pragmatically advocates a thoughtful and responsible programme for the prevention of environmental abuse. Moncrief's (1970) criticism of White's thesis rests on the argument that it was primarily the forces of democracy, technology, urbanization and increasing economic prosperity that were directly related to the environmental crisis. The Judaeo-Christian tradition may have been a necessary – but not a sufficient – condition for Western man's arrogance towards nature.

The main argument against this environmentalist position is that attitudes, metaphysics and ideas do not necessarily induce behaviour but may, on the other hand, themselves be determined by behaviour and changing economic conditions. There are many, Marxists and non-Marxists alike, who would agree with Marx's well-known dictum: 'It is not the consciousness of men which determines their existence but, on the contrary, their social existence which determines their consciousness' (*Preface to a Critique of Political Economy*, 1859). Hence, there is some evidence for the view that it was mercantilism and then later the growth of capitalism which influenced the development of a manipulative and mechanistic philososphy of science (Easlea, 1973; Dijksterhuis, 1961). The rise in public concern about the environment and the popularity of the environmentalist perspective, despite both its explanatory limitations and its inadequacy as a basis for policy, now require an explanation.

The environmental movement: alternative explanations

THE FUNCTIONALIST AND PLURALIST PERSPECTIVES

Systems theory, with its sociological form of functionalism, essentially analyses social problems in terms of strain, stress and anxiety. It is concerned with the relation of parts of the social system to the whole. E. Durkheim used the organic analogy of a homeostatic system with each organ and part of the body contributing to its overall stability. Within this model social problems are a product of systems imbalance or malfunction, with the implied policy implications of repairing the system by reform. In the functionalist and ordered world there is little real conflict of social interest, but only deviation from the consensus. Social movements within this system arise as a consequence of tensions and deviations from the normal ordered state of affairs. Parsons developed this type of explanatory account in his analysis of Nazism and McCarthyism, but it has been a major form of explanation of a variety of movements (see Wilson, 1973) including the environmental movement. Albrecht, for example, accepts the following formalized model suggested by Mauss (1971), as being relevant to the environmental movement:

(1) Incipiences, or the genesis of the movement in response to frustration, need deprivation or whatever; (2) Coalescence, involving the coming together of a more organized and structured whole of the groups and individuals who are dissatisfied with current conditions and seek change; (3) institutionalization, which frequently involves a society-wide co-ordination of the movement in an effort to attain its goals, and organization of the host society to cope with the movement in the form of co-option, or suppression; (4) fragmentation, resulting from either the movement's success or failure to achieve its goals, and (5) the demise of the movement as a viable force in society (1976:148).

Within this functionalist framework the main analytical task is to locate the stresses that have given rise to the environmental movement. Such an account would suggest that the environmental movement was probably initiated in the late 1950s during the height of the Cold War and nuclear testing. There was an alarming realization that radio-isotopes could find their way into milk and hence into the bone marrow. In 1958 Barry Commoner and others set up the St Louis Committee for Nuclear Information. This group provided information for the interested layman. The Federation of Atomic Scientists (now Federation of American Scientists) was set up for similar reasons and its Bulletin urged that the spread of nuclear weapons overseas should be prevented. Rachel Carson's *Silent Spring*, published in 1962 and widely serialized in popular magazines, came just at the right time, adding to the sense of alarm and crisis. From then on during the 1960s a series of horror stories was revealed. Notably, there was the alleged death of Lake Erie, killed by excessive eutrophication resulting from pollution. There was the *Torrey Canyon* incident in March 1967, and there was the Japanese Miniamata tragedy following mercury poisoning of fish. Revelations about the problems posed by nuclear fallout, pesticides and oil pollution were to Barry Commoner symptoms of a generalized problem arising from the impact of a wide range of commodities and products: non-degradable detergents, non-cellulose synthetic fibres, and non-retrievable bottles, while at the same time natural products such as cotton and soap were in decline.

Paul Ehrlich similarly dramatized the population–resource dilemma in 1968 with an alarmist book entitled *The Population Bomb*: 'The battle to feed all of humanity is over', he declared. 'In the 1970s and 1980s hundreds of millions of people will starve to death in spite of any crash programmes embarked upon now. At this late date nothing can prevent a substantial increase in the world death rate, although many lives could be saved through dramatic programmes to 'stretch' the carrying capacity of the earth by increasing food production and providing for more equitable distribution of whatever food is available' (1972:xi). A lively debate then ensued between Ehrlich and Commoner on whether population growth or technology were responsible for the environmental crisis. Commoner's argument rested on the growth of technologically harmful products increasing at a greater rate than population growth, while Ehrlich's case was strongest in relation to the pressure of a rapidly increasing population on resources.

Perceived crises and dramatic events also draw attention to wider problems. Margaret Mead argued: 'The environmental movement was given new life and impetus as a result of the first pictures of the earth as seen from the moon – a small lonely blue ball in space, vulnerable, needing protection from the ravages of technological man' (Sills, 1975:25). It is conceivable that these photographs gave additional popularity to Kenneth Boulding's (1966) metaphor of Spaceship Earth and René Dubos and Barbara Ward's (1972) book, *Only One Earth*. This theme was also taken up by other writers. Garrett Hardin, who makes extensive use of the 'Spaceship Earth' metaphor refers to a passage from Allan Stevenson in 1965: 'We travel together on a little spaceship, dependent on its vulnerable reserves of air and soil . . .' (1972:17).

The importance of the disturbing revelations of the late 1960s was not only that they suddenly uncovered a mass of hitherto unsuspected environmental problems but also that they created a sense of insecurity; alarmism and predictions of catastrophe inevitably aroused fear. Historians have not surprisingly often explained changes in social and economic policies as a consequence partly of serious crises (see Marwick, 1970). The effect of crises is to draw attention to the economic costs imposed by social problems, the loss of tourist revenue from the fouling of a beach after an oil spill, for example. Real and imaginary disasters also produce a lowered threshold to suggestibility as a consequence of fear and anxiety. According to M. Barkum, people are more readily 'moved to abandon the values of the past and place their faith in prophecies of imminent and total transformation' (1974:6). In particular a series of multiple disasters serve not only to destroy the commonly held theories that have served sufficiently well in the past but also, typically, the response to such stress is the rise of charismatic leaders who offer ideas and a philosophy that can be interpreted in a salvationist manner. While there have been no individually recognized environmental leaders in the same mould as Stokely Carmichael or Martin Luther King, there have been identifiable environmentalist philosophies with a few advocates (Commoner, Ehrlich, Roszak etc.) who captured the imagination of their followers.

Barkum's thesis is that millennial movements have arisen during periods of disaster. The Black Death was, for example, an important stimulus to most of the European millennial movements of the time. It is tempting to suggest that race riots, the Vietnam war and environmental alarm precipitated the millennial movements of the 1960s – the hippies, youth and pop culture, and the ecology and transcendental movements. Certainly it would be a mistake to ignore the influence of events outside the environmental sphere of concern. Schnaiberg (1973) suggests a common theme: techniques of participation in resisting social forces, using sit-ins, mass demonstrations, marches, picketing, distributing leaflets and media contact for public interest had been developed in the Civil Rights Movement, then further developed in the anti-Vietnam war movement and finally carried over to the environmental movement.

The functionalist account described above assumes that the natural state is a stable state and conflict of intersts plays little or no part in creating environmental issues. It is this failure to recognize the importance of conflict that has been most damaging to functionalism. Functionalism is inadequate, according to T. B. Bottomore, because 'conflict is an intrinsic part of social life, sustaining, modifying, or destroying the social groups in which it takes place. It cannot be treated satisfactorily as a minor and exceptional form of social relationship, in a brief apologetic appendix to a theory of social solidarity, as has so often been done' (1975:180).

The pluralist standpoint is often associated with functionalism, but it is claimed that environmental problems and policy are subject to many conflicting pressures and interests. Consequently there is no bias towards any ruling group. Any attempt at domination would be checked by the majority through various democratic mechanisms such as elections and many other constitutional and legal safeguards. Pluralism therefore accepts that there must be a consensus of public opinion for social change to take place. It is this reliance upon a commonly accepted interpretation of social problems which makes pluralism particularly compatible with functionalism. The pluralist–functionalist analyses focus typically upon observable issues and the behaviour of participants. Numerous accounts in the politics of environmental planning describe how the participants respond and how decisions are taken (see Chapter 4).

It is worth noting at this point the similarity between pluralism and neo-classical economic analysis. Both work under the same assumptions that decision-making is a product of consensus rather than conflict. For the economist environmental values should be determined by a market consensus. If environmental resources are not marketed then cost–benefit analysis and various surveys enable a market value to be attached and the appropriate intervention carried out. B. Dasgupta comments that the neo-classical approach accepts that 'for a community, the choice of a particular environmental standard was "revealed" by its *collective willingness to pay*, which, according to this view could be ascertained in a variety of ways – through opinion polls, or through variation of charges over a time period' (1978:386) (see also Chapters 2 and 3).

Following Durkheim's (1950) view that even a Society of Saints would have social problems, it has been argued that problems change over time but obey a law of limited numbers. This proposition is supported by Maslow's (1943) hypothesis that society has a hierarchy of needs; when high priority needs such as housing and food are satisfied then lower priority needs can become a focus of political attention (Schon, 1971; Solesbury, 1976). It has been claimed that competing social problems such as poverty, housing and racial tension became less serious in the affluent post-Second World War period. This allowed the increasing problems of the environment to capture public attention (see Chapman, 1969). Perhaps the best known account of competing public issues is the issue–attention model of A. Downs (1972). He suggested that American public interest rarely focuses for very long on any crucial social problem. Instead issues leap into prominence for a short time and then, though they remain largely unresolved, public interest gradually wanes. The model he proposes is based upon public attitudes in general and not the committed behaviour of pressure groups or institutional changes. His explanation of the rise and fall of social issues follows a sequence of five stages:

1 There is a *pre-problem stage* when a social problem exists, often in an extremely serious form, but has not yet caught the public eye.
2 There is *alarmed discovery and euphoric enthusiasm*, often triggered off by a dramatic series of events. At this stage there is often an unrealistic optimism about the possibility of solving the problem.
3 There is an *appreciation of the cost of significant progress*. During this

stage a more realistic assessment is made of the cost involved and sacrifices required by major vested interests.

4 There is a *gradual decline of intense public interest* as the realization of difficulties involved in tackling the social problem grows. Three types of reaction set in: 'Some people just get discouraged. Others feel positively threatened by thinking about the problem, so they suppress such thoughts. Still others become bored by the issue.'

5 There is the *post-problem stage* when the issue moves into a state of prolonged limbo with spasmodic recurrences of interest. It differs from the pre-problem stage in that during the period of intense public interest new institutions, programmes and policies would have been initiated, which ensures that issues in the post-problem stage 'always receive a higher average level of attention, public effort and general concern than those still in the pre-discovery stage'.

Unlike many other social problems he predicted that environmental issues would maintain their interest for a longer period of time for the following reasons:

1 Environmental problems such as air pollution or the oil-soaked seagull are generally much more noticeable and clearly threatening than other social problems.

2 Pollution is less politically divisive because it threatens almost everyone. This makes attacking environmental pollution a safer issue than attacking racism or poverty.

3 Blame for environmental problems can be attributed to a group of 'villains' – the industrialists. Ralph Nader, for instance, gained much support for his campaign against the big giants of industry.

4 The fact that environmental problems can be dealt with by technological solutions rather than having to depend upon political or redistributive change also makes the environmental issue acceptable.

5 The costs of dealing with the problem can be passed on through higher prices to the consumer. This is believed to be more acceptable than the imposition of taxes which would have to be levied to fund other social reforms.

6 The environmental issue may also be prolonged because it could create a big private industrial sector involved in environmental protection. Such organizations would then have vested interests in maintaining the issue.

7 The ambiguity of environmental issues allows almost anybody to claim his or her concern as part of the general environmental concern.

It is not surprising that there was a decline in environmental concern from the early 1970s which coincided with an end of a period of unparalleled economic expansion and social change. In the pluralist perspective this could be simply accounted for by a shift of public concern to other issues. Moreover, in terms of Downs' issue–attention model, it could be claimed that the realization of costs to society of environmental reform were much more obvious when inflation and unemployment were the main preoccupations of the world economy.

The ideas of anti-growth and 'limits to growth' which had been an important concern for the environmental movement were more easily dismissed under these changes in economic circumstances. In the words of W. Beckerman in his defence of economic growth: 'A failure to maintain economic growth means continued poverty, deprivation, disease, squalor, degradation, and slavery to soul-destroying toil for countless millions of the world's population' (1974:9). Society could no longer afford to flirt with the pessimism of environmental disaster. The environmentalist perspective was reinforced by a concern about 'limits to growth' but this has also been subjected to increasing critical analysis (see Chapter 8) and many of the scare stories promulgated during the 1960s were found to be considerably exaggerated.

MARXIST AND MATERIALIST PERSPECTIVES

Marxist interpretations of social movements, problems and policies claim that a true understanding can only be achieved by investigating their relationship with the underlying economic organization of society. This materialist position is put by Friedrich Engels as follows:

The materialist conception of history starts from the proposition that the production of the means to support human life and, next to production, the exchange of things produced, is the basis of all social structure; that in every society that has appeared in history, the manner in which wealth is distributed and society divided into classes or orders is dependent upon what is produced, how it is produced and how the products are exchanged. From this point of view the final causes of all social changes and political revolutions are to be sought, not in men's brains, not in man's better insight into eternal truth and justice, but in changes in the modes of production and exchange. They are to be sought, not in the philosophy, but in the economics of each particular epoch (1950:125).

Much debate exists among Marxists over the degree of autonomy and the type of relationship between the economic base and superstructure, but nevertheless all elements are seen to act within a totality of social relations. In a capitalist society the state and the means for dealing with environmental problems are influenced by the ruling class. Ralph Miliband (1977) suggests three reasons upon which Marxists have relied to justify this assertion. Firstly the state recruits its politicians, civil servants and administrators largely from the ruling class whereas the majority of subordinate classes are poorly represented. Secondly the ruling class wields more power as a result of its economic strength. Thirdly there are structural constraints imposed by an economic organization which is primarily orientated towards the free market. These constraints limit the range of possible policies, and exclude those that would seriously affect the dominant mode of production. Reform may be resisted by the ruling class but nevertheless is accommodated so as to control the worst abuses of capitalism and thus consolidate the social order.

The capitalist system, it is claimed, therefore distorts and constrains the activity of the majority to meet the needs of a few and so preserve the system of private enterprise and its economic rationality. 'Capitalist enterprise', says Milibrand, '*depends* to an even greater extent on the bounties and direct support of the state, and can only preserve its "private" character on the basis of such public help. State intervention in economic life in fact largely *means* intervention for the purpose of helping capitalist enterprise' (1973:17). For the pluralist the intervention of the state is evidence of a dispersion of power within society; for the Marxist, state intervention has been necessary to preserve private enterprise in advanced monopoly capitalism. The pluralist interprets reform as a product of consensus whereas the Marxist sees reform as a product of accommodating the contraditions and conflicts arising out of capitalism.

Instead of an issue–attention model, a conflict–accommodation model would be more appropriate to a materialist understanding of the environmental movement. This model would emphasize the importance of the economic and social base for concern, and how conflicting interests are accommodated through debate, institutional change and legislation. The following stages of a model describe the rise and fall of the environmental movement and environmental issues:

1 There is a pre-issue stage.
2 There is agitation for political action from an articulate social group, usually the enlightened middle class, who have come to perceive the development of a social problem which bears particularly upon their own interests. In response, various proposals are put forward.
3 These proposals clash with the interests of capital. For example, advocacy of a 'no-growth economy' is clearly incompatible with the maintenance of a mixed market economy. These incompatible objectives are debated and fought out at public inquiries, select committees, conferences, and in the mass media and journals.
4 The differences in objectives and interests are accommodated through the development of new institutions, compromise legislation, and the appearance of acceptable explanations and solutions to the problems. Such changes involve dealing with the problem in such a way as to satisfy the vested interests of the conflicting parties.
5 The process of accommodation reduces the threat of the social problem and the issue declines in importance. As accommodation may be only

partially successful, involving perhaps the token response of an official inquiry or permissive legislation, there may be a series of issue cycles with legislation moving from the piecemeal and permissive to effective and compulsory protection of public interests.

On the basis of this model one can see that Downs' explanation of the issue–attention cycle ignores the role of the media, conferences, institutions, legislation etc. in containing the issue without seriously altering the economic and social relations that are at the foundation of the social order. In British politics, Parliamentary select committees, advisory committees, and Royal Commissions play key roles in sorting out the conflicting interests and finding compromise solutions.

The materialist model of society leads to an entirely different view of the environmental movement. The pluralist competition between issues is rejected, and instead it is argued that issues arise as a result of a conflict of interests, usually between the articulate middle- and upper-class pressure group activists and environmentalists on the one hand and the objective interests of capital on the other. Conflict of interests, rather than some generalized social strain, is the key factor in the explanatory account. Pressure from capital also tends to confine issues to safe areas of debate. Some writers, for example, argue that the environmental concern of the 1960s was in part a displacement from the more serious and intractable problems of the Vietnam war, race relations, violence, poverty and urban blight (see Hardin, 1974). The Vietnam war, in particular, demonstrated the abuse and distortions of modern science (see McDermont, 1972), introducing Americans to such notions as the depersonalized computer battlefield – where chemical and electronic sensors could relay information about jungle movements via computers to automatic bombers, which were then guided to the target. Vast areas were also destroyed by defoliants. Anti-Vietnam reaction was accordingly closely associated with both the anti-science and environmental movements. This made the displacement of concern from one to the other all the easier.

The rise of the environmental movement can also be linked to changes in production. The environmental impact of new technological developments had become more widespread, so that powerful interests within the middle and upper classes were less able to take evasive action (Enzensberger, 1974). Nuclear fallout, oil pollution from the *Torrey Canyon*, and pesticides in food were all problems that could not be avoided by geographical mobility, as had been the case with many of the older and more local problems arising from slums, smoke and sewage. An important change since the Second World War has been the increase in leisure time and affluence which has brought a greater contact with the environment. In America, for example, the numbers of people visiting National Parks increased from 33.2 million in 1950 to 150.8 million in 1968, an increase of 450 per cent. Such changes in economic circumstances made environmental concern a much more relevant policy issue.

The materialist position also emphasizes the importance of economic interests in supporting ideologies (comprising beliefs, theories and ideas) that serve their own interest. Environmentalism as such had been no great threat to the business communities since ecologists and environmentalists, for all their vehement attacks on the business communities in the late 1960s and early 1970s, had never linked their attacks with a political philosophy that threatened the stability of the economic and social order. The ecological form of environmentalism, as has already been noted, was closely associated with values that would help reinforce the social order. The transcendental form of environmentalism may have had equally important social implications as Richard Lowry suggests:

The new 'religecology' runs the very great risk of further masking the basic nature of the ecology crisis . . . The collective religious commitment to cleaning up the environment creates a kind of therapeutic community in which all can purge themselves of personal guilt by simple and immediate acts of penitence. Yet, the major activities of life can continue relatively unchanged (see Sills, 1975:22).

The costs of pollution control or resource conservation would be passed on to the public, of whom the poor are most likely to feel the extra cost. These extra costs tend therefore to have a regressive effect. A. Schnaiberg (1975) has illustrated this by delineating the social effects resulting from the energy crisis spiral of 1973–74. Regressive effects included pressure to reduce public expenditure due to increased balance of payments problems, lay-offs, and inability to travel to work. These, he claims, outweigh progressive distributional effects such as any tendency towards greater mass transportation or the impetus given to alternative energy production such as coal-mining. Schnaiberg argues that the social consequences of planned scarcity and demands for a cleaner environment can account for different responses to environmental problems from the rich and poor. The class character of the news-media, he claims, makes this clear:

One needs merely to contrast the recent coverage of environmental problems by the editors of *Fortune*, on the one (and upper-class) hand, and those at *Ramparts*, on the other. A search of the *Fortune* report reveals very little assessment of differential allocation of costs of environmental improvement. The *Ramparts* approach focuses almost exclusively on precisely these differentials, and the related issues of social justice and environmental control. It continuously confronts and attacks the simplistic (and self-serving) view of *Fortune* that environmental control be conceived of as a 'national mission', arguing that the differential control and concern *within* the 'nation' is the crucial lever for environmental change (1973:621).

The Marxist makes two claims in his analysis of the dominant ideas of the mass media and other forms of communication. The first is that the ruling ideas are ideological in the sense that they tend to support the interests of capital accumulation. The second is that they are ideological in the sense of having the appearance of being scientific and empirical but are false and inadequate in comparison with materialist accounts (see Plamenatz, 1970). As the well-known dictum of Marx has it: 'the ideas of the ruling class are in every epoch the ruling ideas, i.e. the class which is the ruling *material* force of society, is at the same time its ruling *intellectual* force' (Marx, 1970(b):64).

The question arises as to why people fail to perceive their true interests and conform to the dominant ideology. Three types of explanation have been commonly given for the origins of this phenomenon (see Easton, 1976). Firstly there is the conspiracy theory of deliberate deception by the ruling class. Secondly there is a theory of self-deception, and thirdly there is the essence/appearance theory. It is this last explanation that seems most likely since the others assume that people are extremely naïve. The essence/appearance theory is much more sophisticated, for it claims that ideology, for example the pluralism studies, describes what is to all appearances truly happening. Descriptions of public opinion, behaviour, and decision-making appear to offer a full and rational picture of the politics of environmental problems. It is certainly easier to make abstractions of this kind than to treat environmental problems in their broader context, and the appearance of reality seems to support the ideological perspective. If one accepts the pluralist account, it is not hard to find political issues that seemingly confirm that a plurality of interests are active in the political arena. It is easy to be persuaded by appearances even if in reality, and despite the appearance of plural activity, capital and other resources accrue to a ruling class.

Whatever the reasons for the origins of the dominant ideology, there are two main reasons why it maintains its dominance. Firstly, the owners of production and their promotional groups have more money for general propaganda. Secondly, the promotion of critical ideas is largely constrained by economic interests. The mass media, for example, are largely supported by advertisers and the commercial interests of publishers.

L. Sellers and D. Jones have argued that reporters are sometimes even prevented by both newspaper managers and editors from writing critical reports – in the financial interests of their paper: although reporters are usually aware of the type of story which is acceptable there are occasionally cases when their critical stories could adversely harm business interests. Sellers and Jones describe one such case which involved censure by the editors:

One environmental reporter on a metropolitan newspaper recalls that soon after the start of the Chevron F-3100 advertising campaign, he attended a respiratory disease convention. Several participants were highly critical of the new gasoline additive. The reporter wrote their criticisms as a sidebar to his convention story. He reported that:

'The City editor held the story for several days. I questioned him about it and he finally red-lined (banned) it with the astounding comments: "Oh hell. This isn't all that pertinent, and the firm has a big advertising campaign with us now. Maybe later." I have done some intensive research of my own on that score and have determined that it was his own second-guessing of management's desires rather than any kind of order from above that promoted his decision' (1973:54).

The media, then, tend largely to affirm rather than challenge the social order. In this respect environmentalism and the media coverage of environmental problems gave rise mainly to an idealist attack on some of the problems arising from the social and economic order. Moreover some of the environmentalist ideas could be used as social levers to promote capitalist enterprise. For example, the idea of population pressure upon agricultural resources helped to accelerate the development of the Green Revolution. Harry Cleaver, Jr., has pointed to the political and economic interests behind this policy:

The Green Revolution has been paid for and staffed by some of the major élite institutions of the American ruling class. The goals of this agricultural strategy based on a new technology are to increase social stability, spread capitalist markets into rural areas, and create new sales and investment opportunities for multinational agribusiness (1972:90).

In a review of the Club of Rome and their *Limits to Growth* study Robert Golub and Jo Towsend (1977) argue that in the 1960s the independence of resource-rich developing countries and population growth threatened the stability of the economic order. Hence the idea of an ecological crisis was supported by certain business interests as a lever for the achievement of greater international co-operation. The stability of effective international controls and regulations would enable planned industrial growth by the ever-increasing number of large multinational companies.

The decline in public concern can also be associated with a reaction by some of the business community to those aspects of environmentalism which involved an extra financial burden. Policies that threaten the source of profit were vehemently opposed, as in a speech by J. M. Roches, the Chairman of the Board of Directors of General Motors:

. . . the short-term political advantages offered by spectacular but unsound consumer legislation can do lasting damage to the very consumers it purports to help. The consumer is the loser when irresponsible criticism and ill-conceived legislation break down faith in our economic system, when harassment distracts us from our modern challenge, when the very idea of free enterprise is diminished in the eyes of young people who must one day manage our businesses. Corporate responsibility is a catchword of the adversary culture that is so evident today. If something is wrong with American society, blame business . . . The dull cloud of pessimism and distrust which some have cast over free enterprise is impairing the ability of business to meet its basic economic responsibilities – not to mention its capacity to take on newer ones (see Schnaiberg, 1973:606).

While business increased its lobbying against environmentalists and in doing so commanded much greater economic resources, the environmental movement lost some of its support. The Ford Foundation withdrew its support for environmental law groups, and labour, which tended to support environmentalists in the early 1970s, increasingly began to side with industry when economic recession set in, largely in fear that further environmental legislation would increase unemployment (Mitchell and Davies, 1978, 26–27; Buttel, 1975).

The decline of the environmental movement can also be attributed to the containment of the issue through political and legislative changes. P. D. Lowe (1975(a)) has shown how the *Torrey Canyon* disaster produced a series of governmental responses, including the setting up of an *ad hoc* committee under Sir Solly (now Lord) Zuckerman to consider the affair. After adverse press publicity responsibility for further investigation was also passed to the Select Committee on Science and Technology which established a sub-committee on Coastal Pollution. Recommendations from this committee made little headway, being stifled by Whitehall bureaucracy, but meanwhile environmental concern was broadening and containment of environmental concern by the existing structure of committees was clearly impossible. So in July 1969, on the recommendation of the Central Advisory Council, a change in government organization was announced: a new Department of the Environment was to be created. In December 1969, the Prime Minister announced further changes: the creation of a permanent Central Scientific Unit on Pollution and a standing Royal Commission on Environmental Pollution.

In the field of environmental planning other committees had been set up, notably the Skeffington Committee. The main proposal of this committee, which reported in 1968, was for greater public participation in planning. This was also to be a principal recommendation of a series of reports by the Royal Commission on Environmental Pollution. The policy of furthering public participation in environmental planning and pollution control has been a recurring theme in legislation, notably the Town and Country Planning Act 1968 and the Control of Pollution Act 1974. The expanded role of public participation in planning accounts for the continued growth of pressure groups after other indications had shown a slackening public interest in the environment. Pressure group involvement rather than their exclusion has been one of the principal means of containment. Through concerned public monitoring it reduces the risk of serious environmental problems arising, and it also reduces the risk of embittered protest when plans are finally settled. Pressure group involvement has also given rise to more effective political leverage (see Chapter 4).

Finally some factors that had been influential in the rise of environmental concern became less prominent. The Vietnam war came to an end and the hippie and youth culture, which had contributed to the environmentalist movement, disintegrated. The precipitous action of OPEC in 1973 no doubt also contributed to a significant shift of emphasis towards energy policy. However, this has helped to maintain the environmental movement, for more recently the fast-breeder reactor and a future dominated by nuclear power has increasingly become the *bête noire* of environmentalists (see Chapter 5).

This chapter has outlined the extent of the rise and partial decline of public concern about the environment. It has also offered a variety of explanations for these phenomena. The question of whether or not environmental issues arise from a plurality of interests, or whether economic interests associated with the development of capital are the most important determinants, has been of central importance. The debate between these two schools of thought is examined further in the following chapters.

2 Environmental Evaluation – Efficient and Just Distribution

In this chapter, an analysis is made of the neo-classical evaluation of environmental problems. Underlying assumptions of the efficacy of the market mechanism and the rational behaviour of participants will be scrutinized. The chapter begins by assessing the 'law and economics' school of thought which has attempted to demonstrate that legal doctrines, procedures and institutions have been influenced by an implicit and sometimes explicit concern to promote economic efficiency. The economist also believes that his analysis can help through improving legal rules to promote even greater efficiency. Nevertheless, a review of common law, one of the main topics for analysis by these economists, suggests that contradictions exist in principle and practice. It will be suggested that common law, and its legitimation by legal and economic theoreticians, tends to support economic interests and fails to promote economic efficiency.

Once the contradictions within the 'law and economics' school of thought have been established, a review is made of the Pigouvian tradition, which accepts the necessity of regulatory agencies acting in the public interest. The most important model here is that which suggests that the optimum level of pollution control occurs when any further reduction would lead to greater costs of control than benefits derived. Much debate among economists has focused on the comparative advantages of standards versus taxes as instruments of pollution control. It will be argued, however, that the efficiency model of pollution control appears to bear little relation to reality, for both standards and taxes are influenced and distorted by economic interests.

One of the main tools of the neo-classical economist in his search for efficiency in both pollution control policy and environmental planning in general is that of cost–benefit analysis. This technique is not, however, neutral in its application. The scope and form of its application will be influenced by economic and other interests. Its reliance upon market indicators for values also means that it tends to reflect and reinforce the distribution of wealth and other resources. In the last part of this chapter the difficulties of undertaking cost–benefit analysis will be discussed and its normative nature demonstrated.

An economic analysis of common law

THE THEORETICAL LIMITATIONS OF COMMON LAW AS A PROMOTER OF EFFICIENCY

The classical economic doctrine that individual self-interest is a natural state of affairs and that it leads to economic efficiency has been promoted with a good deal of enthusiasm. According to R. A. Posner, a notable exponent of this view, 'Participants in the legal process indeed behave as if they were rational maximizers: criminals, contracting parties, automobile drivers, prosecutors, and others subject to legal constraints or involved in legal proceedings act in their relation to the legal system as intelligent (not omniscient) maximizers of their satisfactions' (1975:763). Posner then argues that common law, by determining liability and hence responsibility, enables those engaged in the pursuit of self-interest to maximise the joint value of their activities.

The limitations of R. Coase's (1960) theorem are by now well known. Coase argued that strict liability, which in itself would lead to an inefficient allocation of resources, may nonetheless give rise to an efficient solution if the liable party bribes those concerned to allow the action to continue. Suppose, for example, that A, through the use of certain machinery, is found liable to B for causing a nuisance, and the value to A of using the machinery was £x, and the harm caused to B was £y. Then if £x is greater than £y, it would be worthwhile for A to bribe B by offering him an amount of between £y and £x. Such an amount would satisfy B as it would be greater than the gain resulting from the halting of A's machinery.

The problem with Coase's theorem is that it assumes skilful negotiation operating without cost. However, in reality transaction costs exist which involve obtaining necessary information as well as negotiating, drafting and enforcing a contract resulting from a bargain. This may result in substantial costs, especially if the nuisance is felt by more than just one individual. When it comes to bargaining over ocean pollution or even pollution within urban areas the number of parties involved makes such an operation impracticable. Bargaining may also be inappropriate in many situations which involve, say, the furtive disposal of toxic wastes in a ditch or a decision that affects future as well as present generations.

In reality the basic assumption that individuals are inveterate bargainers and litigators aspiring to 'maximize their own satisfactions' may be questioned. It is doubtful whether people really have this inclination, never mind the time or energy to pursue such single-minded selfishness. Most people, one might claim, are neither knowledgeable about the 'rules' of bargaining, nor equipped psychologically and financially to defend their own interests with the assistance of the legal profession. Nevertheless, let us for the moment go along with this assumption. If in the case above the transaction costs of, say, £z are greater than the difference between £x and £y then a contract will not be forthcoming and there would be an inefficient allocation of resources.

In recognition of the transaction costs problem Posner (1972(a)), and others, such as G. Calabresi and A. D. Melamed (1972), have argued that liability should be determined by considering the joint value or joint cost of continuing or halting the activity in question. In the case above no injunction would have been ordered as this would result in least cost (£y to B) and maximum joint value (£x – £y). Furthermore, the argument goes that if it is unclear which party is the 'least-cost abater' then liability ought to be determined by considering which party is in the best position to negotiate, and hence reduce transaction costs if a contract is forthcoming.

Posner (1972(b)) has tried to show how this principle of balancing the costs permeated the rules governing negligence law and so gave rise to increased efficiency. According to the orthodox legal and historical view, he argues, until the nineteenth century a man was liable for the consequences of accidents irrespective of whether he was negligent. But under the pressure of industrial expansion and *laissez-faire* there was a shift to the position where liability only accrued to those who had failed to take due care. Posner, however, takes a different view. Instead, he sees the change in interpretation of negligence as a response to the increasing demands for economic efficiency – the influence of utilitarianism, one assumes. The failure to take due care concept, he argues, allows the courts to balance firstly, the magnitude of the loss if an accident occurs, secondly, the probability of the accident's occurring and thirdly, the burden of taking precautions that would avert it. He gives evidence that this balancing of costs has taken place, and then argues that efficiency could be further enhanced if accident avoidance were balanced against accident prevention. It might, for example, be more efficient for industrial workers to wear protective clothing than for the firm to pay for extreme safety measures. Posner claims that 'perhaps, then, the dominant function of the fault system is to generate rules of liability that if followed will bring about, at least approximately, the efficient-cost-justified-level of accidents and safety.'

D. J. Storey has tried to refute Posner's view that common law promotes economic efficiency by referenc to its application to river pollution. 'The most important contradiction to Posner's law', he argues, 'concerns the right of riparian landowners to water "in its natural state of purity"' (1976:79). While Storey's empirical claim is supported by evidence in the UK, it is not supported entirely by evidence from other countries. Moreover, Storey gives no reason why the balancing of costs should not be applied to river pollution cases in the UK in the future if the insights of Posner and others are found persuasive. Such possibilities clearly exist with little change in interpretation of definitive statements such as that by Lord MacNaughton in the House of Lords in *John Young* v. *Bankier Distillery Co.*:

A riparian proprietor is entitled to have the water of the stream on which the banks of his property lies, flow down as it has been accustomed to flow down to his property, subject to the *ordinary use* of the flowing water by upper proprietors, and to such further use, if any, on their part in connection with their property as may be reasonable under the circumstances. Every riparian proprietor is thus entitled to the water of his stream, in its natural flow, *without sensible diminution* or increase and *without sensible alteration* in its character or quality. Any invasion of this right causing actual damage or calculated to found a claim which may ripen into an adverse right entitles the party injured to the intervention of the court (1893:698).
(author's italics)

In this standard interpretation of riparian rights the words 'ordinary use', 'reasonable', 'without sensible diminution', and 'without sensible alteration' clearly imply the possibility at least of balancing costs. In the English courts, it is true that there has been to date a strict adherence to the principle of 'natural flow'. For example, in *Brocket* v. *Luton Corporation* (1948) a riparian landowner obtained an injunction against the discharge of sewage effluent. Despite the fact that the defendant spent over £200,000 on effluent treatment, the courts were unsatisfied that the water came to the riparian owner in its *natural* state. The defendant's remedy as a result was to spend £80,000 on buying the bed of the water course and so removing the effect of the injunction.

In America some courts have adopted 'natural flow' principle but others have stressed the economic implications of reasonable use. J. C. Juergens-meyer (1971) has contrasted the two interpretations. Thus in *Mann* v. *Willey* (1900) a downstream owner was granted an injunction to stop the discharge of sewage from a summer hotel, despite the fact that the plaintiff was making no use of the river. On the other hand, in *Lockwood* v.

Brentwood Park Investments Ltd. (1967) J. Coffin argued that four items had to be proved if the plaintiff were to succeed: wrongful interference with flow; substantial diminution; damage which is not trivial; and unreasonable use. In the *Borough of Westville* v. *Whitney Home Builders*, an injunction was refused on the ground of an economic assessment of reasonable use:

Our conception is, rather, that a determination as to the existence of an actionable invasion of the unquestionable property right of a riparian owner in the flow of the water course depends upon a weighting of the reasonableness, under all circumstances, of the use being made by the defendant and of all the materiality of the harm, if any, found to be visited by such use upon the reasonable uses of the water by the complaining owner (1956:244–45).

So the problem with using empirical evidence to refute Posner's law is that the evidence is only partially satisfactory, and it certainly doesn't deal with the question whether or not common law may be reformed to enhance economic efficiency. Perhaps the most obvious question raised by the empirical evidence is: why do the courts not balance the costs in every case, and why is the strict liability rule still of great importance? The answer lies in part in the economic consequences if this were the norm. If every case of common law were dealt with on its own merits the amount of litigation would escalate for all those cases where the least-cost abater was in dispute. If one assumes that all people rationally 'maximise their own interests', then in a complex society this type of additional litigation cost would undermine the apparent economic advantage of balancing the costs. As A. J. Ogus and G. M. Richardson argue, 'the advantage of strict liability is that in the great majority of cases it obviates the need for litigation and enables the parties to proceed with Coasian bargaining, which will be cheaper than forcing the court to indulge in expensive cost-abatement inquiries' (1977:316).

Balancing the costs or the 'least-cost abater' solution may also give rise to blatant cases of injustice. It may, for example, be cheaper for a householder to install sound-proofing insulation than for a manufacturer to reduce his factory's noise levels. It would seem unjust, however, for the manufacturer to avoid liability and for the householder to pay for the sound-proofing. In this particular case the payment of damages might well be the most fair and efficient solution. However, the question of whether damages or an injunction should be awarded gives rise to similar problems to those of deciding between strict liability and balancing costs.

There are two fundamental and complementary principles that are recognized as guidelines for equitable remedies. The first was delineated by R. Evershed in *Pride of Derby* v. *British Celanese Ltd.* He specified the conditions for an injunction as follows: 'If A proves that his proprietory rights are being wrongfully interfered with by B, and B intends to continue his wrong, then A is prima facie entitled to an injunction, and he will be deprived of that remedy only if special circumstances exist' (1953:181). The general principle for awarding damages was outlined by A. L. Smith in *Shelfer* v. *City of London Electric Lighting Co.* Damages would be awarded instead of an injunction: 'if the injury to the plaintiff's legal right is small; if it is one which is capable of being estimated in money; if it is one which can be adequately compensated by a small money payment; if the case is one in which it would be oppressive to the defendant to grant an injunction' (1895:322).

These principles merely act as guidelines and are open to wide interpretation. On the whole, balancing the costs when determining equitable remedies has been uncommon, and the general norm has been much closer to the view of Page-Wood V.C. in *Att. Gen.* v. *Birmingham* when he granted an injunction on the grounds that 'it is a matter of almost absolute indifference whether the decision will affect a population of 250,000 or a single individual carrying on a manufactory for his own benefit' (1958:539–40). On the other hand, the rules of *Shelfer* were, for example, more liberally interpreted in Canada than in England during the early part of the twentieth century. Justice J. Middleton considered it important to balance the costs to the defendant against the cost of the nuisance when determining the remedy of injunction or damages. In *Sub. Nom. Black* v. *Canadian Coppper Co.* he justified the award of modest damages on the ground that:

Mines cannot be operated without the production of smoke from the roast yards and smelters, which smoke contains very large quantities of sulphur dioxide. There are circumstances in which it is impossible for the individual so to assert his individual rights as to inflict a substantial injury upon the whole community. If the mines should be prevented from operating, the community could not exist at all (1917:243).

One way of balancing the costs while maintaining a strict and predictable rule for determining liability would be to compensate the defendant if an injunction is awarded. In practice this has rarely been considered although there has been one recent case in the United States. In *Spur Industries* v. *Del E. Webb Development* (1972) the court awarded an injunction on the condition that the plaintiffs compensated the defendant for any reasonable costs in relocating their cattle foodstuffs business which had resulted in various nuisances including flies and smells. Calabresi and Melamed (1972) argue that this type of settlement could be particularly useful when the court is unsure of the least-cost abater; the plaintiff would not pay compensation costs if he is able to avoid nuisance more cheaply. Moreover a compensatory solution may in certain cases be more just than an injunction alone.

Both the 'Middleton thesis' and the injunction with compensation are possible methods of settling rights with the least-cost abater. However, as has already been argued, this balancing of costs leads to uncertainty and increased litigation. We may summarize the argument so far as follows. If strict liability is the norm and an efficient solution requires continuing activity of the liable party then efficiency may be prevented as a result of the transaction costs necessary to form a contract between affected parties. On the other hand, if the norm is that the award of damages or an injunction is determined by considering the costs to the parties concerned then precedent becomes less important and efficient solutions may be prevented through litigation costs. In both cases, as society becomes more complex, efficiency becomes less likely because transaction costs increase and the determination of the least-cost abater becomes more problematic and costly.

COMMON LAW: ECONOMIC AND POLITICAL INTEREST

The argument that common law leads to efficient settlements is further weakened by a consideration of the context in which the law operates. The difficulties and constraints upon individuals defending their rights in common law are extremely important in this respect. To determine who was negligent or the perpetuator of a nuisance has become more problematic in a mass urban society. In Britain, the problems of proof are exacerbated by secrecy, perpetuated by the Official Secrets Act and statutory legislation which still shrouds the activities of pollution control enforcement bodies. Expert scientific and technical evidence is almost certain to be necessary in order to prove that damage has occurred and that it was caused by the defendant's activity. In the case of isolated accidental damage, this problem is greater still. G. Newson and J. G. Sherratt explain the difficulties facing the riparian proprietor:

In certain cases it can be the greatest good luck that a sample of the river water is taken while the poison is still in it. To take such a sample an observer must act very promptly and must know what to do. It is important, even if the observer arrives too late to take a sample, for the dead fauna to be collected, for accurate observations to be made and noted to show exactly when and where the mortality began, and for a biologist to be summoned promptly to trace, by examination of the river bottom, the extent and situation of the area of damage (1972:13).

Clearly the question of whether the riparian owner is leisured and wealthy is not unimportant in determining his bargaining power and position *vis-à-vis* litigation, if this were necessary to defend his property rights. The costs and time involved in successfully pursuing litigation make it unlikely that the majority of people – given the economic conditions in modern capitalist societies – would seek protection from the courts. The system of legal aid has had little effect, as even those with modest means are likely to have to contribute substantially to the costs of litigation (McLoughlin, 1976). For these reasons, the assumption that participants in the legal profession behave as rational maximizers must be rejected unless one adds the important rider that the participants can only do so within the constraints and circumstances of economic life. For these reasons also property rights are only weakly protected by common law.

Had strict liability been fully enforced then no doubt this would have acted as a considerable brake on industrial progress. If this had been the case one might have expected to see common law being penetrated by the balancing of costs principle as a means of defending industrial and economic power, the reason being that balancing costs, unlike strict liability, enables the defendant to continue his activity if its curtailment would involve greater costs. Balancing costs would also weaken the bargaining power of those affected by the activities of the defendant, for there would be increased uncertainty over property rights – the more so in a society where information is not freely and cheaply available. Litigation costs would increase and the plaintiff would have to determine whether the defendant was likely to be the least-cost abater, an onerous task in the David and Goliath situation of poor individual versus industry.

It is not surprising then that when balancing the costs has been the court's response to complaints – for example, in nuisance law in England since the 1860s and 1870s – this has generally worked against the interests of the working class. Perhaps the most influential ruling in this respect was made in the House of Lords by Lord Westbury, L.C., in *St Helen's Smelting Co.* v. *Tipping* (1865). The judgement upheld the ruling that the company should be responsible for physical damage to trees, hedges, fruit and cattle, but not for substantial discomfort. Material injury was strictly defended whereas amenity loss (including inconvenience and injury to health) was determined by 'the circumstances of the place where the thing complained of actually occurs'. This distinction between physical damage and amenity damage considerably hindered actions in the industrial and urban areas. As property values often rose in polluted areas nuisance proceedings became largely irrelevant to the progress of industrialization, and the consequences of pollution could be ignored (see Brenner, 1974). On the other hand, the consideration of locality with respect to amenity damage helped to protect the environs of the rich. L. J. Thesiger's well-known comments in *Sturges* v. *Bridgman* exemplify the point: 'whether anything is a nuisance or not is a question to be determined, not by an abstract consideration of the thing itself, but in reference to its circumstances; what would be a nuisance in Belgrave Square would not necessarily be a nuisance in Bermondsey' (1879:852).

The efficiency of common law and its distributional consequences are also determined by the range of interests that are protected by law. In Britain, Canada and Australia common law has largely been orientated towards protecting private property *per se*. In the United States, however, rights which may be protected by law have been considerably broadened to meet the changing conditions of the 1960s and 1970s. The law of standing changed markedly after 1965 when *Scenic Hudson Preservation Conference* v. *Federal Power Commission* (1965) held that unincorporated associations could have access to the courts to challenge the exercise of federal power on aesthetic, conservational or recreational grounds, instead of considering economic grounds alone. Since then several statutes have also broadened the types of 'legally protected interest'. For example, the Administrative Procedure Act gives individuals the right to seek redress when 'adversely affected or aggrieved by agency action within the meaning of a relevant statute'. A. O. Thorrold illustrates the relative openness of the American courts to environmental groups:

In a landmark case in 1972, the Supreme Court laid down that the Sierra Club would satisfy standing requirements if it could show that its members trekked over the mountain area in question.

A case of similar importance occurred when the Scientists' Institute for Public Information (SIPI) brought a suit against the Atomic Energy Commission for failure to produce on the Liquid Metal Fast-Breeder Reactor Programme 'Environmental Impact Statement' as required by law. Did SIPI have standing? The court accepted that as a group, one of whose principal aims was receiving and distributing information, they could suffer 'information injury' sufficient to give them standing in the matter (1975(a):11).

Despite the ability of common law to adapt its rules, procedures and criteria for determining liability, it has been argued that these changes have tended to reflect and reinforce economic and political interest rather than a search for economic efficiency. Indeed the failure of common law to adapt to the growing industrialization of capitalist societies was a principle reason for the introduction of statutory regulations to curb the worst forms of pollution. Given the high transaction and legal costs of protecting the environment through private action, it became necessary to form administrations that could promote environmental protection on behalf of the public as a whole. The neo-classical economist has, within the framework of the Pigouvian tradition, suggested that the regulatory agency's function ought to be to control pollution to the point where the marginal costs of pollution are equal to the marginal costs of the abatement.

The model of optimum pollution control and the case for and against pollution taxes

In a simplified model of pollution damage costs and pollution control costs, it is assumed, with the backing of empirical support (see Kneese and Schultze, 1975) that the marginal costs of pollution increase as pollution increases. At the same time, the costs of pollution control increase as the amount of pollution control undertaken is increased (see Figure 2.1). As with common law, there will be transaction costs which form part of the abatement costs, but these will be considerably less if an agency is responsible for controlling large numbers of sources of pollution. For common law, the costs and benefits of each instance of pollution and its effect on property and amenities have to be assessed on an individual basis if an efficient solution is to be achieved. Even for statutory control of pollution the administrative costs of pollution control are likely to be significant. In 1975 they amounted to 26 per cent of the total United States federal pollution control expenditure (Council on Environmental Quality, 1975:530).

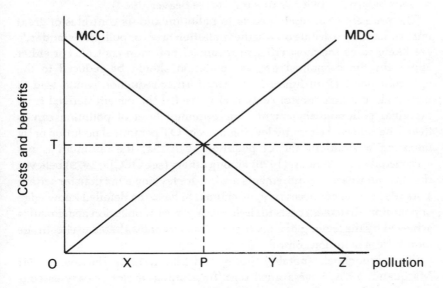

MDC = Marginal damage cost curve

MCC = Marginal pollution control cost curve

Figure 2.1 Model of pollution damage costs and pollution control costs

One of the main difficulties with the model of optimum pollution control is that of assigning economic values to damage caused by pollution. This is a problem that is shared with common law control of pollution and will be dealt with extensively under the heading of cost–benefit analysis later in this chapter. At this point it is merely worth noting that to a great extent the evaluation of pollution damages is dependent upon social priorities and standards of living. For example, it is clearly difficult to put a value on an ancient building threatened by pollution, and the assessment of pollution damage for amenities such as sandy beaches clearly depends upon the social demand for such amenities. Moreover, ignorance of the actual damage caused by pollution often makes it difficult to assign an economic cost to pollution.

The marginal pollution control costs are also hard to measure. If pollution control increases or decreases the efficiency of a production process this must be taken into account. Thus lead substitutes in petrol may add to the cost of petrol and also reduce the fuel efficiency of the automobile. On the other hand, the use of smokeless fuels such as oil or gas instead of coal not only reduces pollution from smoke but often leads to greater efficiency in manufacturing. In the pottery industry, for example, oil and electric kilns were introduced in large numbers for efficiency reasons before the 1956 Clean Air Act (see Beaver, 1964).

The problem of assigning costs to pollution and its control is of great importance in the debate on whether pollution taxes or pollution standards are likely to be the most efficient means of pollution control. For either approach, the economist argues, pollution should be reduced to the optimum point (P in figure 2.1). Any further reduction would lead to marginal pollution control costs that exceeded the benefit derived from marginal pollution abatement. The optimum level of pollution can in theory be achieved either by levying a tax of OT per unit of pollution or by imposing a standard OP of pollution such that the optimum is not exceeded. W. Beckerman (1975) among others (see OECD, 1973) believes that the information requirements are less for levying a tax than for setting a standard. It is not necessary, he claims, to have the detailed knowledge of pollution abatement costs for if the wrong level of pollution abatement is achieved by the levying of a tax then the tax is merely altered to encourage more or less pollution control.

Other economists (notably Storey and Elliott, 1977; Burrows, 1974; Marquand, 1976) have argued that 'fine-tuning' is not as easy as suggested. J. Marquand, for example, points out that 'a firm may incur very substantial expenditure to move from one point to another. It will be impossible for it to deliver minor adjustments in the amount of pollution it emits in exchange for relatively small payments' (1976:838). In order to avoid the 'lock-in' effect of an incorrect tax level, it is claimed that more information is required for setting taxes than for standards.

Even if the marginal social cost of pollution control curve is known in great detail it is still difficult to predict the effect of the tax. Firms may prefer to pay pollution taxes out of revenue expenditure rather than undergo capital expenditure which is more likely to be limited by internal rationing. There may be greater returns on investment from, say, industrial expansion than from pollution control. Thus a firm that invests in pollution control to reduce pollution taxes may suffer an 'opportunity cost' of not investing elsewhere. On the other hand a firm may wish to make additional investments in pollution control as part of its image management policy. Burrows claims that, because of the difficulty of predicting the effect of a pollution tax, the 'lock-in' effect and the additional costs imposed by 'fine-tuning', pollution control policy is better achieved by the application of exogenously determined environmental standards.

The debate over the efficiency of taxes and standards have not been limited to information requirements alone. Economists have claimed that a pollution tax would provide an innovative incentive. Any technical progress would lead to a reduction in pollution control costs and at the same time to a reduction in pollution. The collection of pollution taxes could be used to finance pollution control administration or compensate those affected by pollution.

There are also allocative advantages in a pollution tax. These occur when there are multiple discharges in what may be regarded as the same environment. Firms causing pollution usually have different marginal social costs of reducing pollution. For example, the costs of reducing the biochemical oxygen demands of effluents are much higher in petroleum refining than in sugar-beet refining (Kneese and Schultz, 1975). It makes economic sense for firms with the lowest pollution control costs to undertake most of the pollution control. If firms have to meet the same standard then the overall costs will be much greater.

In a hypothetical example involving two firms A and B which both give rise to x pollution control expenditure (see figure 2.2), when tax OT is levied then an allocative advantage would automatically be achieved. Firm B with the greater pollution control costs would prefer to reduce its pollution only to point P_B and pay more taxes than Firm A. Firm A would want to reduce pollution to P_A and pay much less tax than Firm B. Had both firms been expected to reduce their pollution to the same level P (where $P = \frac{1}{2}P_A + P_B$) then the extra pollution control cost to Firm B would have considerably outweighed the savings by Firm A (see hatched area). The tax system therefore ensures that those firms that can most cheaply reduce pollution do most of the pollution control.

The pollution tax allows the polluter to decide whether to pay more or less tax. If, for example, automobile exhaust fumes were taxed, a car owner might prefer to pay more tax on his petrol if he used his car infrequently rather than spend a lot of money on exhaust control emission

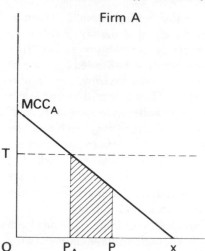
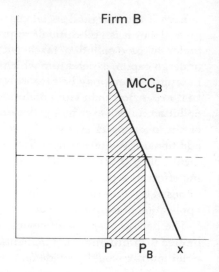

MCC$_A$ = Marginal pollution control cost curve for Firm A
MCC$_B$ = Marginal pollution control cost curve for Firm B

Figure 2.2   Pollution control costs of two firms

devices and pay a lower level of tax on petrol. Those car owners that use their cars more often would prefer to control their exhaust emissions and avoid paying so much tax. Thus the tax system would result in allocative advantages.

Economists such as Beckerman, who have claimed that pollution taxes are more efficient than pollution standards, have been surprised by the resistance to the imposition of taxes by politicians, industry, civil servants and the public. Indeed, where pollution taxes have been introduced they have generally been applied at a level that is inadequate to achieve the desired levels of pollution control (see Foster 1976; OECD 1973). In Britain, the Public Health Act 1937 gave local authorities the right to impose a charge on industrial wastes discharged into public sewers. Most local authorities, however, failed to charge the true cost of treatment (Freeman, 1977). In France, a system of charges was introduced by the 1964 legislation on water management and pollution control. These taxes were also set at an inadequate level (Majone, 1976(a) and (b)).

The failure of pollution taxes and the opposition to them can largely be explained in terms of corporate interests. Pollution taxes introduced under the Public Health Act 1937 were inadequate largely because local authorities wanted to attract industry at a time of high unemployment. Industry was therefore in a strong bargaining position (Freeman, 1977). In France, industrial interests were strongly represented on the basin commissions which were responsible for negotiating the level of charges with the basin agency (Majone 1976(a) and (b)). Generally, industry prefers a system of standards because it is easier to delay meeting them and to avoid prosecutions. Tax avoidance is likely to be less easy than the abuse of standards. Litigation, which has been a common technique for postponing the application of a standard in America, would be less likely with a system of taxes. In any case, a firm would still have to pay a tax while litigation is proceeding.

A pollution tax would force industry to pay a charge straight away, whereas the cost of meeting a standard is only incurred during and after the process of installing abatement equipment. Moreover, the firm has to pay a charge on the pollution that remains after treatment which would not be the case when a standard is applied. It is not therefore surprising that industrialists have resisted the imposition of pollution taxes. Ideological rhetoric such as the accusation that pollution taxes are a 'licence to pollute' has often been used to attack the tax proposals.

Instead of the achievement of efficient pollution through the application of taxes or standards, history has shown industry's great resistance to effective legislation and enforcement of the law. In the nineteenth century, the most effective pollution control legislation, the Alkali Act 1863, came about largely because of the threat to the large landed estates of Lord Derby and other landowners. Following the Act, and in less than two years, the quantity of waste acidic fumes emitted was reduced from 13,000 tons to forty-three tons. Manufacturers also gained from the legislation in that new and profitable uses were found for the condensed hydrochloric acid. Legislation protected the industry by legitimating low levels of pollution which could otherwise have been a cause of law action.

Although there has been a growth of state activity in the twentieth century, there has also been an increase in the number of partnerships between government and industry. Corporate interests have been well positioned to influence the development of pollution control policy at early and crucial stages in its development. H. J. Steck (1975) has illustrated how American advisory committees, such as the Advisory Council on Federal Reports and the National Industrial Pollution Council, have played an important role in ensuring that corporate interests are protected.

In Britain, the Clean Air Act 1956 was riddled with loopholes which enabled industry to develop its own independent fuel policy. There was a seven-year exemption period for converting to smokeless fuels. The adoption of smoke control areas (rather than smokeless zones) was the discretionary responsibility of local authorities. This allowed industrial pressure and the threat of unemployment to be applied if necessary at the local level (see Foulkes, 1970).

The close relationship between industry and the Alkali Inspectorate, which is responsible for controlling complex air pollution emissions, has been well documented by J. Bugler (1972) and M. Frankel (1974). They claim that this alliance between industry and the inspectorate has led to few prosecutions and a poor record of enforcement. Water pollution control in Britain similarly suffers from extensive abuse of standards by industry and a low level of prosecutions (see Storey, 1977 and Sandbach, 1977(a)). In the *Un-Politics of Air Pollution*, M. A. Crenson (1971) demonstrated the power of corporations in influencing the development of pollution control policy. Those cities with strong industrial corporations were best able to hinder the development of air pollution regulations. They were also better able to influence the form that regulations took when they were eventually implemented.

Such delays and modifications to pollution control policy in the interests of industry have been common in both America and Britain. One further example is that of automotive emissions control in America. Controls were introduced in California on 1961 model cars. They were applied in the first instance to hydrocarbon emissions, but in 1966 were made more restrictive and also extended to carbon monoxide emissions. In 1964, car manufacturers campaigned to prevent implementation of effective controls. There is some evidence that industrial collusion took place because an anti-trust suit alleging collusion was later brought by the federal government in 1969 and this was settled by a consent decree in the same year. Car manufacturers agreed to comply with deadlines only when the State Motor Vehicle Pollution Control Board declared that there were already at least two practical systems for meeting the required standards (see White 1976(a) and (b)).

In 1970, the Clean Air Act established comprehensive federal standards for carbon monoxides and hydrocarbons to be implemented by 1975 and for nitrogen oxides to be implemented by 1976. Five years after the Clean Air Act had been passed, little had been achieved that could not have been achieved without legislation. H. Margolis refers to a comment made by Senator Muskie (the promoter of the Clean Air Act 1970) to the presidents of the car companies when they requested a five-year extension of the standards:

The fact is that insofar as the automobile is concerned you are in no different position as the result of the passage of the Clean Air Act than you would have been if the Clean Air Act hadn't been passed. The standards you are now meeting, you agreed to meet in 1969. . . . I am frustrated, frankly (1977:15).

Despite Muskie's frustration at the failure to force industry to improve its pollution control measures, deadlines for the introduction of standards have been extended by the US government on numerous occasions. The Clean Air Act Amendments 1977 postponed the enforcement of standards of hydrocarbon emissions to 1980, and carbon monoxide and nitrogen oxide emissions until 1981. In addition, the standard of nitrogen oxide omissions was relaxed.

Delaying the imposition of emissions standards and relaxing the nitrogen oxide emissions standard were legitimated in part by the oil crisis in 1973 and the economic depression, but also by cost–benefit studies which suggested that the total damage costs estimated at $20 billion would be exceeded by $1 billion if the cost of the Environmental Protection Agency's standards current in 1972 were complied with (see Peskin, 1975). Cost–benefit analysis has played an enormous part in influencing pollution control policy and environmental policy in favour of market considerations and now deserves close scrutiny.

Studies aimed at assessing the market value of an environmental resource or the damage caused

Four distinct stages are involved when undertaking a cost–benefit analysis: identifying possible effects on the environment, costs, benefits, risks and uncertainties; attributing economic costs and benefits; assessing the effect of time and future uncertainties; deciding upon the criteria for comparing projects – namely, cost/benefit ratio, benefit minus cost, or the internal rate of return. Cost–benefit analysis has tended in practice to be associated with a rather narrow approach where only those elements that can be easily translated into cash terms are included for comparison. Because of costs and the technical difficulties of investigation, it has been argued, it is desirable to ignore certain effects on the environment.

IDENTIFYING EFFECTS ON THE ENVIRONMENT, COSTS, BENEFITS, RISKS AND UNCERTAINTIES

Typically, cost–benefit analysis in transport studies exclude effects other than those upon users of transport facilities. They also tend to identify definite effects rather than probable effects. Travel costs on a road network, in Department of Environment analyses, comprise: (a) vehicle-operating costs; (b) working and non-working time costs; (c) accident costs. The assessment of these costs is extensively used in road planning to select a particular scheme from various others (Transport Policy, 1976). Cost–benefit analysis has been criticized for its restricted assessment of the variables involved in any problem; it is claimed that ignoring less easily quantifiable environmental and social effects leads to misleading conclusions. Thus P. Self criticized the legendary Roskill cost–benefit analysis of the proposed schemes for London's third airport on the grounds that the 'cost–benefit figures are incredible, not only because of the disparate basis of the items included, but because of the important items excluded' (1970:254). Two alternatives to the cost–benefit analysis framework for identifying effects of any scheme are policy analysis and risk analysis.

A. Williams (1972) suggests that some have been tempted to reject cost–benefit analysis on the grounds of so many studies being wrongly conceived; poorly understood, and misguidedly acted upon or not acted on at all. According to Y. Dror (1967) policy analysis is distinguished as follows:

1 Much attention would be paid to the political aspects of decision-making and public policy-making (instead of ignoring or condescendingly disregarding political aspects) . . .
2 A broad conception of decision-making and policy-making would be involved (instead of viewing all decision-making as mainly a resource allocation) . . .
3 A main emphasis would be on creativity and search for new policy alternatives, with explicit attention to encouragement of innovative thinking . . .
4 There would be extensive reliance on . . . qualitative methods . . .
5 There would be much more emphasis on futuristic thinking . . .
6 The approach would be looser and less rigid, but nevertheless systematic, one which would recognize the complexity of means–ends interdependence, the multiplicity of relevant criteria of decision, and the partial and tentative nature of every analysis . . . (quoted by A. Wildarsky, 1969:190).

Risk analysis has also developed as a means of decision analysis offering a holistic approach to evaluating environmental consequences where uncertainties predominate. There are two key methods: fault-tree and event-tree analyses. The interrelations between the components of an operating system are in each case shown by a tree structure so that pathways to disaster may be traced. Event-trees start from undesirable initiating events, whereas fault-trees start with undesirable final events and work backwards. The most difficult factors to account for involve human error, predictions of changes in the world in which the technology functions, confidence in scientific and technological knowledge, the operation of a safety system as a whole, and 'common mode failure' where various safety factors have a common fault such as a defective metal (Fischoff, 1977).

In the case of nuclear power stations, unpredictable human error was shown when a fire was started in one of the world's largest nuclear power plants, the Browns Ferry. The fire was started by a technician checking for an air leak with a candle, a direct violation of operating procedures. The fire got out of control because of delays in sounding the alarm. Unanticipated changes in the operating environment are illustrated by the great blackout of 1965 which drew attention to back-up electrical power sources which are necessary if a reactor should fail and need to be shut down. The 'common mode failure' was again illustrated by the Browns Ferry fire which caused the core to overheat and also damaged the electrical system, so preventing the shut-down of the plant. Disaster was only averted when make-shift machinery, usually used to operate control rods, was used to pump water to cool the reactor core with water. Further problems exist in assessing risks of sabotage and predicting consequences of a loss-of-coolant accident in the absence of any full-scale simulation of the total safety system (Fischoff, 1977).

ATTRIBUTING ECONOMIC COSTS AND BENEFITS

Cost–benefit analysis as traditionally understood depends upon establishing prices for environmental resources and the consequences of development projects. Its adherents have attempted to establish techniques and procedures for setting-up comparable estimates of prices. Some of the difficulties and pitfalls are illustrated by (a) property price indicators; (b) travel costs; (c) techniques of measuring air pollution damage.

(a) *Property price indicators.* Changes in property prices may be used in evaluating costs of amenity loss and pollution. For example, it has been claimed that if people value peace and quiet, then this will be reflected in the housing market; prices should, it is argued, be lower in noisy areas than in quiet areas (see Hedges, 1972). The much debated Roskill Commission's cost–benefit analysis for the third London airport included an extensive assessment of the costs to households displaced and the noise costs of those remaining in the neighbourhood. Estimates of effects on property prices have also been undertaken in assessing air pollution damage (Anderson and Crocker, 1971), and also in assessing the benefits brought by recreational sites (Byers, 1970).

In the Roskill study, environmental costs were based on estimated depreciation of property, removal expenses, and 'consumer surplus' or the value above the market value at which a family would be willing to sell. Estimates of depreciation were calculated by investigating property prices around Gatwick and Heathrow. Calculations were made, after consultation with estate agents, of differences in market prices between equivalent properties suffering varying amounts of aircraft disturbance.

This kind of approach to evaluating costs and benefits has been much criticized, not least on the grounds that it is very difficult to disentangle disadvantageous environmental effects on house prices from social benefits such as being near a better transport network. The extra housing demand created by more jobs resulting from a particular project or development programme also distorts the issue. It is consequently little wonder that in certain circumstances road traffic noise appears to have had no significant effect on property prices despite the indications from psychological and sociological studies which suggest that people are more sensitive to road noise than to aircraft noise (see Pearce, 1976). In one study in North Birmingham, house prices tended to be higher on the noisy Queslett ringroad than the quieter local roads. In another study in America, a survey of rents paid for similar apartments with different levels of noise produced no apparent evidence that the occupants' annoyance was reflected in rent levels (Sharp and Jennings, 1976).

The market value of property or land may be a very poor guide to policy where there is conflict over various possible uses of land. Thus agricultural land valued at between £50 and £500 per acre (in 1972) might be worth £5,000–£15,000 per acre for urban use. If land values were the sole guide for planning policy then there would be little protection against the use of grades 1 and 2 agricultural land for urban development (Boddington, 1973). Unfortunately, the influence of property prices with high financial returns on offices, conference centres, hotels and marinas have often led to their development at the expense of much needed low-income housing (Ambrose, 1975).

Self has stressed the importance of adopting certain standards and rules of conduct which act as constraints on the evaluation process. For example, the social ideal of maintaining healthy rural communities may be a perfectly adequate justification for maintaining an unprofitable railway or bus service. Furthermore, priorities should be given to the preservation of grades 1 and 2 agricultural land; and certain urban areas should be designated as conservation areas, pedestrian routes or precincts and noise abatement zones. Such designations should be made on the grounds of principle rather than crude economic determinism. In practice, town and country planning is often based upon simple assumptions about desirable goals and their realization. Broad delineation of such objectives may have distinct advantages over narrowly construed numerate analysis (see Self, 1975). On the other hand, the economist will argue that trade-offs between competing desirable objectives may still be necessary, and unless one is willing to give infinite value to the preservation of agricultural land or old buildings, some price must be agreed.

Reliance upon market values is likely to lead to problems of equity and social distribution. Differences in income, education, occupation, age, etc. will affect mobility which will lead to differential changes in the housing market (see Nuaneri, 1970). In two studies on the London airports at Heathrow and Gatwick, it was found that depreciation in house value was four times greater for 'high-class' property than for 'low-class' property. Consequently, only small values would be attached to amenity loss in working-class sections of the community (see Rothman, 1972). This problem of distributional values lies at the core of cost–benefit analysis. In principle, one could adopt a weighting system. For example, one could ensure that the costs to the poor count for more than the costs to the rich. However, as Self has remarked 'clearly there are almost as many views upon the precise weight to be attached to these "distributional" or "generational" values as there are people in Britain' (1970:245). The normative nature of cost–benefit analysis and the distributional implications therefore means that it is very susceptible to distortion by economic interests.

The use of householders' surplus 'or the amount residents would need to be bribed to compensate them for the loss of particular environmental amenities' has some advantages over the use of house property values. It avoids the inclusion of property values which may reflect other than environmental influences. It might also give some idea of the resistance to proposed plans as shown by the respondents who place infinite values on their homes or in some other way refuse to conform to the questionnaire. In some instances, however, it may be very difficult to demonstrate to those being interviewed the implications of a particular change in nuisance. For example, most people would not know what an increase in noise of 10 dBA would signify. Moreover, survey results have been shown to be highly dependent upon the way the question is posed.

In the Roskill study there was a sample survey of households that would have been displaced by the third London airport, and people were asked the following question: 'Suppose your house was wanted to form part of a large development scheme and developer offered to buy it from you, what price would be just high enough to compensate you for leaving this house (flat) and moving to another area?' For those that would be affected by noise but would not be displaced, the following question was asked: 'What is the minimum sum you would accept to reconcile yourself to the increase in aircraft noise to which you are, and in the future will be, subjected?' In the Roskill study, only 8 per cent of respondents indicated that no amount of money would compensate for their being uprooted. In this situation, the interviewer recorded an arbitrary figure of £5,000.

In another study on the third London airport, people were asked the following question: 'Suppose you discovered that house prices in this area were higher than prices in similar areas five or more miles away. Say that in those areas you could get a house comparable to this one and make £100

profit after all expenses, would you seriously consider moving? *If no,*
what would the difference have to be to make you seriously consider
moving?' To this type of question aimed at estimating the consumer
surplus attached to a home, 38 per cent indicated that no amount of money
would make them move (Plowden, 1970).

Mishan has argued 'it may be that a good interviewer would have
elicited a finite sum, though well in excess of £5,000 – perhaps £50,000 or
£5 million?' (1970:228). No doubt there is some truth in this, but
subjective evaluations in a survey situation are unlikely to bear much
relation to the same evaluations made under conditions of market exchange if it were possible (Self, 1975). Moreover, the 'householder
surplus' approach has distributional biases similar to those of a market
price approach. Again, differences in income, job, class, etc. influence
mobility and willingness to move.

(b) *Travel costs.* In the Roskill study on the third London airport, savings
in travel-time costs were of crucial importance in establishing the choice of
airports. Travel-time costs at 1968 prices were made up of business air
passengers' time (valued at 555 pence per hour); adult leisure air passengers' time (valued at 55 pence per hour); childrens' time (valued at 13
pence per hour); adult accompanying persons' time (valued at 39 pence
per hour); and paid drivers' time (valued at 128 pence per hour). It was
these travel-time cost elements that above all else were most important in
the Commission's dismissal of Foulness as a suitable site. If the travel-
time cost item had been removed, an entirely different order of ranking
would have resulted (table 2.1). Instead of Foulness having the greatest
disadvantage of £120 million, it would have had the greatest advantage of
£33 million.

It is not surprising then that the public inquiry focused on the value of
travelling time. Questions of when a holiday started, or whether or not
'business' time should be costed in terms of average income and em-

Table 2.1   *The Roskill study on the third London airport (from the Roskill
Commission Report)*

All discounted to 1975	Cublington £m	Foulness £m	Nuthampstead £m	Thurleigh £m
Travel-time costs	887	1,041	868	889
Total net costs	2,264.6	2,385.2	2,273.9	2,266.3
Total net costs minus travel-time costs	1,377.6	1,344.2	1,405.9	1,377.3

(*Source:* Newton, 1972:68 and 69)

ployers' overheads were crucial and yet largely unresolved. It could be claimed that in this sort of analysis the distinction between costs and benefits is often artificial. Time spent travelling to work or on holiday may well be considered enjoyable rather than an economic cost. In an analogous example, work may sometimes be considered a burden and sometimes a pleasure (Self, 1975). Buchanan was the only member on the Roskill Commission to dissent from the results of the cost–benefit analysis which favoured Cublington. He argued as a matter of principle that any of the inland sites would be an environmental disaster and favoured Foulness on both local and regional planning grounds.

If travel-time costs are considered an important factor there is inevitably a problem of weighting which is not a technical matter alone, and slight variations in values may produce very different results. Government transport policy in Britain has relied on cost–benefit analysis for inter-urban road schemes and all urban transport schemes. The major part of the benefits, some 80 per cent on average, usually accrue from time savings. The remaining benefits are attributed to accident savings (see table 2.2). Dislocation costs resulting from compulsory purchase and adverse amenity effects on new and existing roads are usually ignored. Such emphasis upon travel-time costs sways the argument against proposed by-pass roads for villages which suffer considerable environmental damage yet do not significantly hinder the speed of traffic. The case for a

Table 2.2 *Average benefits from a road improvement scheme*

	%
Accident savings	20
Vehicle operating cost savings	0
Working time savings:	
Cars	26
Light goods vehicles	11
Heavy goods vehicles	11
Buses	3
Non-working time savings:	
Cars	23
Buses	6
Total	100

(*Source:* Transport Policy, 1976:99)

by-pass, which probably involves a circuitous route, would not look favourable from the point of view of saving time, and therefore money.

The same situation exists in America. The AASHO Red Book, the official guide to cost–benefit analysis of road projects, also stresses the importance of travel-time cost and ignores most of the external social and environmental costs. Hence labour-intensive transportation systems such as cycle tracks tend to be regarded unfavourably. M. Everett (1977) has shown how cost–benefit analysis could be used to favour such schemes if the desirable effects they have on the community were taken into account. These could include, for example, increased opportunities for exercise, outdoor recreation and relaxation. In addition, such a scheme would involve a reduction in noise pollution, community disruption, and the isolation of non-drivers as a result of road-building projects.

In the Archway road-widening scheme, a cost–benefit analysis was conducted in 1973 by Scott, Wilson, Kirkpatrick and partners. Opponents of the scheme criticized the study for its bias in favour of the the car-driver. The working time of a car-driver was estimated at £1.68 per hour, a bus user at only £0.88 per hour, and the non-working travelling time of pedestrians at the rate of a mere £0.17 per hour for adults and £0.06 for children. 'In plain English', G. Stern argued, 'a bus-user is reckoned to be worth half as much as a car-driver, while a mother loaded down with shopping and two children only rates one-fifth as much attention as the car superman' (1977:35). The DOE (now Ministry of Transport) has argued that leisure time spent walking or waiting involves greater costs than similar time spent on a vehicle and accordingly values reductions in walking and waiting time for non-work trips higher by a factor of two than the value of 'in-vehicle' time. Nevertheless working time is considered to be very much more important than leisure time. The Department's recommended values in 1976 are shown in table 2.3.

A study by D. A. Quarmby (1967) in central Leeds suggested that the cost of bus travel time should be more highly valued than car time and that walking and waiting time should be valued at two or three times in-vehicle times. This would suggest much greater attention should be paid to pedestrians and buses than was given in the Archway road-widening scheme or even in the DOE guidelines. Once again there is the question of whether or not travel time should be considered as a cost or a benefit, and hence the importance attached to time-cost savings. Self asks: 'If they do mind, why do so many motorists sit patiently on the most crowded roads on a Sunday when there are so many alternatives open to them? Why do so many people make crowded journeys to work on the roads when they could exercise some influence for employment to be located in less-crowded centres?' (Self, 1975).

Whereas cost–benefit analysis has favoured the motorist by empha-

Table 2.3   *Value of time spent in travelling*

	Pence/hour
Working time	**1975 Values**
1. Car drivers	331
2. Car passengers	287
3. Rail passengers	357
4. Bus passengers	168
5. Underground passengers	313
6. HGV occupants	155
7. LGV occupants	139
8. Bus drivers	166
9. Bus conductors	158
Leisure time	
1. In-vehicle time	35
2. Walk/wait time	70

(*Source:* Transport Policy, 1976:99)

sizing the time saved through building better roads, time-cost analysis could equally well be employed to emphasize the futility of encouraging the motorist at the expense of other means of transport. Ivan Illich amusingly explains how inefficient the car may be made to appear:

The typical American male devotes more than 1,600 hours a year to his car. He sits in it while it goes and while it stands idling. He parks it and searches for it. He earns money to put down on it and to meet the monthly instalments. He works to pay for petrol, tolls, insurance, taxes and tickets. He spends four of his sixteen waking hours on the road or gathering resources for it. And this figure does not take into account the time consumed in other activities dictated by transport: time spent in hospitals, traffic courts and garages; time spent watching automobile commercials or attending consumer education meetings to improve the quality of the next buy. The model American puts in 1,600 hours to get 7,500 miles: less than five miles per hour (1974:30–31).

The other major quantifiable benefit accounted for in transport cost–benefit analysis is the cost per road accident. Departmental estimates are necessarily rather arbitrary (see table 2.4) and are obviously a focus for debate (see Transport Policy, 1976). The only significant changes in Departmental cost–benefit analysis during recent years have been a consideration of the effect on the whole road network rather than just the proposed new road, and the assessment of benefits over a thirty-year period rather than just one year. The importance of considering the whole transport network lies in the effects of a new road on transport flow rates for existing roads, and hence the influence on

Table 2.4   *Cost per road accident*

| | | | January 1976 price levels | |
	Urban	Rural	Motor-way	All
	£	£	£	£
Fatal	41,900	47,600	52,000	44,000
Serious	2,750	3,800	3,810	3,060
Slight	450	810	870	520
Average cost of an injury accident	1,810	4,240	4,120	2,360
Cost of damage only accident	220	270	310	230

The cost of each accident involving a fatality on motorways is higher than that for other roads because the accidnets that occur involve a larger number of casualties. The chances of having an accident on motorways are lower than on other roads.
(*Source:* Transport Policy, 1976:100)

travel-time costs. Estimating over thirty years also offers a more realistic assessment of the benefits arising from a new road.

Stern's rather colourful assessment of cost–benefit analysis as applied to transport policy unfortunately contains more than a grain of truth:

The basis for cost–benefit analysis can now be seen; by forecasting 'prove' that traffic will increase even if there is no road space or fuel available. Then ignore all factors except a few, and give these weights reflecting one's preconceptions. More specifically, weight the time of car and lorry drivers very heavily, and virtually ignore the mobility of others. Ignore deaths, noise, fumes, pollution and destruction on the scale of war. In some cases, it must be admitted, officials do allow for noise and deaths. They assess the value of a life by funeral costs, earning capacity and a few thousands to cover grief, etc (1977:36).

There are beginning to be signs that a broader approach to roads policy will be adopted as a result of pressure from environmental organizations, but as yet little action has been taken. Local authority road transport policy is formulated in annual Transport Policies and Programmes (TPP) statements. Although most councils make some reference to environmental considerations, these are usually couched in very general terms. However, some county councils do appear to be interested in using a 'points' evaluation system whereby points are awarded to road safety, environmental consequences, and the interests of pedestrians, public transport users, comercial vehicle users, business drivers, non-car users and commuters. These points could then be translated into cash figures and combined with data based upon current cost–benefit analysis. While the weighting of such points would again be of a non-technical nature and should be open to wide debate, they would help to make up a more realistic assessment of costs and benefits resulting from transport projects.

The travel-cost technique of cost–benefit analysis has also played an important part in attempts to evaluate recreational resources, an area of research stimulated by studies of river-basin development in America. In a review of such studies, G. H. Peters distinguishes between three possible approaches:

(a) The summation of travel costs of all visitors to an area, to arrive at an imputed evaluation of benefits. Travel is here regarded as a cost which must be paid and the total of the latter can be held to be relevant.
(b) The use of a 'consumer surplus' value, derived on the basis of a comparison of travel costs of users drawn from various distances from the recreation site.
(c) The derivation of a 'demand curve' for use of a particular site using travel cost data as a basic source of information (1970:205).

The 'demand curve' approach is the most comprehensive of the three approaches and has been associated with the work of Clawson (1959) and Knetsch (1963). Visit rates to a recreational centre are measured as a percentage of population in different zones, each containing 1,000 people and represented as concentric circles drawn around the centre. Distance travelled is then converted into travel cost. This may include a value for the time spent in travelling and the cost of transportation. In addition, any entry fee is added to the cost of the distance travelled. From this data, tables can be compiled of the total costs of visiting a recreational area and visits per 100,000 in each zone. Using regression analysis, one can calculate the number of probable visits given various changes in charge for the recreational site. A demand curve for the recreational resource can then be drawn in order to estimate the additional financial benefit and so arrive at an estimate of total social benefit.

A study of Grafham Water by R. J. Smith and N. J. Kavanagh (1969) illustrates the technique. People trout-fishing on Grafham Water were charged £1.00 per visit in 1967. A total number of visitors (21,143) gave a financial return of as many pounds in the season. Travel costs were worked out on the basis of those car costs defined by the Automobile Association as 'running costs' namely 1.575p per mile. The figure could have been as low as 0.83p per mile if petrol costs only were considered, or as high as 4.17p per mile if the full depreciation and maintenance costs were included. In this study, no account was taken of the travel-time costs of the journey. On the basis of one person travelling in each car (fishermen were regarded as solitary types and no attempt was made to investigate the number of passengers per car), travel costs per 100,000 population were calculated for eight zones of population (table 2.5). From these figures a demand schedule was worked out (table 2.6) and a demand curve (figure 2.3) drawn. The consumers' surplus or the amount anglers would have been willing to pay over and above the £1.00 fee per visit, £18,801, is

Table 2.5   *Travel costs from the Grafham Water study*

Zone	Length of return journey (miles)	Travel cost (pence)	Total cost (pence)	Visits per 100,000 population
A	23	36	136	589
B	69	110	210	359
C	115	181	281	81
D	161	253	353	35
E	230	362	462	9
F	322	507	607	2.8
G	414	652	752	1.2
H	506	797	897	1.2

(*Source:* Newton, 1972:151)

Table 2.6   *Final Clawson demand schedule for the recreation site, 1967*

Change in fishing charge from present level of 100p (in pence)	Actual charge (in pence)	No. of visits
0	100	21,143
20	120	15,837
40	140	12,270
60	160	9,734
80	180	7,865
100	200	6,447
120	220	5,347
140	240	4,477
160	260	3,755
180	280	3,194
200	300	2,737
220	320	2,345
240	340	2,014
260	360	1,786
280	380	1,499
300	400	1,295

(*Source:* Newton, 1972:15)

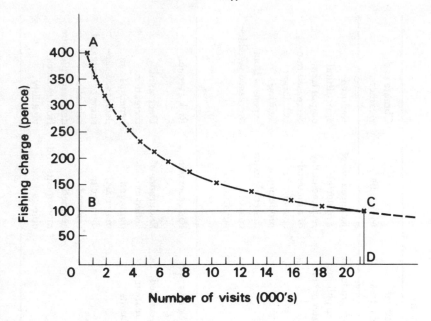

Figure 2.3   Demand curve from the Grafham Water study

(*Source:* Newton, 1972:152)

represented by the area ABC. The total social benefit of £39,944 is then calculated from the addition of revenue from fees and the consumers' surplus (21,143 + £18,801).

The Clawson demand approach is not without its critics. Indeed it has many of the snags of previously mentioned techniques. Empirical work by R. J. Smith (1971) on the benefits of trout-fishing on Grafham Water suggests that time spent on travelling had an important influence on visit rates. But others have doubted whether travel-time should be included, as many people positively enjoy travelling to a recreational site (Mansfield, 1969). Then there is the problem of isolating influences from other nearby recreational sites. Decisions to visit one site may be influenced by the proximity of other sites and the possibility of making most use of travel-time and costs.

A more difficult problem to overcome is the question of whether or not people choose their houses so as to be close to a recreational site. Some studies have demonstrated the obvious, namely that land prices reflect amenity value. For example, Beardsley (1972) has suggested that land values at the perimeter of Cape Cod National Seashore account for over 70 per cent of national economic benefits associated with the area. Another

Table 2.7 *Damage classification scheme with examples*

DAMAGE CATEGORY

	Human health	Fauna	Flora	Natural resources	Materials	Climate and weather
Financial loss	Productivity losses; health care costs including increased research costs to avoid pollution; premature burial costs	Lost animal and fish production	Reduced crop production; reduced forest growth	Lost production from polluted water or soil	Reduced life of a material; reduced utility of a material; cost of producing a material; extra cost of a substitute	Reduced agricultural output from decreased rainfall; larger lighting expenses from decreased sunshine
	Risk aversion	Risk aversion	Risk aversion	Risk aversion	Risk aversion	Risk aversion
Loss of amenity	Cost of Suffering; cost of bereavement; cost of limitations imposed upon an individual, his family and his society	Reduced pleasure from fishing and hunting; reduced wildlife populations	Reduced pleasure from horticultural and forestry losses	Decreased recreation benefits	Endurance of soiled or damaged materials; damage to selected aesthetic monuments and objects	Decreased recreation benefits from decreased sunshine or increased rainfall; decreased pleasure from reduced visibility

(*Source:* OECDm 1976:50)

study demonstrated that property doubled in value when a new park was created (Council on Environmental Quality, 1974). Because recreational sites influence land and property markets, these must be considered as part of the consumers' surplus, and so the Clawson method breaks down. An estimate of inflated house/land prices would have to be included if this reflected the influence of a nearby recreational site (see Anderson, 1974). However, the problem remains of determining the influence of recreational and other factors on the market value of housing. There may also be a distributional bias in the analysis, recreational resources nearer wealthier suburbs being given greater value than similar resources nearer poor communities.

Finally, there is the problem of evaluating a resource in terms of non-users. Many 'non-users' would be outraged if a natural beauty spot were spoilt or an historic monument destroyed, even if they had never visited it. The value of a resource clearly transcends that of its immediate users, but it would be extremely difficult to say by how much if a trade-off had to be made between losing an amenity and gaining economically by some project or other (see *Changing Directions*, 1974).

(c) *Air pollution damage.* Pollution damage results not only in the loss of amenity but also in tangible and measurable financial losses (see table 2.7). The Beaver Committee Report of 1954 classified the costs in two categories:

The *direct* costs include laundry and domestic cleaning, painting and repair of buildings; the corrosion of metals, which entails the cost not only of replacements but also of providing protective coverings, etc.; damage to goods; additional lighting and extra hospital and medical services, etc.; and secondly, the *loss of efficiency* includes, for example, the effects on agriculture of damage to soil, crops and animals, interference with transport, and reduced human efficiency due to illness (1954:11).

The Beaver Committee's estimates of air pollution damage in the UK of £230 million per annum were confined to the effects on property and health. Amenity costs were excluded. More recent estimates in the early 1970s which include amenity damage costs put the losses in the UK at £1,190 million per annum (see table 2.8). Local studies of air pollution damage in the Greater Manchester area alone have indicated that losses to all grassland (agricultural, permanent, recreational, cemeteries, etc.) amount to an estimated £500,000 per annum (Saunders, 1976). The costs of air pollution in the US for 1968 have been estimated to be health, $6.1 billion; residential property, $5.2 billion; materials and vegetation, $4.9 billion; giving a total of $16.2 billion damage (Council on Environmental Quality, 1973).

Table 2.8   *Estimated current total damage costs due to air pollution in the UK*

| Item | Costs (£ million/annum) | | | |
| | Economic | | Social | |
	Mean	SD	Mean	SD
Painting	–	–	6.3	2.5
Laundry, dry cleaning, etc.	0.5	0.1	164	60
Exterior cleaning of buildings	–	–	1.5	0.2
Window cleaning, etc.	5.0	0.2	–	–
Corrosion and protection of metals	42	28	–	–
Damage to textiles and paper	33	4.5	–	–
Agricultural production	195	110	–	–
Amenity – damage from:				
point sources	–	–	100	33
motor vehicles	–	–	3	1
Health	130	63	510	243
Rounded totals	410	130	(780)	(252)
Grand total			1,190	

Figures rounded to nearest whole number. ( ) = incomplete estimates.
The high levels of standard deviation (SD) clearly indicate the uncertainty and lack of reliable data of physical estimates of damage.
(*Source:* Saunders, 1976:94)

Although the effects of air pollution appear more tangible than those from development projects there is still a problem of specifying the effects and then putting a price on them. For example, there have been wide differences in estimates of health damage resulting from sulphur dioxide. In some studies of environmental health damage, bronchitis alone is attributed to air pollution, other studies attribute many more effects such as emphysema, arteriosclerotic heart disease, the common cold, asthma, and even deaths due to motor vehicle air pollution. There are also problems of attributing effects to one pollutant only. Harmful effects of smoking, for example, may be intensified in the presence of air pollution. Variations in the way people cope with pollution may also affect the amount of damage caused (OECD, 1976). In the UK, studies suggest that sulphur dioxide accounts for between 20 and 50 per cent of mortality and morbidity due to bronchitis and emphysema, and smaller values for other illnesses. Annual costs associated with this damage to health have been estimated to vary between £21 million and £63 million (Saunders, 1976).

Differences in opinion on the costing of health damage due to pollution are reflected in the great variation in damages awarded by the courts. In Japan, victims of mercury, arsenic, cadmium, and sulphur dioxide pollution have been able to recover damages. The amounts recoverable have also increased substantially over time. In America, awards granted in noise nuisance cases brought against airport authorities have been highly variable (OECD, 1976). Objective assessments of morbidity costs are problematic. It is disputed, for example, whether or not health service treatment (which may be more or less relevant to curing the patient), loss of productivity and various intangibles such as the quality of life should be included in the assessment, and if so what weighting they should be given.

The costs to physical materials are complicated by over-specification, the substitution of less sensitive materials and the use of protective materials which help to reduce maintenance and replacement costs. In agriculture, less sensitive crops may be substituted, with costs dependent upon the degree of adaptation possible. Climatic and global effects are poorly understood, which makes economic assessment even more problematic.

For many critics, the problems of assigning costs and benefits to environmental consequences of pollution and development projects are insurmountable. Furthermore, the techniques used can contribute to misleading conclusions. Given the shortcomings discussed, it may be more expedient in many cases to adopt a much more descriptive and broader analysis of environmental consequences when considering trade-offs in the policy-making process. If cost–benefit analysis is used, its outcome is very dependent upon the goals set and the determination of certain values such as travel-time. This makes cost–benefit analysis particularly prone to influence by powerful interest groups. Hence in its general application cost–benefit analysis tends to serve the ruling class in a capitalist economy. The difficulties discussed are, however, still not at an end, for costs and benefits will change as time goes by, and it is necessary to consider some of the uncertainties of the future.

ASSESSING THE EFFECT OF TIME AND FUTURE UNCERTAINTIES

According to T. Newton, the passage of time will affect the assessment of the costs and benefits resulting from any particular project in three respects:

1 changes in the market prices of benefits and costs;
2 the relatively greater desirability of consumption in the near future to consumption in the more distant future;
3 the possibility of alternative productive investment of the funds used in a public project (1972:25).

Differential inflation, involving relative changes in prices, should be taken into account. It is possible, for example, that with the expansion of population and rising *per capita* incomes, the demand for environmental amenities and natural resources will rise steeply in relation to other prices. This might well apply to forestry and timber production. On the other hand, a world shortage of timber by the end of the century may be counteracted by the development of satisfactory substitutes. However, it is necessary to recognize the importance of the political as well as the economic reasoning behind forestry promotion. In Britain, the Forestry Commission was established during the First World War, when it was realized how dependent the country had become on imports. To avoid importing wood, when merchant shipping was desperately needed for bringing in food supplies, meant the felling of large areas of indigenous woodland. The Acland Report, which became the basis of forestry policy, stressed the need to increase the acreage of indigenous forest, irrespective of possible low returns on capital, for the political reason of self-sufficiency in case of war. Moreover, despite studies that show a lower return on capital from forestry than from hill farming, forestry provides more employment. It is for these two reasons that forestry has been encouraged although the rate of return on capital falls well short of the minimum rate which is normally required for public sector investment (Whitby *et al.*, 1974).

During the 1960s the Ministry of Transport developed techniques for comparing alternative road schemes. In 1967, the Highway Economics Unit introduced a manual, commonly referred to as T5/67 (Ministry of Transport, 1967), which was later superseded in 1973 by another known as COBA (Department of the Environment, 1973). T5/67 was concerned merely with pay-back percentage over the first year of use, whereas COBA suggested that benefits should be assessed over a period of thirty years. Reliance on travel-time costs and losses from accidents remain the key determinants, but current policy is now more biased towards roads, where traffic flow may be expected to build up over a period of time rather than reach a peak level almost immediately (Sharp and Jennings, 1976).

Major problems in forecasting and evaluating benefits exist even within the limited context of COBA. Forecasting traffic flows involves uncertainty about conditions in twenty or thirty years' time. Regional economic policy, the availability of fuel, and development of other forms of transport will all play an important part in determining future traffic forecasts. In assessing the costs of a road scheme, it is not always possible to determine a fair market value of land required. Loss of historic buildings and good agricultural land may or may not have a reliable present-day market value, but their value in thirty years' time is even harder to estimate.

Future benefits from investment are usually discounted (that is, given smaller and smaller values) over a period of time. The actual rates of discount will be determined by the 'social time preference' and/or by the 'social opportunity cost rate'. The former emphasizes society's choice between present and future consumption as well as estimates of future values in a more or less prosperous society. The latter reflects the opportunity cost of investment funds used for financing other projects with a more immediate return on capital. Uncertainties abour relative rates of inflation, etc., may lead to the enumeration of a range of discount rates. The actual rate chosen is clearly important in terms of trade-offs between scarcity for future generations and the present-day demand for cheap exploitation of environmental resources. Sensitivity analysis through operations research would then be undertaken to assess the sensitivity of policy options to slight changes in the rates of discount. There is little general agreement over selecting a discount rate and the range of values is usually set around existing interest rates.

CRITERIA FOR COMPARING PROJECTS

The costs and benefits, having been enumerated and adjusted for the effects of time and uncertainty, are then presented in a suitable form for comparison. Before making a comparison, however, a decision should be made about what criteria are to be applied. There are two common criteria – the Kaldor-Hicks and Pareto criteria. The Kaldor-Hicks criterion requires that the net benefits of a project exceed the net costs. The Pareto criterion has a stricter requirement that a project be selected only if no one is adversely affected. The Pareto optimum exists when no one can be better off without somebody else being worse off. This second criterion is almost impossible to meet since most projects of any size will adversely affect at least a minority of people.

Having decided upon the criterion, three forms of comparison are commonly used: the benefit/cost ratio; the benefit minus cost which is shown as 'net present value'; the internal rate of return, or the discount rate, which just equates the present value of costs with the present value of benefits. Different ways of comparing projects may account for a different order of ranking. Whitby has illustrated how this can happen with a theoretical example of four projects A, B, C and D (Whitby *et al.*, 1974). Project A, which might be a clean air programme, involves large initial capital expenditure and continuing annual operating costs. After ten years the investment is valueless and the flow of output ceases. Project B, which might be a road, involves a small annual cost for five years which then doubles when the project starts to produce from the sixth to the tenth year. Project C, which might be a flood control system, incurs annual costs and provides a revenue every two years. Project D might be a forestry project which involves high initial expenditure, a small expenditure in the eighth year and no return until the thirtieth year (see table 2.9). The cost–benefit analysis, with different discount rates and forms of comparison, is

Table 2.9   *Time-streams of benefits and costs*

Project	Year		1	2	3	4	5	6	7	8	9	10	30	40
A	Benefits	£	0	0	100	100	100	100	100	100	100	100	–	–
	Costs	£	500	10	10	10	10	10	10	10	10	10	–	–
B	Benefits	£	0	0	0	0	0	200	200	200	200	200	–	–
	Costs	£	50	50	50	50	50	150	150	150	150	150	–	–
C	Benefits	£	0	100	0	100	0	100	0	100	0	100	–	–
	Costs	£	45	45	45	45	45	45	45	45	45	45	–	–
D	Benefits	£	0	0	0	0	0	0	0	0	0	0	2,000	0
	Costs	£	100	0	0	0	0	0	0	30	0	0	0	0

(*Source:* Whitby et al., *Rural Resource Development*, 1974:29)

displayed in table 2.10. In each case there is a different ranking of projects in terms of return on investment. This example is a warning of the care required in deciding which forms of comparison are used when presenting the results, and the possibility of manipulation to suit the interests of one or other of the parties concerned.

Table 2.10   *Efficiency benefits and costs*

	A		B		C		D	
	Value	Rank	Value	Rank	Value	Rank	Value	Rank
Present value of benefits £	577.4	–	470	–	292.6	–	114	–
Present value of costs £	551.4	–	424.5	–	276.3	–	114	–
B/C (10%) £/£	1.047	3	1.107	1	1.059	2	1.000	4
B/C (8%) £/£	1.58	2	1.150	3	1.068	4	1.98	1
B-C (10%) £	20.0	2	45.5	1	16.3	3	0	4
Internal rate of return %	10.9	3	15.0	2	15.9	1	10.0	4

(*Source:* Whitby et al., *Rural Resource Development*, 1974:31)

Cost–benefit analysis, then, is open to distortions. Inevitably some biases will creep in, such as concentrating on data that are easiest to treat, as well as in the evaluation of the costs, accidents, etc., and in the choice of criteria or form of comparison. The way that cost–benefit analysis is undertaken, then, involves both political and sociological considerations. A good illustration of the political features of cost–benefit analysis occurred when it became a centre of debate in relation to the choice of London's third airport. It has also become important to environmentalists who recognize that cost–benefit analysis has been used as a lever to develop and expand trunk roads at the expense of alternative public transport systems. Had they not been so biased, no doubt the massive private financial interests of the road lobby, spearheaded by the British Roads Federation, would have conducted a campaign to change the form of techniques in its own interest. As it was, the environmental lobby succeeded in securing in December 1976 the setting up of the Leitch Committee (1978) to review forecasting and cost–benefit techniques used in the planning of roads. This Committee reported in 1978 and made recommendations to improve the process of cost–benefit analysis.

The report suggested that analyses should be calculated, not as at present mainly in terms of road users, but instead on a much wider basis, including social, economic and environmental factors, so as to take into account the interests of groups affected directly and indirectly. The Friends of the Earth welcomed the report as 'another major blow against the power and influence of the road lobby' (*The Times*, 11 January 1978). But in fact, the recommendations were little threat to the road lobby.

The Leitch Committee's task can be seen as one of accommodating the critical assault on cost–benefit analysis by recommending slight modifications. The recommendation that more information should be included when making trade-offs in transport policy would appear to be an important advance, but these measures fail to come to grips with the main feature of cost–benefit analysis which has been to make environmental decisions commensurate with the market economy. Self's criticisms of the Roskill Commission cost–benefit analysis remain as apposite today as they were then. He argued that cost–benefit analysis strengthened 'the existing tendency to convert genuine political and social issues into bogus technical ones' (1970:251) and complained of 'the grotesque attempt to place all factors on the same monetary basis' (1970:253). It was, however, these two elements of cost–benefit analysis that made this form of decision-making an appropriate tool for ensuring compatibility between public policy-making and the market economy.

Cost–benefit analysis suffers from defects of a low order and a high order (see Edwards, 1977). Low-order problems include the range of effects to be evaluated, technical difficulties of calculating the equivalent market price of public goods, the discount rate, and the type of cost/benefit ratio. Such difficulties allow the technique to be manipulated to support a variety of interests. Cost–benefit analysis will therefore tend to serve the interests of powerful groups. Nevertheless such manipulation can be countered by environmental groups and others who may try to change the 'rules of the games' to favour their own interests. A well-organized community action group could, for example, in principle demand that cost–benefit analysis attach greater value to housing with a low market value so as to avoid inequitable planning proposals.

High-order problems of cost–benefit analysis are associated with the neo-classical assumptions upon which it is based. Neo-classical economics provides a model of environmental management which ignores the reality of class conflict and differential power. Instead there is the questionable, assumption that price equals value where price is determined by individual preferences operating in a market with perfect competition and perfect knowledge of 'costs' and 'benefits'. However, price is not determined by individuals with *equal* power to maximize their own preferences. The ruling class of capital owners are still, despite union and labour organization, in the strongest position to determine the price of labour, material inputs and manufactured goods. Market price is not therefore equivalent to any intrinsic value but a distorted value which serves the interests of the ruling class. Cost–benefit analysis, by relying upon market price, imputes a value to resources and public goods, such as clean air, which supports the determination of price under the social order of capitalism. Hence the neo-classical economic assumptions upon which cost–benefit analysis rests serve the ideological function of providing an apparently rational, although defective, basis for public decision-making.

3 Environmental Evaluation – Behavioural and Holistic Assessments

In Chapter 1, the unreliability of public opinion surveys was discussed in relation to the growth of the environmental movement. It was pointed out that surveys of attitudes and preferences were a poor guide to strength of commitment to policy objectives. Nevertheless there has been a growth of behavioural analysis in geography and related subjects, some of which is claimed to be of value in the decision-making process. This chapter begins by reviewing the relevance of a behavioural focus to environmental evaluation.

Another aid to environmental planning, especially in America, has been environmental impact analysis. In Britain there is as yet no statutory obligation to produce detailed environmental evaluations as a step in the policy-making process, although in practice cost–benefit analysis and some kinds of survey partially fulfil this role. Environmental impact statements have been commissioned on an *ad hoc* basis for some major projects, including the Loch Carron and Loch Broom production platform sites, the Redcar steel works, the Nigg oil refinery and the Flotta oil terminal (see Wathern, 1976; Cairns, 1978). In the United States, following the Environmental Policy Act of 1969, decision upon all major federal projects with significant effects upon the environment must be guided by a detailed Environmental Impact Statement (EIS). Canada, Australia, Germany and France have also adopted the EIS procedure. A review of this procedure and how it might be applied in Britain will follow a discussion of behavioural analysis of environmental values.

Behavioural analysis of environmental values

The environment takes on different values according to the form of physical environment, to the economic organization of society, to rules, customs and social expectations, as well as to the goals and values of individual members of society. Three types of perceptual evaluation can be distinguished: operational perception, inferential perception, and responsive perception.

OPERATIONAL PERCEPTION

This may be equated with goal-orientated behaviour. In other words, aspects of the environment take on significance according to activities in which people participate. R. Lucas (1972) has shown how canoeists and motor-boat enthusiasts have different perceptions of wilderness in the Boundary Waters Canoe Area of the Quetrico Provincial Park in Ontario. The motor-boat enthusiasts were less discriminating and considered a much larger area to be wilderness. Such differences in perception, preferences and attitudes to the environment may, it is claimed, be helpful in zoning by keeping the motor-boat users away from areas considered by canoeists to be wilderness. The implication of this type of reasoning is that present preferences should be maximized. Thus those who are too poor to make use of the recreational resource will not have their preferences considered in the policy recommendations. Policy derived from declared preferences of current resource users has a function of reinforcing the social order rather than radically altering it.

INFERENTIAL PERCEPTION

This is rather similar to operational perception but the emphasis is not so much upon isolated activities as upon behaviour determined by roles within the social and economic organization of society. The meaning of the environment and the values placed upon it bears an important relation to the social patterns of living. Sociological and anthropological literature discusses the differences in perception that are attributed to socio-economic factors. This type of behavioural study, unlike the first category, is more meaningful because it does not treat behaviour in isolation from the social order.

M. Douglas (1972) has shown how two tribes, the Lele and the Bushong, held different views about the climate in the same area of the Belgian Congo (now Zaire). The two tribes celebrated their cold and hot seasons at the opposite points of the calendar. The Lele considered the dry season as unbearably hot, while the Bushong and the Belgian administrators in the region both agreed that this period was pleasantly cool and they dreaded the onset of the first rains. From meteorological records made by the Belgians there appeared to be no objective differences that would make one group disagree so strongly about the climate. The difference of opinion was explained as follows. The Lele suffered more during the dry season because it coincided with a heavy period of agricultural work. The Bushong, living across the river, had a more complex agricultural system and worked steadily throughout the year. Douglas considers that the Belgians obtained their impressions of hot and cold periods from their contacts with Leopoldville, the colonial capital, where the temperature readings showed a noticeable difference between the seasons.

Similar distortions in environmental perception are commonly found in map drawings. Exaggerated importance is often given to those features that are most socially relevant. Typically, maps are ethnocentric. Yi Fu-Tuan (1974) cites the example of sketches made by Eskimos of Southampton Island in 1927 before any 'accurate' map had been produced. These maps were later found to be very accurate according to most details, but the area with the greatest population, the Bell Peninsula, was exaggerated in size. The maps also varied according to sex and occupation. The Aivilik hunter included greater detail and accuracy in the island's outline as well as the harbours and inlets of the neighbouring coastline of Hudson Bay. The women, in contrast, did not express their knowledge in outlines. Their maps tended to consist of separate points, each of which indicated the location of a settlement or trading post. These were equally accurate with respect to distance and relative direction.

RESPONSIVE PERCEPTION

Despite the relativity of perception as discussed under the headings of operational and inferential perception, certain aspects of the environment appear to be more readily visualized than others. According to Kevin Lynch's classic, *The Image of the City* (1964), our perception of our surroundings tends to emphasize paths, edges, nodes, districts and landmarks. Some distortions occur in a process of simplification. Thus nearby streets appear parallel when in fact they diverge. According to one recent study Parisians tend to see the Seine, which actually forms almost a half circle, as a much gentler curve than it really is (Milgram and Jodelet, 1977). The *Gestalt* psychologists also pointed out the simplifications we make in perceiving and understanding the environment.

While it is clear that the physical structure of the environment influences responsive perception and attitudes to it, there is a mutual interaction between economic and social organization and physical form. In his study of house form, A. Rapoport (1969(a)) attempts to demonstrate how the form of dwellings is closely related to physical features of the environment such as temperature, and also to social organization, religious beliefs and attitudes towards nature. In a particularly striking example, he contrasts the *pueblo* and *hogan* house forms. The Hopi Indians living in the *pueblo* and the Navajo in the *hogan* inhabit a similar geographical region (South-Western United States), have similar climates, and a somewhat similar economic and technological organization based upon agriculture. He argues that they differ mainly in world views, religion, attitudes towards nature and social organization.

The *pueblo* house form (see figure 3.1) is communal in structure. It is a multi-storeyed cluster of interlocking rooms. The clusters are additive and expressive of a highly organized and egalitarian society. Within the centre of the cluster there is usually an open space or plaza where dance ceremonies take place. The *hogan*, on the other hand, is a family abode looking rather like a tent (see figure 3.2). *Hogans* are usually clustered with matrilinearly related families living in close proximity.

Each house form is designed to suit a climate of hot days and cold nights, and has a structure with small surface areas in relation to volume; this tends to prevent heat gain during the day and heat losses during the night. The house form also reflects cultural values. The sacred rooms in the *pueblo*, called *kivas*, are usually centrally located at the heart of the building and so are most protected. The *pueblo* is carefully orientated to face the sacred directions of east and north, and the close and harmonious attitude towards nature is reflected in the way the *pueblo* fits unobtrusively into the landscape.

The *hogan* structure is also influenced by religious activity which takes up to one-third of the active time of the Navajo. The sun is very important so the *hogan* always faces east; and the bodies of the dead are always removed through the north door. The space within the *hogan* is split up according to compass bearings. Women tend to occupy the south part, and men the northern part. The much more aggressive attitude towards nature is reflected in the more obtrusive style of the house form. The Navajo are more individualistic than the Hopi, but nevertheless *hogans* are never sited where they could interfere with the rights of others with respect to grazing or water. *Hogans* are for this reason very rarely sited less than two or three miles from water. Respect for others is also shown by the fact that timber for building is rarely cut within one mile of someone else's dwelling.

One can begin to generalize from Rapoport's example of house form and understand how house forms within industrially developed nations reflect and reinforce the varying values attached to community, kinship, mobility, technological innovation, private space, the influence of experts such as architects and engineers, as well as the underlying influence of capital and its ownership. In Britain during the twentieth century, the suburban family home with a garden has been a dominant house form save for a brief period after the Second World War when technological optimism and architectural idealism led to the development of high rise flats (see

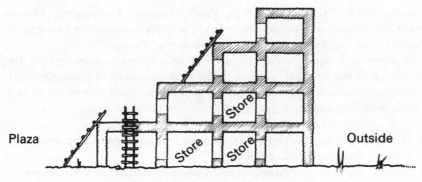

Figure 3.1 Ideal section through *pueblo* terrace (not to scale)

(*Source:* Rapoport, 1969:69)

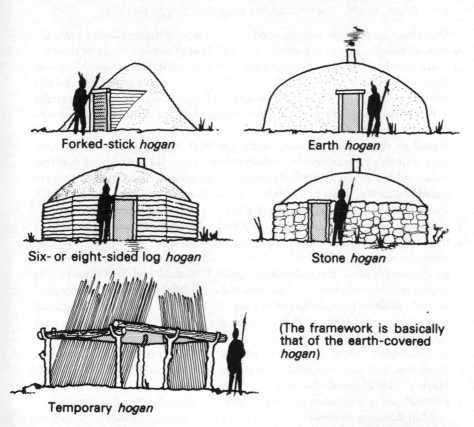

Forked-stick *hogan*

Earth *hogan*

Six- or eight-sided log *hogan*

Stone *hogan*

Temporary *hogan*

(The framework is basically that of the earth-covered *hogan*)

Figure 3.2 Different types of Navajo *hogan* (note the basic similarity of design, despite differences in technique, building materials, etc.)

(*Source:* Rapoport, 1969:73)

Rapoport, 1969(b); Taylor, 1973). The Alternative Techonology Move-ment's environmental values, in contrast, became expressed in a variety of house forms expressing the needs for self-sufficiency.

Various techniques have been used in an attempt to demonstrate the relevance of behavioural analysis to the understanding of environmental perception, attitudes, values and preferences. These will now be discussed under the following headings:

1 Drawings, maps, sorting tasks, and content analysis of literature, art, history, science, travel, diaries, etc.
2 Survey approaches where attitudes are solicited by direct questions, and checked for internal consistency and structure.

DRAWINGS, MAPS, SORTING TASKS AND CONTENT ANALYSIS

Drawings have been widely used to obtain information about environ-mental values. The psychologist F. Ladd (1967) made a study of how the black youths of Boston envisaged their environment. She asked children to draw maps of the Mission Hill area of Boston and also tape-recorded her conversations with them. The maps and recordings revealed that the White Mission Hill Project was *terra incognita,* and detail of this area was virtually absent. One of the black boys, Ralph, who went to a superior school in the neighbourhood, while diminishing the size of the project area, put five educational insitutions in the area. It is suggested that this indicated his perception of education as an escape route from the segre-gated life he led. Other boys felt at home in quite a restricted area which they knew well and their maps were far less balanced than Ralph's.

It is possible to use an outline map and ask participants to fill in areas or to place on the map certain features. By having a fixed outline one can compare results, as there is a common fixed scale. A homomorphic map is an aggregate of all the individual maps. P. Gould and R. White (1974) have used this technique to illustrate the combined location preferences of school children from different regions in England and Wales. National homorphic maps show preferences for the southern area, an area in East Anglia and the Lake District, with a noticeable dislike for London. Local homomorphic maps of preference tend to represent a shared national viewpoint and a zone of local desirability (see figures 3.3 and 3.4). D. W. Harvey (1972) used the technique to produce a map of investment possibilities in Baltimore housing as seen by three landlords in 1971.

Map drawing surveys have also been used by environmental planners. B. Goodey (1971), with the aid of the Birmingham Post, asked people in Birmingham to construct maps that conveyed the main impressions they had of the area. By combining hundreds of responses he was able to build

Figure 3.3 Map showing areas of greatest residential desirability
(nationwide sample questioned)

Note: Residential desirability of different regions was measured on a scale from zero to one hundred. The values recorded were then used to construct residential perception surfaces. The contours connect similar points of perceived desirability. If the gap between the contours is large then this indicates that the perception of residential desirability changes only gradually over that area.

(*Source:* Gould and White, 1974:82)

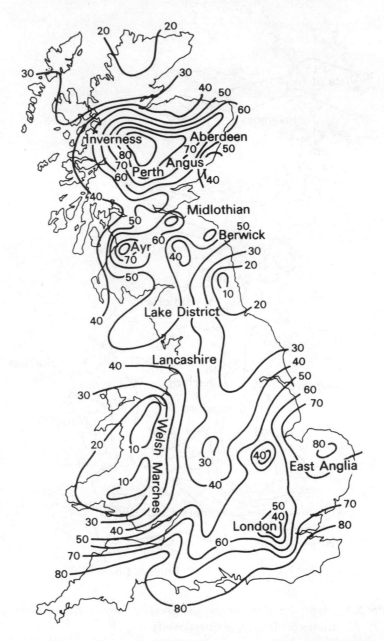

Figure 3.4 Map showing areas of greatest residential desirability for inhabitants of Inverness

(*Source:* Gould and White, 1974:80)
(See Note to Figure 3.3)

up a composite mental map which tended to emphasize such areas as the Cathedral Yard and the Bull Ring, but played down the importance of some tall features. The maps collected and the large numbers of comments about the area were claimed to be very valuable to the planners concerned with the future appearance of the city. R. M. Downs and D. Stea claim that cognitive mapping is of practical use to investors as well as public planners: 'Given the fundamental link between cognitive maps and decisions as to what to do where, cognitive maps are a target for advertisers with products and places to sell. Real estate agents, land speculators, travel agents, resort operators, shopping centre developers, and local chambers of commerce are all trying to alter the way that we think about the world around us' (1977:25).

One alternative to map drawing is that of sorting. People are tested for their ability to locate photos, well-known places, street names, etc. In this way geographical knowledge can be tested in a deliberate and planned manner. In one photographic recognition test, Parisians were tested for their knowledge of Paris. This particular study demonstrated the influence of historical geographical boundaries on spatial recognition. There appeared to be a boundary between known and unknown parts of Paris which follows part of the route of the lost city wall, the Férmiers Généraux (Milgram and Jodelet, 1977).

Content analysis of literature, maps, science, art, travel diaries, etc. may also be used to reveal examples of environmental perception. The Ancient Greek historian Herodotus, for instance, imagined the combined size of Africa and Asia to be far less than that of Europe. The Greek and Roman writers tended to refer infrequently to the extent of the deserts. The Qur'an did likewise in contrast to the Bible's more repetitious descriptions of the deserts. R. M. Elson's investigation of more than 1,000 textbooks used in the first eight years of American schooling in the nineteenth century led to the following conclusions about contemporary environmental attitudes:

Thus the nineteenth-century child was taught that nature is animated with man's purposes. God designed nature for man's physical needs and spiritual training. Scientific understanding of nature will reveal the greater glory of God, and the practical application of such knowledge should be encouraged as part of the use God meant man to make of nature. Besides serving the material needs of man, nature is a source of man's health, strength, and virtue. He departs at his peril from a life close to nature. At a time when America was becoming increasingly industrial and urban, agrarian values which had been a natural growth in earlier America became articles of fervent faith in American nationalism. The American character had been formed in virtue because it developed in a rural environment, and it must remain the same despite vast environmental change. The existence of a bounteous and fruitful frontier in America, with its promise not only of future prosperity but of continued virtue, offers proof that God has singled out the United States above other nations for His fostering care. The superiority of nature to man-made things confers superiority on the American over older civilizations. That uncle Sam sooner or later will have to become a city dweller is not envisaged by these textbook writers, although their almost fanatical advocacy of rural values would seem to suggest an unconscious fear that this might be so (1964:39–40).

OPINION POLLSTER TYPE OF APPROACH

In the Rotheram study (1973), people in six different areas were interviewed by a working group who had formulated a list of public priorities that needed attention. The study was based on job evaluation techniques which require a series of comparisons between two factors at a time. Using these techniques a random sample of the Rotheram population ranked the importance of sixteen different priorities. The results stressed the public's view that traffic safety and visual amenity of the town, covering factors such as dereliction and appearance of buildings and streets, were high on the list for improvement (see table 3.1). It is interesting to note that the working group had not included these factors in their short list of ten priorities.

In a similar study by H. G. Frederickson and H. Magnas (1972), people in Syracuse, New York, were asked to rank different social and environmental priorities. In this study, however, the influence of location and

Table 3.1   *Survey on public priorities for improving the environment*

Factor	Score
Traffic safety	11.5
Air pollution	10.6
Pavement and roads	8.4
Dereliction	8.4
Vehicles parked in street	8.0
Condition of buildings	7.3
Condition of walls and fences	6.6
Litter	6.5
Street furniture	5.6
Noise	5.5
Car parking in town centre	5.5
Trees, shrubs and grass	4.9
Private gardens	4.7
Overhead wires/aerials	4.1
Advertisements	2.4

(*Source:* the Rotheram study, 1973:19)

socio-economic status was also investigated. Suburban as opposed to urban dwellers attached more importance to water pollution, adequate water, welfare and traffic tie-ups, but less importance to employment, housing, maintenance of streets and parks and recreational facilities (see table 3.2). The study also showed that those in a higher income bracket considered water pollution to be more important, and concluded that the more affluent, better educated and younger respondents felt more directly affected by water pollution. However, the distinctions were not so clear-cut when people were asked whether they were prepared to pay various amounts of tax towards controlling water pollution. One of the problems with this type of study is the frequent unreality of the survey situation. One way of reducing this problem is to conduct the survey at the sites where resources are used.

Table 3.2   *Relative priorities to different social concerns assigned by urban and suburban residents in Syracuse, New York*

Priority assigned by urban residents	*Priority assigned by suburban residents*
Education	Education
Police protection	Police protection
Employment	Water pollution
Housing	Employment
Water pollution	Adequate water
Maintenance of streets	Welfare
Welfare	Maintenance of streets
Adequate water	Housing
Parks and recreational facilities	Traffic tie-ups
Traffic tie-ups	Parks and recreational facilities

(*Source:* Frederickson and Magnas, 1972:274)

Lucas's (1972) study of wilderness perception and use in the boundary waters canoe area is an example of this approach. The routes chosen by motor-boat users and canoeists were mapped, and questions were asked in different places as to whether or not that particular place was considered to be wilderness. Wilderness perception maps were then constructed for each recreational use. The study showed that roads were almost never in 'the wilderness' and that heavily used areas were less often considered as wilderness. Motor-boat users were less demanding about their standards of 'wilderness', which was often considered to exist immediately after leaving the town. Lakes with buildings were considered as wilderness even if there were many other boats. One lake called Moose Lake was considered to be an area of wilderness by 58 per cent of the motor-boat users but by none of the canoeists.

The use of such surveys as a guide to policy must be regarded with great scepticism. In a study by R. W. Kates (1962) on the behaviour of residents of a flood plain, despite first-hand experience and extensive mass media reports, residents often had a very inaccurate idea of the likelihood of floods.

Another way of trying to avoid some of the unrealities of survey situations is to ask people to voice opinions after being exposed to a variety of information and persuasive argument. The Department of the Environment's consultative documents and questionnaires released during early stages of by-pass road planning are examples of this type of approach. For example, in November 1973, the DOE published a consultative document on the Canterbury Southern By-Pass (A2) Alternative Routes. Exhibitions were also held on four days during November. Details of traffic forecasts and the pros and cons of three alternative routes were briefly outlined. Total length, estimated costs and benefits, number of properties to suffer demolition and agricultural land taken, with lists of advantages and disadvantages, were summarized in tabular form. After digesting the available information, the public were requested to fill in a questionnaire indicating various preferences concerning not only a choice of route but also the criteria considered most important for planning. These criteria included: agricultural interests; amenity and recreation; cost; demolition of property; effect on property close to, but not physically affected by the proposed road; noise and pollution; traffic needs; any other factors.

This sort of survey, it might be argued, is partly designed as a public relations exercise, and even the most sophisticated of questionnaires have tended to give very unreliable results (see Ashby, 1976). Unfortunately most of the behaviourist studies of this sort have tended to confuse actual environmental problems such as the extent of pollution with prejudices and preconceptions of these problems. R. Rieser gives an example of how attitude studies can bear little relation to objective conditions:

As part of a field course, several other students and I carried out a study of the perception of the disturbance suffered by people living along a stretch of heavily used road. At one end were Victorian artisan cottages fronting directly on the road. A mile further along there were spacious Edwardian villas set well back from the road. The working class in the cottages reported they were unable to use their front rooms because of the traffic noise. The middle class in their villas reported no such inconvenience. Yet when asked to rate how disturbed they were by the traffic the middle class, who objectively were much better off, consistently rated their disturbance higher than the working-class respondents (1973:54).

The type of behaviour analysis referred to by Rieser, which obscures objective conditions, is often justified by the notion of cultural relativity. There is a popular notion that reality is entirely a construction of society.

P. L. Berger and T. Luckman (1967) have been particularly influential in supporting this notion. A. L. Mauss (1975) speaks of a 'consensual reality' where social problems exist, not as objective conditions, but as a product of the behaviour of social groups. Marxists on the other hand have recognized the difference between scientific or objective statements and ideology. In the example cited by Rieser the behavioural analysis is a form of ideology which distracts attention from the objective reality of traffic disturbance.

Behaviourists have more often than not assumed that preferences and attitudes are a reliable guide for policy-making. Whereas it is more true to say that many aspects of behaviour result from the structure of society. Isolated behavioural studies therefore tend implicitly to accept the social order as given and are ahistorical in design. The idea of society as a non-mutable entity is an absurd notion but nevertheless serves as a convenient conservative ideology. By focusing on attitudes in isolation, the behaviourist obscures the objective conditions.

It is not difficult to see what sort of policy implications might arise from D. Royse's (1969) study which showed that the upper classes tend to dislike the suburban settings which are preferred by the lower classes. The upper classes, on the other hand, were shown to prefer lower density housing which appeared to be of no importance to lower status groups. Such studies merely obscure the nature and extent of deprivation, and even ligitimate existing conditions by demonstrating reputed preferences for them.

Environmental behaviour studies have tended to ignore such issues as discontent of workers over working conditions and control over their working environment. They have also largely diverted attention from the fact that workers are more affected by pollution and other environmental problems (see Commoner, 1973; Woodcock, 1971; England and Bluestone, 1973; Deutsch and Van Houten, 1974). The popularity of behavioural studies can be analysed in terms of the support they offer to the *status quo* and ruling class. Their appeal in the environmental planning field can largely be attributed to a substitute for true representation in decision-making, and to a means of legitimating what might otherwise be unpopular policy.

One of the techniques of environmental evaluation which attempts to be more comprehensive than the cost–benefit analysis and yet more objective than behavioural analysis is that of 'environmental impact analysis'. In development proposals, especially those involving significant and diverse environmental and social consequences, it is necessary, so it has been claimed, to make a holistic appraisal of all potential impacts. The next section will explore the operation of and limitations of this approach in practice.

Environmental impact statements, reviews and analysis

UNITED STATES

Early attempts at cost–benefit analysis in the United States were often of very dubious value. Elements that were difficult to price were sometimes overlooked, as were distributional effects at national, regional and local level. It was, in short, the recognized failure of previous practice which led to the adoption of the environmental impact statement (EIS) procedure in the National Environmental Policy Act of 1969 (NEPA). An EIS was to be required for all 'major federal actions significantly affecting the quality of the human environment. The statement itself should identify and develop methods and procedures 'which will ensure that presently unqualified environmental amenities and values may be given appropriate consideration in decision-making along with economic and technical considerations'. In NEPA (Section 102 2(c)) the EIS had to be detailed and contain statements upon:

1 the environmental impact of the proposed action;
2 any adverse environmental effects which cannot be avoided should the proposal be implemented;
3 alternatives to the proposed action;
4 the relationship between local short-term uses of man's environment and the maintenance of long-term productivity;
5 any irreversible and irretrievable commitments of resources which would be involved in the proposed action should it be implemented.

Federal EIS legislation has been interpreted by the development of guidelines issued by the Council on Environmental Quality, state authorities and federal departments. The courts have also played a major part in interpreting legislative objectives. Similar EIS procedures have been adopted under supplementary state legislation. By 1975 some twenty-four states had established EIS requirements of their own (Council on Environmental Quality, 1975). In the case of the California Environmental Quality Act 1970 (CEQA), the procedure of Environmental Impact Review (EIR) has been applied to private developments requiring a local authority licence, as well as to those developments initiated by state authorities. Hence the Californian EIR covers a wide range of development projects and in effect can be demanded for any project with significant environmental consequences. In some of the other states there are much less comprehensive measures. In Nevada, for example, it is limited to specific activities such as electric power plant siting.

Under NEPA the first consideration is whether or not an EIS is required, and this depends upon interpretation of 'major federal actions . . .'. An EIS may be necessary for projects, regulations, grant allocations and programmes such as those involving insect control. Under the 1972 Federal Water Pollution Control Act, all discharge applications have to be licensed by the Environmental Protection Agency. The system of permits is subject to an EIS. Consequently many non-federal projects such as nuclear power stations and new housing developments are subject to EIS procedures (Meyers, 1976).

The CEQ issued detailed guidelines on 23 April 1971. These guidelines were revised in August 1973 and again in the spring of 1975. According to the CEQ a decision upon whether or not an EIS is required should be taken 'with a view to the overall, cumulative impact of the action proposed, related federal actions and projects in the area and further actions contemplated. Such actions may be localized in their impact, but if there is potential that the environment may be significantly affected, the statement is to be prepared. Proposed major actions, the environmental impact of which is likely to be highly controversial, should be covered in all cases . . . an environmental statement should be prepared if it is reasonable to anticipate accumulatively significant impact on the environment from federal action' (Council on Environmental Quality, 1975:696).

The CEQ guidelines are further supplemented by federal agency guidelines. For example, the Federal Power Commission consider only hydro-electric schemes of more than 2,000 hp to be worthy of an EIS (Wathern, 1976). However, despite amplification by CEQ and federal agency guidelines, the courts have played a major role in deciding whether or not an EIS shall be undertaken. The courts have decided that the following did not require an EIS: Operation Snowy Beach, a mock winter amphibious exercise in Maine's coastal Reid State Park; the widening of a fourteen-block portion of Mt Vernon Road in Cedar Rapids, Iowa; the construction of a 4.3 mile, one-lane gravel road through a portion of Monongahela National Forest in West Virginia. On the other hand the courts have ruled for an EIS on the following projects: the Cross-Florida Barge Canal; the Giltham Dam project on Arkansas' Cossatot River; a continuous barge waterway from the Upper Mississippi and Ohio valleys to Mobile, Alabama, on the Gulf of Mexico; and the channelling of sixty-six miles of river in North Carolina (Greis, 1973).

Some of the court decisions had a dramatic impact on the volume of work on EISs. For example, it has been said that the Calvert Cliffs decision in 1971 led the Atomic Energy Commission to expand its staff concerned with EIS procedure from 20 to 200. In 1972 the Greene County case similarly led to the Federal Power Commission's increasing its EIS staff from 22 to 75 (Thorrold, 1975). By 1978 about 7,300 EISs had been prepared by federal agencies. The cost of producing EISs in 1975 alone was $162 million. The statements usually take between three and nineteen months to prepare (Stoel and Scherr, 1978).

Once it has been decided that an EIS is required, a draft impact statement is produced. CEQ guidelines have helped to clarify the scope of the EIS. Environmental evaluation should consider comparative benefits, costs and risks of alternative proposals as well as the proposed action. Trade-offs between the long term and short term must also be considered. The EIS is not, however, as narrowly construed as cost–benefit analysis has been in practice, for guidelines dictate that the following have to be included:

1 A description of the proposed action, a statement of its purposes, and a description of the environment affected, including information, summary, technical data, and maps and diagrams where relevant, adequate to permit an assessment of potential environmental impact by commenting agencies and the public . . .
2 The relationship of the proposed action to land use plans, policies and controls for the affected area . . .
3 The probable impact of the proposed action on the environment.
    (i)   This requires agencies to assess the positive and negative effects of the proposed actions as it affects both the national and international environment . . .
    (ii) Secondary or indirect, as well as primary or direct, consequences for the environment should be included in the analysis . . .
4 Alternatives to the proposed action, including, where relevant, those not within the existing authority of the responsible agency . . .
5 Any probable adverse environmental effects which cannot be avoided (such as water or air pollution, undesirable land use patterns, damage to life systems, urban congestion, threats to health or other consequences adverse to the environmental goals set out in Section 101(b) of the Act) . . .
6 The relationship between local short-term uses of man's environment and the maintenance and enhancement of long-term productivity . . .
7 Any irreversible commitments of resources that would be involved in the proposed action should it be implemented . . .
8 An indication of what other interests and considerations of federal policy are thought to offset the adverse environmental effects of the proposed action . . .
(Council on Environmental Quality, 1975:701–702).

Federal agency guidelines have supplemented those of the CEQ. For example, in April 1971, the Department of Transportation issued its own procedures for the preparation of an EIS. Detailed directions are given on what information should be included, namely the 'type of facility, length, termini, basic traffic data, right-of-way width, major design features, a general description of the surrounding terrain, land use, existing highway facilities, the need for the proposal, the benefits to the state, region, and community, an estimate of completion time, and an inventory of economic factors, such as employment, taxes and property values' (Flowerdew and Cooke, 1975:7–8). Estimated costs, engineering factors, transportation requirements, and environmental consequences, especially anticipated effects on urbanization and migration, of proposed and alternative projects are also considered important to the EIS. Similar details of what should be included for short-term uses in comparison with long-term effects, irreversible and irretrievable commitments of resources, and the other CEQ guidelines have been outlined.

Once a draft federal EIS has been completed it is circulated to other federal agencies for comment and must be made available to the general public. After a minimum period of ninety days allowed for comments, the federal agency prepares a final EIS. The EIS is then filed with the CEQ and a period of at least thirty days must pass before development may proceed. During this time anyone not satisfied with the EIS may take the agency to court in order to seek modifications. The EIS may be challenged over points of detail, and on whether or not sufficient attention has been given to alternative proposals, or opposing views. Its anlaysis of possible environmental effects and its summary of the scheme may also be criticized.

Environmental groups and others cocerned with defence of their neighbourhoods have been able to use the EIS as a legal and political instrument to delay and even cancel projects that they dislike. Clearly federal agencies have to be very careful to present their material in a way that will cause the least delay from environmental groups. In the early years after NEPA delays often occurred due to administrative inefficiency in completing EISs early in the planning process. The Department of Transport, moreover, was obliged to make EISs on projects that had been approved before NEPA but either had not begun or had not been completed. For this reason a large number of EISs had to be submitted within a very short period, and delays were inevitable. In recent years delays caused by litigation have been more confined to environmental grounds than administrative incompetency (Council on Environmental Quality, 1975).

The inflexible EIS guidelines, which must be followed in each case irrespective of the project, have been much criticized. In many cases the rigid requirements have led to cumbersome, uneven and inadequate research reports (see Elkington, 1977; Bardach and Pugliaresi, 1977). The CEQ (1975) admits that many EISs have been inordinately long, with too much description and too little analysis. In May 1977 an Executive Order was issued by President Carter directing the CEQ to issue regulations to correct some of these faults. If the EIS procedure is adopted in Britain it is much more likely that a Ministerial decision on the appropriateness of an EIS would suffice and the degree of litigation prevalent in the United

States would be avoided. It is also questionable whether or not the EISs have been sufficiently comprehensive. While the American system deals with most of the physical and ecological implications, many aspects, such as socio-economic considerations, are not included. For example, in an early critique, J. B. Sullivan and P. A. Montgomery (1972) showed that 34 per cent of a sample of EISs for highway projects failed to consider the issue of community disruption. More recently, however, EISs have begun to recognize the importance of considering social and economic effects (Friesema and Culhane, 1976).

There were early fears that the EISs would have little effect on final policy decisions. D. Greis argued in 1973 that 'in spite of initial optimism, and a court decision every ten days for three years, not one project with adverse environmental effects had been stopped by NEPA and the EIS requirement' (1973:302). On the other hand, H. P. Friesema and P. J. Culhane (1976) claim that federal agency decisions have been modified on about half the occasions when an EIS has been undertaken. D. W. Fischer (1974) and others have suggested the possibility that the EIS, like cost–benefit analysis, could be turned into a self-servicing agency tool. M. R. Greenberg and R. M. Hordon have suggested this could arise out of the difficulties in satisfactorily meeting the answers to six questions pertinent to the formulation of an EIS.

1 What environmental impacts are likely to result from alternative development patterns?
2 Do we have indicators of environmental damage and standards for these indicators which reflect the threshold beyond which serious and possibly irreversible environmental damage may result?
3 Have enough data been collected to determine the present and probable future environmental status given alternative development plans?
4 Will mathematical simulation models adequately specify environmental impact?
5 Will agencies responsible for preparing and evaluating impact statements attempt to avoid any manifestations of internal disagreements or disagreements with other agencies regarding impacts?
6 Will the court system be able to adequately weigh information of varying quality and quantity from a widely divergent set of disciplines and from persons with different value systems? (1974:164–65).

When the adequacy of the EIS procedure is analysed in the light of these questions the possibility arises that they may be used to serve vested interests. However, in defence of the EIS procedure, the CEQ has cited several examples when projects have been abandoned as a consequence of an EIS. In the Sixth Report of the CEQ, it is argued that the Corps of Engineers decided to stop work on over a dozen proposed projects because of unfavourable EISs. Moreover, the Corps has modified many more projects as a result of the EIS requirement. The Department of Transport have claimed that scores of major projects have been abandoned or modified on the basis of the EIS process. The Atomic Energy Commission has abandoned two major radioactive waste disposal proposals, one at Lyons, Kansas and the other on the Savannah River in South Carolina, because of the possible undesirable environmental effects identified by the EIS process. Finally, the CEQ cite an example whereby the EIS process affected building projects of the General Services Administration:

In 1974, when the Kennedy Library Corporation proposed construction of the Kennedy Library and Museum just below Harvard Square, GSA, which was to build and maintain the structure, issued a draft EIS. It focused attention on the traffic and other adverse effects on the area. As a result, the Library Corporation decided against the proposed museum site and is examining several other alternatives while planning to keep the Kennedy archives on Harvard University property (1975:631).

These examples of the influence of the EIS process must be seen in the context of autonomous federal responsiblity. For once an adequate EIS has been prepared it is up to the federal agency to decide upon the course of action. Judicial review of agency decisions can only ensure that the proper legal procedures have been taken. The CEQ acts only as an environmental adviser to the President and is not an ombudsman, as is often popularly believed. The EIS procedure can help to make federal agencies more sensitive to environmental considerations. It forces agencies to articulate their decisions and opens previously closed administrative procedures to public comment. But in the end the policy decision rests with the federal agency itself and not the public, the courts or the CEQ.

CALIFORNIA

The advantages and shortcomings of environmental impact analysis are illustrated by the experience of its operation in California. Before 1972 there was much debate about whether Environmental Impact Reviews should apply to the private as well as to the public sector. Environmental groups helped to define the scope of the act by litigation, and in 1972 the Supreme Court ruling in *Friends of Mamouth* v. *Board of Supervisors of Mono County* eventually established that the intentions of CEQA were that private as well as public projects should be preceded by an Environmental Impact Review (EIR). This ruling threw the powerful construction industry into chaos and a moratorium of 120 days was declared by local governments so that they could adapt to the problems of preparing and processing EIRs. During this period the State Secretary for Resources was asked to devise procedures for preparing EIRs. The first guidelines were issued in February 1973 and were put into effect in March. The guidelines have since been reviewed and extended on several occasions (Catalano and Reich, 1977).

The CEQA guidelines differ slightly from NEPA guidelines. Perhaps the most significant difference is the greater emphasis on leaving the public agencies to balance the environmental costs and benefits rather than attempting to do this in the EIR. The Californian guidelines also allow rather more public participation in EIR formulation than is the case under NEPA (Flowerdew and Cooke, 1975). Since the *Friends of Mamouth* decision the annual number of EIRs has been about 3,800 – two-thirds of these have involved private projects, and one-third public projects (see table 3.3).

Table 3.3   *Approximate number of EIRs prepared annually by type of project or activity**

	No.	%
Private housing and land sales	1,380	37
Industrial projects	390	10
Commercial projects	740	20
Public works projects by local jurisdictions	770	20
Public works projects by state agencies	200	5
EIRs prepared on policies, plans and ordinances	230	6
Miscellaneous institutional projects (principally schools and hospitals)	90	2
TOTAL	3,800	100

* These figures are derived from records during the period 1973–75.
(*Source:* State of California Office of Planning and Research, 1976:19)

In the years 1972–75 there was extensive discussion and criticism of the EIR procedure from developers, public agencies, legislators and the general public. The main advantage of the Act had been that projects, both public and private, were scrutinized for any adverse impacts. A thorough analysis of this procedure was made by the Assembly Committee on Local Government (1975). It noted that for approximately 30 per cent of projects approval was granted without any special conditions of mitigating adverse impacts. Eight per cent of the proposed projects were rejected, and of these almost half were rejected on environmental grounds. The remainder required some modification. Of all the adverse impacts identified by EIRs some 25 per cent were required to be modified. The Assembly

Committee believed that the EIRs had made it necessary for local government to make more effective and accountable decision-making.

Despite the alleged achievements of EIRs there were some very obvious bureaucratic shortcomings. Firstly, the EIRs tended to be too technical and lengthy. They failed to discriminate adequately between more and less relevant information. Analysis was consequently often either too mundane or too superficial. Secondly, the assessment requirements did not vary according to the scale and type of activity of the proposed project. Thirdly, environmental assessment was often carried out late in the project design process. Fourthly, there was uncertainty as to whether the analysis complied with legal requirements. Fifthly, the intergovernmental review stage infrequently led to any improvement in the quality of the EIR. Sixthly, the environmental assessment procedure had been insufficiently integrated with land use planning and decision-making procedures.

For most projects the cost of an EIR and the delays that followed this procedure were small in comparison with total project costs. Costs of environmental documentation were typically less than 1 per cent of the total project cost. However, for utility projects the costs of delay were significant because of rapid inflation in the construction industry. In the case of ten utility projects the costs associated with environmental documentation were only 0.05 per cent of the total project cost, but delays attributed to the assessment of four of these projects resulted in costs amounting to 6 per cent to 11 per cent of total costs, depending upon which construction cost index was used (State of California Office of Planning and Research, 1976).

As a result of the *Friends of Mamouth* decision and the financial consequences of documentation and delay there was mounting pressure from industry for legislative changes (see Jackson, 1975). The forest practices controversy was particularly important in this respect because the logging industry supported by labour groups conducted an impressive campaign against EIRs. They emphasized costs, delays and consequent unemployment in the northern coastal counties that were already suffering from economic depression (Wandesforde-Smith, 1977). In 1976, Assembly Bill 2679 came on to the statute books and substantially modified the CEQA. The main result was that EIRs were to be shorter, with greater focus on critical problems. Senate amendments also declared that local public agencies were permitted to approve a project, despite adverse environmental impacts, when:

1 The project is changed or altered to mitigate the effects and the changes or alterations are within the agency jurisdiction to approve or have already been adopted by the proper jurisdiction.

2 Enforcement of existing statutory law will prevent the ill-effect.
3 Economic, social, or other conditions make it unfeasible, impractical, or unreasonable to mitigate the specified effect (California State Assembly Office of research, 1977:2).

In order to reduce the number of EIRs Senate amendments adopted a Negative Declaration procedure. This procedure enabled the sponsor of a project to avoid undertaking an EIR by declaring in the design of the project how any potential adverse impacts were to be eliminated. N. Hill describes how this procedure could work in practice:

Using this approach a city or county planning staff would analyse a project. If they found one or two significant effects that could be eliminated by modifications in the project, they would alert the project's sponsor. They would inform him of the potential significant effect and of the way in which his project could be modified to eliminate the effect. When all the significant effects were reduced to insignificance, a negative declaration could be prepared instead of an EIR. In many cases, the project's sponsors have gratefully modified their projects in order to qualify for a cheaper, faster and less controversial Negative Declaration. Using this approach county planning staffs have reported that they have achieved more environmental protection in their offices than they had ever been able to achieve through the formal EIR process (1977:4).

Negative Declarations should allow considerable short cuts by private and public bodies. Nevertheless adaptation to the new legislation has in the first instance been slow. Hill suggests that this can be explained partly by the resistance of administrative and bureaucratic bodies to change, but also by fears that law suits might considerably delay starting a project, so causing greater costs than those of preparing a full EIR.

There are still considerable delays and problems of policy integration. For large projects, in particular, there are often insurmountable problems of meeting declared objectives on unemployment, industrial location, agriculture, conservation, pollution control, energy and other policies. This problem of policy integration has not been surmounted by the use of EIRs. The consequent delays led to the Dow Chemical company's abandoning in 1977 a $500 million petrochemical complex in the Sacramento–San Joaquin Delta (Wandesforde-Smith, 1977). There is still consequently considerable financial interest in modifying the EIR procedure and improving its policy integrating function.

There is little doubt that the EIS and EIR procedures described above have been of great interest to other countries. In November 1974, the OECD recommended that its member countries should 'establish procedures and methodologies for forecasting and describing the environmental consequences of significant public and private projects likely to have a major impact on the quality of the environment; exchange information on environmental effects which would help them to forecast and describe the environmental effects of proposed programmes or projects' (Council of the Organization for Economic Co-operation, 1974). The World Bank and the US AID agency have shown considerable interest in investigating social and environmental impacts of proposed projects prior to funding (see Bisset, 1978).

The EEC has also indicated a strong interest in environmental impact assessment and its Environmental Programme 1977–81 includes a study on how such procedures might be adopted. Of EEC countries, Germany, by Ministerial decree of 22 August 1975, made it obligatory for environmental impact assessment to be undertaken for measures taken by federal authorities, local authorities, public organizations and foundations which are directly responsible to the state (Bulletin of the European Communities, 1976). In France environmental impact surveys became necessary from January 1978 for all public projects involving costs of at least 6 million francs (Elkington, 1978). In Eire, following the Local Government (Planning and Development) Act 1976, EISs can be required by the Minister for Local Government on any private project having a value of more than £5 million (Lee and Wood, 1978).

BRITAIN

In Britain, proposals for adopting formal environmental impact analysis for major projects have been made by the Royal Commission on Environmental Pollution in their report on Nuclear Power and the Environment as well as the Town and Country Planning Association. The advantages and disadvantages became an issue of some importance at the Windscale Inquiry into British Nuclear Fuels' application to build a nuclear reprocessing plant. EIA has also been the focus of two reports published by the DOE in 1976 (Catlow and Thirlwall, 1976; Project Appraisal for Development Control Team at Aberdeen University, 1976). These reports were commissioned following two other reports issued by the Dobry (1974) inquiry into the development control system. The inquiry expressed the view that there should be much greater information produced for the public on the social and environmental consequences of development proposals than had formerly been the case. It suggested that EIA might be useful in this respect and so lead to more informed planning. The DOE research reports on EIA that followed the Dobry inquiry have dealt specifically with questions of land use planning, and in this sense its scope has so far been rather narrowly investigated in the British context. The adequacy of other areas of policy-making which might have serious environmental consequences has as yet not been considered in relation to EIA.

The first DOE report by J. Catlow and C. G. Thirlwall attempted to look at the framework within which the EIA might work. Their recommendations were that county planning authorities in England and Wales and Regional and Island Councils in Scotland should be responsible for undertaking the EIA. The ensuing report would then be considered by the planning authority together with any comments on the report by those affected by the development proposal. There would be a reasonable time before any decision was made. The suggestion was for a twelve-month period instead of the eight weeks allowed under the General Development Orders. The EIA was not seen as a way of avoiding current planning procedures, but as supplementary and would only be applicable to between twenty-five and fifty projects in any one year, these projects being ones 'where the nature of the development, taken in conjunction with the existing environmental conditions, is such that large scale and complex environmental impacts will occur which are difficult to comprehend and analyse except by a systematic process in which the necessary specialist skills are employed' (1976:67).

Given a fairly sophisticated land use planning system in Britain, and a wealth of environmental legislation dealing with pollution and town and country planning, the EIA would consequently fit into the established system rather than replace it. It would be a tool for providing additional information rather than for imposing a new administrative framework for decision-making as was the case in America. How such analysis might be used within the existing development control procedures was also reviewed by the Project Appraisal for Development Control team at Aberdeen University. An indication of the procedures that might be adopted is shown in table 3.4.

The Aberdeen study was concerned in particular with the desirable characteristics of EIA, and the type of project to which it might be applied. It was concluded that EIA could usefully be applied to those developments with a large land-take; those of contentious nature; those having significant impact on the physical environment, on local employment or on the level of service provision; and those of a 'national' or 'regional' significance. Moreover, EIA could be of use when departing from approved plans (Elkington, 1977).

Although the DOE research reports have come out in favour of adopting EIA procedures, some serious objections have been made. First, it is arguably quite possible to use the present planning system to stimulate the information necessary for planning decisions without adopting a special EIA. Some, such as D. Lock (1976), have suggested referring complex development proposals to a planning inquiry commission which became possible following the 1971 Town and Country Planning Act, but has yet to be used. A planning inquiry commission would have advisers

Table 3.4   *An appraisal under existing development control procedures*

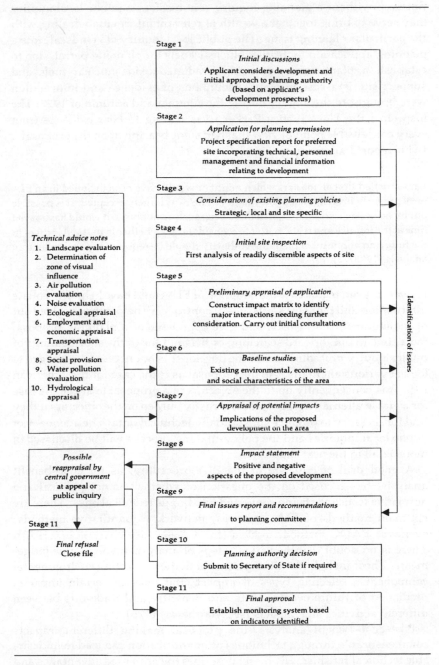

Technical advice notes
1. Landscape evaluation
2. Determination of zone of visual influence
3. Air pollution evaluation
4. Noise evaluation
5. Ecological appraisal
6. Employment and economic appraisal
7. Transportation appraisal
8. Social provision
9. Water pollution evaluation
10. Hydrological appraisal

Stage 1
Initial discussions
Applicant considers development and initial approach to planning authority (based on applicant's development prospectus)

Stage 2
Application for planning permission
Project specification report for preferred site incorporating technical, personnel management and financial information relating to development

Stage 3
Consideration of existing planning policies
Strategic, local and site specific

Stage 4
Initial site inspection
First analysis of readily discernible aspects of site

Stage 5
Preliminary appraisal of application
Construct impact matrix to identify major interactions needing further consideration. Carry out initial consultations

Stage 6
Baseline studies
Existing environmental, economic and social characteristics of the area

Stage 7
Appraisal of potential impacts
Implications of the proposed development on the area

Stage 8
Impact statement
Positive and negative aspects of the proposed development

Stage 9
Final issues report and recommendations
to planning committee

Stage 10
Planning authority decision
Submit to Secretary of State if required

Stage 11
Final approval
Establish monitoring system based on indicators identified

Possible reappraisal by central government at appeal or public inquiry

Stage 11
Final refusal
Close file

Identification of issues

(*Source:* Clark, 1976:92)

and would be able to call witnesses, and if necessary commission studies. But even without a planning inquiry commission, a public local inquiry may serve to bring together a wealth of relevant information dealing with the particular planning issue. The public local inquiry at Windscale into a planning application by British Nuclear Fuels for planning permission to establish a plant for reprocessing irradiated oxide nuclear fuels and support site is a case in point. Mountains of evidence and information were brought to the inquiry during the summer and autumn of 1977. The inspector, the Hon. Justice Parker, was willing to hear evidence from every conceivable point of view that had some bearing upon the proposals. In his report Parker comments:

I am satisfied that all matters which might or would have been included in an EIA were properly investigated at the inquiry. This was largely accepted. It is possible but by no means certain that, had there been such an analysis, it would have saved time at the inquiry and it is a matter for consideration whether in particular cases in the future an applicant or planning authority should be required to prepare such an analysis (1978:73).

However, even in this case the adoption of EIA could have helped to collate information and pinpoint key issues of controversy before they evolved out of the inquiry itself. This would give opponents of a planning proposal more time to put forward searching criticism. One of the shortcomings of public inquiry procedure is that the developer is not necessarily obliged to look at various alternatives to the proposal as is the case for the American EIS. It is consequently up to the objectors of a proposal to argue the case for a viable alternative. This places a costly burden on the objectors if they find it necessary to produce substantially technical data. The adequacy of public local inquiries and the policy-making process will be discussed in more detail in the next chapter.

A good deal of criticism of the EIA procedure, as for cost–benefit analysis, has focused on the question of whether or not political and normative issues are being converted into bogus technical ones. There are six main methods of EIA: matrices; networks; quantitative methods; overlays; PADC method; models (for a review see Clark *et al.*, 1978). There is no doubt that the various steps of analysis involve value judgements. These include identifying major activities; selecting environmental components; selecting types of impact; the risks of certain impacts; prediction of future events; costs and benefits; and trade-offs between different activities and impacts (see Matthews, 1975).

Like cost–benefit analysis, the proposal making different impacts commensurable through techniques of quantification can lead to undesirable technical fetishism. R. Bisset describes the professed advantages and limitations of the best known quantitative method – the Environmental Evaluation System (EES) – and some of its kindred types:

Those who advocate quantification see it as a means of reducing the amount of and complexity of data obtained during impact analysis and, consequently, making the task of decision-maker(s) easier. EES exemplifies one of the main problems of wholly quantitative methods. All impacts are related to each other by differential weighing. In this method 1,000 weighting units are distributed amongst 78 environmental and social parameters likely to be affected by a development. Anthropologists might query the value judgements which result in 'adequate species diversity' receiving 13 of these units and 'Indians' receiving 14 (1978:3).

Bisset goes on to argue that quantitative methods often 'enhance dubious scientific predictions by using complex technical jargon and data'. Such methods lead to legitimation of contentious development projects by diverting and mystifying potential opposition. Unfortunately critics of EIA (and cost–benefit analysis) have very often failed to go beyond a tirade of polemical abuse, and have merely suggested that decision-making involving trade-offs should be based upon intuition which often amounts to confused and muddled thinking (see, for example, the popularized analyses of Brookes, 1976, and Eversley, 1976). What critics have less often explored are the very assumptions behind attempts to make impacts commensurable.

At the heart of capitalism lies the notion that everything has an exchange value or a market price. Pollution must have a price and must be traded with other costs and benefits that derive from business activity. Market values and exchange values exist so that profit can be made. Environmental impact analysis, like cost–benefit analysis, offers a technique for attaching a price to environmental and social impacts that have previously not been exchanged in the market. The question of what price is attached to what consequences is a matter of bargaining, but as with commodity goods, capital owners and the ruling class are better able to ensure that the process of evaluation, or the mechanisms of the market, operate in their interests. The next chapter will explore this argument in more detail while looking at alternative concepts of pressure groups and power.

4 Pressure Groups and Power

In the last two chapters we have seen how techniques of planning have tended to reflect and reinforce the social order of capitalism. In this chapter we will consider how interest groups influence the outcome of environmental planning or the lack of it. The study of pressure groups and power makes little sense except in relation to structures of constraint. Such constraints may be economic, political or ideological. Pressure groups operate within structures but they also seek to alter structures in accordance with their own interests. There exists what S. Lukes calls a dialectic of power and structure:

Social life can only properly be understood as a dialectic of power and structure, a web of possibilities for agents, whose nature is both active and structured, to make choices and pursue strategies within given limits, which in consequence expand and contract overtime. Any standpoint or methodology which reduces that dialectic to a one-sided consideration of agents without (internal and external) structural limits, or structures without agents, or which does not address the problem of their interrelations, will be unsatisfactory. No social theory merits serious attention that fails to retain an ever-present sense of dialectic of power and structure (1977:29).

Much of this chapter will serve to reinforce Lukes' remarks, for there is still a widespread belief among the corporate planning movement that local authorities can act as environmental managers in a way that is virtually free from constraint. This naïve view fails to recognize the influence and constraint of the economic and social structure. In Britain, for example, local authorities in the inner city areas have found it virtually impossible to avoid the development of urban decay as a result of the market processes that have been operating since the Second World War. These market constraints are compounded by the New Towns Programme which has also attracted industry and people out of the inner cities (see Young, 1977).

It is necessary therefore to look not only at how pressure groups are able to influence and control the political agenda but also at how they seek to modify the policy-making institutions and their rules of conduct so that they operate in their own interests. We shall look at the pluralist view of pressure groups and compare this with a Marxist view.

According to R. Dahl (1961), one of the principal exponents of the pluralist perspective, every citizen has the right and possibility within a pluralist society to seek access to the political process in pursuit of his own preferences. Any disputes are settled within the context of a planning system which has a consensus of support. The pluralist justifies the existence of élites, whether they be civil servants, executive members of pressure groups, or elected politicians, in terms of representation. Élites compete for support as politicians compete for votes. A. Downs (1957) draws the analogy with liberal economic theory where private enterprise produces what is demanded. It is argued that competition between élites, as between businesses, leads to what is demanded by consumers. As with commodities, nobody will buy the policy recommendations of a pressure group unless there is a popular demand for them. M. Parenti outlines the pluralist/élitist position as follows:

No evidence is found supporting the claim that a corporate 'power élite' rules over an inarticulate mass. If there are élites in our society, they are numerous and specialized, and they are checked in their demand by the institutionalized rules of the political culture and by the competing demands of other élites, all of whom represent varying, if sometimes overlapping, constituencies. Conflict is multi-lateral and ever-changing, and the 'bulk of the population consists not of the mass but of integrated groups and publics, stratified with varying degrees of power' (Rose, 1967:16), and endowed with a 'multitude of techniques for exercising influence on decisions salient to them' (Polsby, 1963:118) (1970:112).

In this assessment, the power and resources that pressure groups can command derive largely from their public support. According to T. B. Bottomore (1966) élites and the theories that justify them amount to government by representation and cannot really lead to democratic government by people. Moreover, élite theory and pluralism can only be justified theoretically if it can be proved that there is equality of opportunity to influence planning. If this were not so there would not be a free circulation of élites and there would not be a true plurality of interests in policy-making.

From a Marxist standpoint, the division of labour under capitalism influences the development of an élite class, prevents significant mobility between classes and so maintains a non-egalitarian society. The romantic idealism of Marx in *The German Ideology* elegantly expresses the point:

. . . As soon as the division of labour begins, each man has a particular, exclusive sphere of activity, which is forced upon him and from which he cannot escape. He is a hunter, a fisherman, a shepherd, or a critical critic, and must remain so if he does not want to lose his means of livelihood; whereas in communist society, where nobody has one exclusive sphere of activity but each can become accomplished in any branch he wishes, production as a whole is regulated by society, thus making it possible for me to do one thing today and another tomorrow, to hunt in the morning, fish in the afternoon, rear cattle in the evening, criticize after dinner, in accordance with my inclination, without ever becoming hunter, fisherman, shepherd or critic (Bottomore and Rubel, 1963:110–11).

Power, according to some Marxists, derives from 'the capacity of a social class to realize its specific objective interests' (Poulantzas, 1973:104). Within a capitalist society it is the ruling capital-owning class that is most able to realize its own objective interest. This, however, does not prevent oppressed groups from 'seizing power'. But it does mean that this task is difficult, since structural constraints operate in favour of the ruling class and against oppressed groups. These constraints on policy-making are seen not as abstract political constraints, as the pluralists believe, but as political constraints that are related to economic interests. The fact that lower-class groups fail to participate in decision-making activities is consequently of no surprise to the Marxist but provides strong evidence against the pluralist claim that power is fragmented and that all interests can therefore participate in policy-making.

The Marxist analysis emphasizes the objective substantive achievements of different classes instead of merely focusing on the behaviour of those involved in the planning process. Concentration on participants' behaviour has serious theoretical weaknesses, for power and influence may be exercised without any observable behaviour (see Lukes, 1974). Weak interest groups will tend not to raise issues when expectations of successfully resolving them in their favour is small. Hence groups with power may enjoy their position because of the passive acceptance of the state of affairs, or as G. C. Moodie has suggested, 'the absence of pressure may therefore be of little significance – it could, conceivably, mean either that the potential pressure is so great that it need not be applied, or that the aggrieved group has no leverage' (1970:65). Westergaard and Resler (1976) claim that a behaviourist view of power would neglect the domination of a paternalist employer over a passive and unorganized labour force or of a totalitarian government which had exterminated all effective opposition. The behaviourist perspective would only come into play when the labour force became organized or there was some questioning of the legitimacy of the dominating groups: a situation where the power of one group over another had become less strong. Likewise environmental planning is often the outcome of the lack of overt conflict and resistance to proposals. This can be due to the distribution of resources within society, which presents alternative ways of satisfying objective interests, rather than to a lack of interest on the part of affected parties.

The pluralist study of environmental pressure groups

In *Anonymous Empire: A Study of the Lobby in Great Britain*, S. E. Finer is of the opinion that 'mostly the lobbies seek to get their way by advice or, at the best, by persuasion. But should they fail, and the issue be serious, or the association be obstinate or angry, it can employ a number of techniques, each involving lesser or greater degrees of "pressure"' (1969:24). The first major studies of environmental groups by R. Gregory (1971) accepted this behaviourist focus. Gregory himself looked at the ways in which different groups argued about the values of amenity. The persuasiveness of amenity groups was set against the case of the developers. The values of amenity were determined by the outcome of the dispute and the arguments and techniques of the different groups. R. Kimber and J. J. Richardson (1974(a)), following Gregory's work and similar studies, have suggested that the use of various resources by pressure groups make it more or less likely that they will be successful. These resources are: access to information and advance intelligence; liaison with administrators, politicians and legislators; rational argument and the merits of the case; relationships with the mass media; resources such as wealth, leadership skills and cohesiveness; sanctions.

The claim that the success of pressure groups may be enhanced by mobilizing resources bears a strong resemblance to management theory. The utilization of money, labour, the communications media, institutional networks, etc. enable a pressure group (industry) to sell its ideas. J. D. McCarthy and M. N. Zald argue that social movement organizations (SMOs) are able to do just this: 'grievances and discontent may be defined, created, and manipulated by issue entrepreneurs and organizations' (1977:1,215). The analogy with the market does not stop here: 'perceived lack of success in goal accomplishment by a SMO may lead an individual to switch to SMOs with alternative strategies or, to the extent that products are substitutable, to switch to those with other target goals' (1977:1,229). McCarthy and Zald even go so far as to talk about a social movement industry (SMI). Competition between pressure groups and their ability to win campaigns are regarded as equivalent, then, to free enterprise competition under capitalism. The pressure groups that succeed are those best able to mobilize resources:

SMOs depending heavily upon such resource mobilization techniques must resort to slick packaging and convoluted appeal to self-interest in order to make their products more attractive. This should be especially true within competitive SMIs. The behaviour in the early 1970s of environmental groups, which depend heavily upon isolated constituents, appears to illustrate the point. Many of those SMOs took credit for stalling the Alaskan pipeline and attempted to link that issue to personal self-interest and preferences in their direct-mail advertising. Slick packaging is evident in the high quality of printing and the heavy use of photogravure (1977:1,231).

A great number of pressure group studies have focused on resource mobilization and an analysis of the success or failure of pressure group tactics. What follows is a description of some of these resources. Much stress has been laid on access to information and advance intelligence as they are often a prerequisite to making a rational and well-argued case at the right time. Moreover, access to information may reveal important issues that would otherwise remain dormant. The British lorry drivers' revelation of details about illicit cyanide tipping to members of the Conservation Society in 1972 illustrates this point. The leak of Cabinet secrets concerning the shelving of a new family allowance scheme in 1977 is another example.

In the case of local planning matters advance warning of proposed planning applications may be of much assistance to amenity groups such as the CPRE county branches (see Ringrose-Voase, 1970). On the other hand, the local planning authority may well give little forewarning of controversial planning proposals which they themselves sponsor. Kimber and Richardson (1974) cite the case of Harrogate, when controversial plans were submitted to the planning committee only four days before it met. Other developers will also try to keep secret their intentions if it will facilitate success in planning applications. For example, Gregory (1974) argues that attention to the siting of the M4 before the decision was publicly announced occurred only when the surveyors were noticed in action. In the same way, Rio Tinto Zinc's mineral investigations during the late 1960s in the Snowdonia National Park were shrouded in secrecy (Searle, 1975).

Environmental pressure groups may collect information themselves or commission reports from sympathetic experts. The Royal Society for the Protection of Birds and the British Trust for Ornithology collected information on bird deaths which was used to determine the effects of certain agricultural chemicals (Lowe, 1975(b)). Among pressure groups, official and private organizations, key individuals may act as 'gatekeepers' exerting control over the information available to other groups. Secretaries of societies can play an important part here in influencing the strategies adopted by their own and other societies.

Access to information, and the possibility of making use of this information, depends upon liaison with other bodies such as administrators, politicians, legislators and the mass media. P. Lowe (1977) has pointed out that voluntary groups are playing an increasingly important part as mediators between the public and planners. He refers to the Kent County Council's decision in 1975 to conduct most of its consultation through the Kent Federation of Amenity Societies. Given this structuring of public participation, representation and exclusion of groups by the federation become important for many diverse interests within the county. S. J. Dolbey (1969), in her study of the politics of Manchester's water supply, demonstrated how appeals to National Trust members in the House of Lords helped to block a Private Bill. The Bill was promoted by the Manchester Corporation in 1962 to enable it to take water from Ullswater in the Lake District. At this time 932 peers were on the roll, of whom 120 were members of the National Trust.

Liaison with administrators is a dominant feature of many environmental groups such as the CPRE, which spends a considerable amount of time submitting evidence to committees and commenting on white papers and reports in an attempt to influence the outcome of legislation or Departmental policy. The National Smoke Abatement Society (now National Society for Clean Air) had gained a considerable reputation as an authority on air pollution when the Beaver Committee was set up after the 1952 smog disaster. Three members of the society were appointed to this committee of twelve. The society's links with the MP Gerald Nabarro were important in influencing the eventual clean air legislation of 1956. The National Smoke Abatement Society had also developed the idea of smokeless zones through liaison with newspapers and television. The effectiveness of the National Society for Clean Air has continued to rest on its authority and expertise. Its advice on the implementation of legislation is sought by local authorities and various statutory bodies, many of whom are members of the society and contribute substantially to its funds.

Such close administrative links are, however, rare, although it is not uncommon for members of societies to sit on Government Committees. For example, when the Ministry of Housing and Local Government set up the Gosling Committee on Footpaths in 1967 four out of the eleven members were on the CPRE executive committee (Lowe, 1975(b)). Allison has argued that the status and prestige of pressure groups are often enhanced by electing well-known personalities to official positions. His analysis of pressure groups stresses the professional and titled qualifications of their officers. Thus the Conservation Society's officers, including Vice-President, in 1969 showed:

Titles	5	15%
Doctors	5	15%
Professors	10	30%
Civil awards	7	22%
None of these	5	15%

(Allison, 1975:122)

The problems of presenting a solid rational case opposing certain proposals or promoting new ones is not as straightforward as it might appear. Experts have often to be approached. The arguments of the 'opposition' must be understood and successfully countered. Viable alternatives must also be put forward using persuasive arguments backed up by reliable and detailed information. Access to such information and its presentation may impose heavy costs, and it is in this aspect of planning that the wealth of pressure groups and their contacts with professionals willing to give advice freely or at little cost are undoubtedly of great importance.

The Wing Airport Resistance Association's (WARA) opposition to the siting of the third London airport at Cublington illustrates this point. It had to undertake a critical analysis of the cost–benefit study by the Roskill Commission and also argue for the advantages of Foulness over Cublington. The overall costs to WARA were £57,240, of which 76 per cent was for legal and professional expenses, 16.3 per cent for publicity and public relations, and 7.3 per cent for administration (Kimber and Richardson, 1974(b)). In another case the costs to the CPRE for the fight over the Manchester Water Order for Ullswater and Windermere during the period from 1961 to 1966 amounted to some £11,000. This opposition had involved the attention of the local planning authority, both Houses of Parliament, a special conference, a public inquiry, two Ministries and finally the Cabinet. The costs of fighting an issue in the courts or at a public inquiry may of course prevent some affected groups from taking action, especially if attendance during working hours involves loss of income. Lack of financial resources could therefore cause ineffective presentation of a case or indeed prevent the case ever being made.

On the whole sanctions are rarely used, but perhaps the commonest threat available to pressure groups is that of causing delays through outright opposition to a planning proposal. Given the extensive possibilities of delaying planning decisions in the United States through litigation, this tactic may be more common than one might expect. In Britain, Kimber and Richardson cite the example recorded in the Civic Trust News Letter of March 1972: 'In June 1969, one of the more active branches of the CPRE, the Sheffield and Peak District Branch, threatened to oppose the proposed expansion of a cement works in the Hope Valley and thereby cause a very considerable delay to the company concerned. By making this threat the Branch managed to gain important concessions from the company, which enabled the Peak Planning Board to impose conditions on the planning permission that the company would otherwise have contested' (1974(a):221).

The use of direct action in an attempt to prevent changes in land use has not been uncommon. The first national amenity pressure group, the Commons Preservation Society founded in 1865, took direct action in its attempts to preserve the common land in London. On one occasion in 1866, 120 workmen were employed during the night to remove two miles of fencing that had recently been erected to enclose Berkhamstead Common (Eversley, 1910). In the early 1930s the rambling mvement organized mass trespassing on Kinder Scout in the Peak District to draw attention to their case for access to the countryside.

During more recent years some of the new pressure groups such as the Friends of the Earth have adopted direct action tactics. Greenpeace, an international organization, has adopted techniques of hindering whaling operations and seal culls by cruising in boats between the hunters and their intended victims. But it is the anti-nuclear power policy demonstrations that have marked the most militant opposition from environmentalists and others. On 25 September 1977 some 60,000 demonstrators descended on the uncompleted fast-breeder reactor site in Kalkar, Germany. The demonstration went by peacefully, but the security operation necessary in case of trouble was enormous. Some 7,500 police surrounded the site, cars and coaches were searched at the borders, French and Dutch demonstrators were turned back, and paratroopers searched the trains travelling to Kalkar (see *Undercurrents*, 1977:25,2). Anti-nuclear demonstrations at Malville in France a few months earlier had not taken place so peacefully. One demonstrator was killed and several police were seriously injured.

This view of 'power resources' assumes that their availability and use depend upon public demand, and that pressure groups responding to some issue will therefore automatically be able to mobilize 'power resources'. What this school of thought manifestly fails to realize is that different classes have different opportunities of mobilizing resources to achieve their objective interests. The pluralist account assumes equal access to these resources, but this assumption is very obviously incorrect. The working classes on the whole have less opportunity to take time off from work to pursue their own interests, and have less access to telephones and other resources which would help them in a protest campaign. Legislation and land use controls tend to help protect the environment for élitist groups and deny opportunities for enhancing the quality of the environment for the rest (see Healy, 1976; and Neuhaus, 1971). Lack of the same opportunities to pursue their interests does not prevent people from taking action but it does make the task much harder. Alternative tactics to those described by Kimber and Richardson would also be more likely to result in success. Power is easier to mobilize by collective action through well-established unions or political parties, which can bring pressure to bear so as to neutralize the power of opposing interests. This is not, however, the subject of a pluralist account.

The pluralist account of pressure groups is not confined solely to a discussion of tactics. The concept of pluralism is itself a relative notion, since there can be more or less public representation and participation. Consequently one of the main concerns is that decision-making should be as open as possible and should at least have the appearance of being representative. One of the main worries of pluralist thinkers in Britain has been the extent to which national environmental policy can be scrutinized by representatives of the public, either at public inquiries or within Parliament. The question of public accountability and representation has been a central political issue in the controversies surrounding motorway inquiries and nuclear power planning. The adequacy of public inquiries and parliamentary control will now be discussed. It will be shown that the type of response made by the government has gone a long way to satisfy pluralist criteria but leaves the influences on motorway planning and nuclear power policy virtually unchanged.

PUBLIC INQUIRIES

The public inquiry system has its origins in the enclosure movement of the nineteenth century. During the latter part of the enclosure movement Private Bills had become increasingly necessary for farmers who wished to enclose and work land which was not privately owned. The Private Bill procedure was cumbersome for what was seen as a routine affair, especially when there was no opposition to enclosure. The enclosure procedure was made less cumbersome by a provision of the Enclosure Act 1845 which introduced an order for a government department to hold an inquiry which could settle land ownership rights, and only if there was opposition would the Private Bill procedure be reverted to. Here was the first case of land use planning control being delegated from Parliament to the executive. This type of order was extended to other policy areas such as public health in 1848 and local government from 1858. The Commons Act 1876 made it obligatory for the Inspector at a public inquiry to hear anyone who wished to speak, and also laid down procedural rules. In the twentieth century public inquiries were introduced under town and country planning legislation as well as legislation dealing with electricity production and distribution, water resource development, roads, etc.

The Private Bill procedure is now very rarely used by promoters of land use change although it is still used when the alternative is a complex series of public inquiries. In the case of the Cow Green Reservoir project in the Tees Valley, the Cleveland Water Board promoted a Private Bill to avoid the public inquiries otherwise necessary under the Water Act 1945, the Land Acquisition (Authorization Procedure) Act 1946, and the Commons Act 1899. (Grove-White, 1975). The crucial stage of a Private Bill is during the committee stage following the second reading. Here four or five members of the House of Commons or House of Lords will sit and hear both sides of the case if the Bill is opposed. In a semi-judicial capacity the committee then recommends that the Bill be supported or opposed.

The costs to the objectors of opposing a Private Bill during the committee stage are particularly onerous, running usually into several thousands of pounds. For example, when the North Wales (Hydro-Electricity) Protection Committee opposed the North Wales Hydro-Electric Power Bill for nine days in May 1973, they incurred costs of £3,000 (CPRE Bulletin, 1973). Apart from the committee stage, the opposers of the Private Bill must try to seek support in the House during the second and third readings when debating support and voting becomes crucial.

Today most of the land use planning has been completely delegated from Parliament to the minister concerned. However, for certain types of project there are further procedures whereby objectors may appeal to Parliament if dissatisfied with the Minister's decision after a public inquiry. For example, special Parliamentary procedures may be set up under the Water Act 1945 and the Water Resources Act 1963, whereby a joint committee of both Houses of Parliament sit in judgement on the planning application and can reverse the Minister's final order (Grove-White, 1975).

Almost all controversial planning proposals are the subject of a local planning inquiry. There must, however, be evidence of controversy. Thus there was no public inquiry over the application to build a nuclear power station at Heysham, near Lancaster, despite the fact that it has been the only nuclear power station to be built close to a large population area. In this case there were few objections at the time of the proposal. Some planning proposals may go unnoticed while the energy of potential opposition is directed elsewhere. The oil production platform application at Loch Kishorn is an example. This application was approved without a public inquiry although the inquiry inspector at the Drumbuie public inquiry considered its beauty to surpass that of Drumbuie itself. The Loch Kishorn application was submitted just one month after the Drumbuie application for an oil production platform had been rejected following a long and expensive public inquiry. It is more than likely that the objectors, led by the National Trust for Scotland, had grown weary after this long and much publicized case (see *Guardian*, 24 September 1975). Moreover, the National Trust for Scotland was not directly concerned as it did not own land at the Kishorn site.

Local inquiries are also requested by a Minister when a developer appeals against the decision of a local planning authority, or when a local planning application is sufficiently controversial to cause a significant number of objections, irrespective of whether or not the local authority gives approval to the application. In both cases the Minister acts as final arbiter, and the inquiry can be seen as an administrative mechanism to help him reach an appropriate decision. The question of whether public inquiry procedures should follow judicial practices has been a continuing source of debate. The Franks Committee of 1957 recognized that openness, fairness and impartiality should be encouraged, whereas the discretionary nature of an inquiry and its role of aiding the Minister in making the final decision are administrative decisions. During a visit to the Selby Coalfield in mid-1977 Peter Shore, the Secretary of State for the Environment, re-affirmed the importance of the public inquiry in terms of both efficient administration and fairness to the public:

. . . first, I believe that as a result of our inquiry processes we can make better informed decisions which fit the facts and which fit into national, regional and local objectives; second, our inquiry system enables us to hear and to have answered the legitimate anxieties of people who have the right to express their concern; third, the public examination of these large questions assist us in achieving a measure of consent when final decisions are made . . . My concern is to try to strike the right balance between efficiency and speed in decision-making on the one hand and on the other to satisfy myself on the issues and to see to it that the public are convinced of the fairness of the decision-making system (*Journal of Planning and Environmental Law*, 1977:695).

In a series of court cases from the Errington case of 1934 to the Fairmont decision in the House of Lords in 1976 it has been held that public inquiry procedures should be just. In the latter case a compulsory purchase order was quashed on the grounds of violation of natural justice at an inquiry. However, in December 1977 the High Court rejected an application by two members of the M42 Action Committee seeking to quash approval of the M42 Scheme given by the Secretary of State for the Environment. The petitioners had contended that they were not able to cross-examine Departmental witnesses on the methods of forecasting traffic-flows. They also claimed they were unable to answer evidence arising after the inquiry which was taken into account by the Minister. The judge, while arguing that the refusal to permit cross-examination of witnesses was a denial of natural justice, also claimed that if every document produced at a public inquiry had to be proved inquiries would take much longer: 'The likely result would be for the public inquiry system to collapse', and the judge, Sir Douglas Frank, QC, decided that 'there must come a point at which the rights of objectors end and the freedom of the Minister to implement his policy begins' (see Grove-White, 1978). This judgement has clouded the extent to which natural justice must be permitted within the public inquiry procedures.

In the motorway inquiry controversies, objectors found that they could not question the assumptions on which policies were based, but instead that debate was confined to discussing the merits of alternative routes. For example, at a local public inquiry into the Denton relief road (the M67) in 1975, the DOE's inspector was asked to disregard any evidence submitted in relation to the need for the motorway (*Guardian*, 10 December 1977). The Town and Country Planning (Inquiry Procedure) Rules 1974 and Highway (Inquiry Procedure) Rules 1976 legitimated the doctrine that national policy matters are for Parliament scrutiny alone and have consequently restricted the scope of objectors' challenges to proposals. It is worth bearing in mind that the Private Bill procedure of old never constrained the rights of an objector to argue against the need of a proposed project.

The disruption by opponents of motorway policy at the Aire Valley, M25, M3, Eastleigh and Archway Public Inquiries was based upon the following grounds for dissatisfaction. First, objectors argued that national policy matters should not be excluded because there had been no national policy formulated and debated in public – what emerged as transport policy was merely a product of Departmental planning and the assumptions it chose to accept (see Adams, 1977; Sharman, 1977; Tyme, 1978). Although there had been a White Paper in 1970, *Roads for the Future*, which had been the basis of national policy, much had changed since then. There had been the energy crisis of 1973 and a widespread public reaction against motorways which its critics felt ought to be considered in national policy.

Secondly, motorway objectors found it intolerable that they could not challenge the techniques involving forecasting and cost–benefit analysis on which local and national policies were based. Lord Foot (Chairman of the Dartmoor Preservation Association) referred to a road inquiry in Plymouth in 1974: 'we were presented with a multiplicity of forecasts and extrapolations as to what would be the traffic-flows in the years 1980 and 2000 coming from all kinds of different sources. Plymouth City Council had their own extrapolation which differed fundamentally from those of the Department of the Environment – and, indeed, one witness from the Department of the Environment was in favour of one extrapolation, while another was in favour of a different one. It is absolutely intolerable that objectors to a scheme who say, 'there is no need for this' should not be allowed to challenge not the policy, but the assumptions of that which the Department of the Environment choose to make' (House of Lords, debate, 2 July 1976).

Following many disruptions to the M3 inquiry, the inspector, Major-General Raymond Edge, conceded the need for a cost–benefit analysis of the objectors' alternative proposal to upgrade the existing by-pass (*The Times*, 24 August 1976). The distinction between national policy and information establishing the necessity of a particular project was clearly made by the *Expenditure Committee on 'public expenditure on transport'* (House of Commons Paper No. 269). It recommended in its first report in 1974 that 'the right to challenge the need for a transport scheme at a public inquiry should be firmly established. It should allow consideration of different pricing structures and of the traffic forecasts which underline proposals. It should not, however, embrace the question of directing passengers or freight on to a particular form of transport; this is a matter of policy, to be decided by Parliament' (1974:xvii). In response to objections that forecasting and cost–benefit techniques were unreliable the government diffused the objectors' ill-feeling over this issue by setting up the Leitch Committee in December 1976 to inquire into the justification for motorways and trunk roads, and into the official traffic forecasts upon which they are based (*The Times*, 31 January 1977).

The third ground for objection was that the inspectors at local inquiries were appointed by the Department that had called for the inquiry. The Department was, metaphorically speaking, both judge and jury of its own case. The anti-roads lobby wanted to see the appointment of the inspector made by the Lord Chancellor (see House of Lords debate, 2 July 1976). The fourth ground for complaint was that those who object on amenity grounds, and are not statutory objectors, can only be heard at the discretion of the inspector. All these objections to the operation of public inquiries were closely associated with a pluralistic conception of planning. The demands were for better representation so that policy-making could better reflect a plurality of interests.

The response by government has been to investigate the objections which were made during the period of disturbances at motorway inquiries and to adopt slightly new procedures. These go a long way to satisfying the demands for greater public participation and apparent fairness which are the hallmarks of pluralist prescriptions. The Department of Transport and the Department of the Environment in conjunction with the Council on Tribunals set out these changes in a White Paper in April 1978 (Report on the Review of Highway Inquiry Procedures, 1978). The administrative purpose of the public inquiry was confirmed, and at the same time the White Paper made recommendations for improving fairness. For example, the Lord Chancellor would be asked to appoint public inquiry inspectors as requested by environmental groups. More information on proposed plans would be made available. In this there was total agreement with the Leitch Committee which reported in October 1977.

In future, it was stated, a new covering note would be circulated on the policy and reasons for the public inquiry as well as information on the assumptions made in planning and on the general background to the road programme. Pre-inquiry procedural meetings would be adopted to agree a programme for hearing objections, deciding upon relevant policy matters, and resolving some questions of fact. In other words objectors will have access to the same information for considering future road proposals as the Department of Transport, and this will be available well in advance of the public inquiry. Moreover, alternative routes will receive much greater attention.

The government was still unwilling to meet the costs of objectors at public inquiries unless they were successful in their case, but nevertheless recommendations went a long way towards increasing the level of information on which policy decisions were to be debated. What the government was unwilling to do was to allow the public inquiry to become a forum for debating national policy on trunk roads or for challenging the methodologies such as the principles of forecasting and cost–benefit analysis. These were to be issues of Departmental concern; the Minister responsible for such policies, it was argued, was accountable to Parliament and hence the public at large.

At the Windscale inquiry into THORP, an exception was made to the national/local policy demarcation because the inquiry became a forum for discussing broad issues of national energy policy as well as the implications concerning nuclear proliferation, hazardous pollution, and terrorism. In this particular issue the government responded to the pluralistic demands of open debate at a local level, but this made some sense as there were certainly no grounds for claiming that a national policy already existed. The Secretary of State for the Environment has also promised a separate 'local' public inquiry which will allow wider relevant issues to be considered when a decision is needed on whether or not to proceed with a fast-breeder reactor. In other areas of energy policy objectors have been less successful at raising questions of national concern. Only three power station applications have been rejected by a Minister in the twenty years since the creation of the CEGB in 1957 (these were at Holme Pierrepoint (oil-fired, 1961), Stourport (nuclear, 1970), and Connah's Quay (nuclear, 1972)). In none of these cases was the rejection based upon grounds of need, but instead all were based upon land use priority considerations (Flood and Grove-White, 1976).

In 1973, the North Wales (Hydro-Electric) Protection Committee opposed a Parliamentary Bill to give CEGB powers to construct a storage reservoir scheme at Llanberis in Snowdonia National Park. As it was a Private Bill, policy issues were discussed, but the objectors failed as a result of a decision taken years previously that storage space was needed somewhere in the generating system (CPRE Bulletin, 1973). This sort of case is comparable to the motorway application which is part of a larger national scheme.

In making a distinction between national and local policy matters the government was merely following the long-trodden path recognized by the Franks Report (1957) on Administrative Tribunals and Inquiries. In this report it was clearly argued that broad policy 'is something for which a Minister is answerable to Parliament alone' and 'should not be automatically open to debate in a restrictive forum of the inquiry'. This power of exclusion 'would avoid useless discussion of policy in the wrong forum, but the manner of its exercise would itself be open to criticism in the right forum – Parliament.' There is much sense in this local/national policy distinction. In 1977, for example, there were twenty-seven public inquiries into big road schemes in England. It would understandably have been a great waste of time and money to debate the same issues of national policy, forecasting and cost–benefit techniques at each inquiry. The problem now in the pluralist perspective is to what extent national policy is accountable to Parliament and the public.

PARLIAMENTARY CONTROL OVER ENVIRONMENTAL POLICY

In theory Ministers are accountable to Parliament, but in practice Parliamentary scrutiny of the executive has left much to be desired, Ministerial accountability may be examined through questions in the House of Commons, but discussion of environmental policy is usually confined to debates on Bills, Green and White Papers and the adjournment debate. The technical complications of energy and transportation forecasting tend to limit informed discussion to only a few members of Parliament. In a House of Lords debate in February 1976, which touched upon traffic forecasts, the government spokesman, Baroness Stedman, felt obliged to admit: 'I do not profess to understand or be able to translate the mathematical formula referred to by the noble Lord, Lord Avebury' (see *The Times*, 29 July 1976). T. O'Riordan also pointed out that in an adjournment debate on nuclear reactors only fifteen members spoke, and all but three were members of the Select Committee on Science and Technology. The extent of Parliamentary scrutiny was, in this case, clearly dependent upon Select Committee procedure.

While nuclear power policy had been discussed by the Select Committee on Science and Technology, no such committee had reviewed motorway policy. Moreover, according to J. Tyme, the anti-motorway campaigner, who was writing in November 1975:

It is now clear that Parliament has never had the opportunity to debate or approve the enormous financial, economic and land-use commitment which the nation is being compelled to make in the form of the planned 3,100 mile motorway/trunk road network. A careful scrutiny of Hansard since 1967 reveals that only in that year did any vote take place on a motion put to the House. That was on 22 February 1967 when it approved £1,000 million on inter-urban construction. No vote was taken on Dr John Dunwoody's motion (24 February 1967) that 'an extended motorway plan should now be produced', nor upon Mr Mulley's White Paper of May 1970. Even more startling is the discovery that the all-important Road Strategy Paper of June 1971 was not even the subject of Parliamentary questions, and the Secretary of State deprived the House of any opportunity to debate it by refusing to publish it as a White Paper (Hansard, 6 July 1971). Furthermore, no debate whatever on the motorway and trunk road network has taken place in Parliament since 1971 (1975:321).

One of the ways in which Parliament has responded to the lack of informed Parliamentary debate has been to set up Select Committees staffed by Members of Parliament. There is no doubt that these committees have some influence, though limited, on government policy. A. Palmer, Chairman of the Select Committee on Science and Technology, thought that their report on nuclear reactors had an important influence on the government's decision to dismiss the CEGB's preferred policy of adopting the American-styled light water nuclear reactors. This Committee has also on occasion challenged departmental evaluations. In 1975, for example, it pointed out the falsity of the Department of Energy's conservation statistics. It claimed that some of the reduction in energy consumption labelled as conservation was in fact due to the industrial recession (*The Times*, 27 May 1976). The CPRE has argued that Select Committee scrutiny of policy should be extended: 'it should become standard practice for public authorities such as those for electricity supply, water and motorways to submit regularly to Parliament detailed draft statements of long-range policy and for Parliament, in turn, to create select committees with specific responsibilities for scrutinizing each' (Grove-White, 1977).

The problems which Select Committees face are numerous and there are serious constraints upon extending Parliamentary scrutiny of policy in this manner. First there is the question of time. Select Committees often cannot meet for more than two and a half hours a week and the topics covered are limited by the MPs available and the time they can devote to a Select Committee. Other *ad hoc* Parliamentary committees and study groups set up to monitor and advise face similar constraints. In the field of roads policy there is a Commons All Party Roads Study Group, but in 1976 they had become completely overloaded with work. The CPRE, who were concerned with motorway policy, were told that it would be at least a year before they could be seen to discuss policy (*The Times*, 29 July 1976). One possible way of alleviating pressure on Select Committees would be to delegate the committee functions to the political party in power. This would also help to avoid the pitfalls of all-party Select Committees where agreement is often only possible for trivial non-party matters (see National Executive Committee of the Labour Party, 1978).

Pluralist critics of national policies have also seen secrecy as a major constraint on the possibilities of Parliamentary scrutiny. For example, in 1972 the Department of Industry refused to allow the Select Committee on Science and Technology to see the Vinter Report (see Flood and Grove-White, 1976). This was a report made by a civil servants' working party on thermal nuclear reactors. The Minister has the right in this situation to prevent information, prepared as a guide to policy, from being scrutinized by a Select Committee.

It is ostensibly for the above reasons that public faith in Parliamentary scrutiny of policy has been undermined. It is for these reasons also that pressure groups have sought to disrupt local public inquiries and to use them as a platform for national policy debate. C. Hall, director of the CPRE, writing in July 1976, argued that such disruption 'will continue until Parliament takes control of the executive; gives us a roads programme of convincing proportions based on proven need and not obfuscated by dubious and impenetrable techniques of forecasting and evaluation; and provides a forum either in specialist committees of its own or elsewhere in which the need for particular roads can be adequately examined with the public playing a full part' (*The Times*, 29 July 1976).

During 1977 and 1978 the government made several responses to the criticisms above by making national policy-making more open to scrutiny and public debate. In the field of transport policy annual White Papers were to be published setting out national policy. These could be debated by Parliament and by environmental pressure groups. The first of the White Papers, called *Transport Policy*, was published in 1977. The second White Paper (*Policy for Roads: England 1978*) considered that national policy was being adequately dealt with, and felt safe to argue:

Highway inquiries can now take place against the background of the statement of national roads policy, in the context of transport policy as a whole, in this White Paper and in the Transport Policy White Paper . . .
Local highway inquiries about particular schemes cannot sensibly be about national transport policies, which are for Government and Parliament. Nor can they usefully deal with methodologies such as the principles of traffic forecasting: these also need to be examined at the national level, and the Government's policy is that they should be subject to continuous monitoring by an independent and expert body, such as the Leitch Committee or its successor the Standing Advisory Committee (1978:13).

Naturally objectors to roads policy still find fault with the degree of accountability to Parliament that White Papers accord. The Council for the Protection of Rural England, for example, suggests that objectors should be allowed to petition Parliament against an administrative order which is of major public concern. Parliament, if it so wished, could then seek recommendations from an *ad hoc* Select Committee (C. Hall, letter to *The Times*, 14 April 1978). Precedents for such a procedure exist for various developments under the Statutory Orders (Special Procedure) Act 1945. For example, the Dartmoor Preservation Association in 1967 petitioned Parliament against the Meldon Reservoir Order (Dartmoor Preservation Association, 1967).

Some politicians favour standing Select Committees to act as watch-dogs over the executive departments of government. One such committee could oversee the roads programme. This type of accountability is wel-comed by Anthony Wedgewood Benn and others, but is deeply opposed by Parliamentarians such as Michael Foot (see Fenton, 1978). Whether there has been sufficient movement towards accountable planning and policy-making continues to be debated, but the main argument of objec-tors still seems to rest mainly on the view that wide representative discussion and debate will lead to policy that reflects public opinion (see Adams, 1977).

In the field of nuclear power policy government has, it appears, diligently responded to pluralist requests for public participation and open government (see Bugler, 1978(b)). It has been the subject of a major report by the Royal Commission on Environmental Pollution, and the question of whether or not a nuclear waste reprocessing plant should be extended at Windscale has been widely debated at a public inquiry and within Parliament. The Friends of the Earth played an important part in ensuring that the debate was extensive. They can claim to have substantially influenced the decision in favour of the Windscale inquiry, an inquiry that was to become the longest, most costly and most highly publicized local public inquiry. Firstly, it encouraged newspaper coverage while the Secretary of State, Peter Shore, was deciding whether or not to 'call in' the application. Secondly, it prepared a petition signed by 26,000 disapprov-ing of a statement made by Shore in the House of Commons claiming that an earlier inquiry by the local authority had shown that the residents of Cumbria wanted development of a nuclear reprocessing plant. Finally and conclusively the Friends of the Earth and several other groups obtained legal support from the lawyers' ecology group in sending a letter to Shore stating the possible illegality of the planning procedure in Cumbria. Two QCs, Messrs G. Dobry and D. Widdicombe, pointed out that the local council had specifically excluded itself from investigating safety issues such as the long-term build-up of radio-activity in the sea, and security issues relating to the operation of the proposed plant. These matters, it was argued, should have been dealt with under Section 29 of the Town and Country Planning Act 1971. It was this letter, supported also by eminent

MPs (G. Rippon, A. Blenkinsop and S. Ross), which finally persuaded Shore to call in the application and hold a local public inquiry.

There were obviously other influences on the Cabinet's decision to hold an inquiry despite opposition from the Treasury, Ministry of Defence, the Department of Trade and Industry and the Foreign and Commonwealth Office. The *Daily Mirror* caused a certain amount of anguish when on 21 October 1975 it revealed that extension of reprocessing would enable British Nuclear Fuels Ltd. (BNFL) to reprocess waste from Japan. The *Mirror* referred to the proposal as leading to 'the world's first nuclear dustbin'; Parliament debated the Windscale proposal in the House of Commons in December 1975; and Benn, the Secretary of State for Energy, announced his suggestion that there should be an open public debate on the Japanese contract. Hence there were various pressures upon the government to give the Windscale affair a public forum for debate. In the event, a local public inquiry was chosen, but this was not bound by the usual constraints of only considering the implications of local land use planning.

The inquiry was lengthy and legalistic. The Friends of the Earth alone spent something like £50,000 in presenting their case against BNFL, but most of this was on legal fees. Opposition groups played along with the inquiry procedures in exemplary fashion, recruiting numerous eminent experts in nuclear physics and energy policy. The whole inquiry was conducted like court proceedings on an academic debate. Uncertainty and disagreement among experts was profound and the central issues of how a new reprocessing plant would influence future energy policy, nuclear proliferation, pollution, and terrorism were never settled with any degree of confidence.

After the inquiry had finished pressure was again put on the government for Parliament to debate the inquiry report. An Early Day Motion calling for a debate before publication was signed by over two hundred MPs. In the end, the Windscale inquiry report was debated on two occasions in March and May 1978. Needless to say the report was favourable to BNFL's application and Parliament supported the recommendations. The groups opposed to the application were incensed that their views, many of which had not been adequately refuted, had not been considered in the inquiry report. A stream of letters appeared in *The Times* complaining about the way evidence had been misrepresented or blatantly ignored.

Opposition groups were, however, still remorselessly tied into the pluralistic assumptions that debate and yet more debate would ensure fair treatment (see Breach, 1978). The Town and Country Planning Association thought that there would have been a different outcome had Parliament debated the plan more fully before the inquiry stage. They also favoured the use of environmental impact analysis before an inquiry. The Friends of the Earth organized a demonstration in London, but by and large there was a complete tactical failure of opposition groups to mobilize any major source of power. The trade unions, with the exception of the Yorkshire miners' opposition to BNFL on purely a coal-based interest, remained largely aloof from the whole affair.

The environmental lobby in Britain (and elsewhere) in its apolitical stand has failed to comprehend the implications of Windscale, nuclear power policy or motorway policy within any coherent political or socio-logical perspective. They have been duped into the dominant political ideology of pluralism whereas in fact the pressures to develop nuclear power, waste reprocessing at Windscale and a motorway network are closely related to the nature and demands of modern capitalism. In the next section (and in Part III) we shall explore this argument further and analyse pressure group activity in terms of economic interests and class.

A Marxist framework of analysis

R. Goodman's book *After the Planners* brilliantly illustrates the failing of pluralist mechanisms of public participation or advocacy planning in America. Goodman argues that planning goals are subordinate to cor-porate interests. Of particular importance in this respect are the financial interests of the roads lobby:

That Washington's spending to help states build highways is one of its most expensive budget items is hardly unrelated to the fact that seven of the country's ten largest corporations produce either oil or cars, and twenty of the thirty-five wealthiest people have gained their abundance from the same kind of production. In addition, the biggest single market for steel in this country is connected with highways; one fifth of all the steel produced is used for either cars or highway construction . . .

So strong are the business interests guiding Washington's highway programs that when Congress called for a $6 billion cut in government spending in 1968 in order to continue the blood-bath in Vietnam, its $12.3 billion 1968 Highway Act added still more mileage to the highway program. And the year before, while Congress was cutting its poverty funds by $300 million, its new Model Cities program by $350 million and its meager $40 million rent supplement to $10 million, an attempt to cut back highway money was quickly defeated. The experience of highway programs, like urban renewal, is another frightening forecast of what to expect when business, government and the planners are marshalled to solve urban problems (1972:113–14).

Whereas Goodman shows how the planner in America is a party to the alliance between politician and industry, the British planner is in a slightly different position. He is not a consultant with a fixed contract but an employee of central or local government. Nevertheless, the interests of capital can be equally influential on the policy outcome. M. Hamer's study *Wheels Within Wheels: A Study of the Road Lobby* demonstrates the power of the road lobby and its financial supporters. The British Road Federation, founded in 1932, is the most important organization within this lobby. Hamer identifies six major areas of support: the motor industry; the bus operators; road haulage firms; the motorists' organizations; the road construction industry; the oil industry. He argues that the road lobby exerts considerable influence over the information supplied to the government and has close contacts with the Civil Service. But unlike the road lobby, he argues, 'cause groups, such as the anti-motorway lobby, do not have their own teams of accountants and statisticians, and thus are unable to offer government technical service or information. This makes it difficult to establish the close contacts that provide a real measure of influence' (1974:24).

The influence of private enterprise upon government is illustrated by a leak to the *Guardian* of a Civil Service document dealing with the road haulage industry. Despite W. Rodgers, Secretary for Transport, assuring Parliament that no consideration was being given to lorry weights, it is clear that this was untrue and that there were proposals being circulated 'to improve the public image of the road haulage industry'. The document suggested that a public inquiry was 'a way of dealing with the political opposition' to heavier lorries. Mr Peeler, who wrote the document and circulated it to a dozen senior civil servants, states:

We welcome the idea of an inquiry as a means of getting round the political obstacles to change the lorry weights. Given that the more straightforward approach is politically unacceptable, I have no doubt that . . . the inquiry would be a worthwhile investment . . .
. . . The establishment in the public mind of a clear and overwhelming case on balance for heavier weights is seen as the main end of the inquiry.
. . . It should provide a focus for the various road haulage interests to get together, marshal their forces, and act cohesively to produce a really good case which should not really establish the main point at issue but should do good to their now sadly tarnished public image . . .
At the end of the day, recommendations would be made by impartial people of repute who have carefully weighed and sifted the evidence and have come, one hopes, to a sensible conclusion in lines with the Department's view. Backed by such a recommendation, the Government of the day will be in a stronger position to take action (*Guardian*, 30 October 1978).

The report is quoted at length because there is no clearer indictment of the pluralists' emphasis upon public debate and participation as an end in itself. Indeed there is no clearer example of how public participation is recognized as a lever to support an economic interest.

One of the major features of modern capitalism is the concentration of economic and technological power. This concentration of power favours the capitalist class in several respects. Control over information and planning is strengthened as the possibilities of independent and critical assessment become more problematic. In the case of nuclear power and motorways a near monopoly of expertise resides in the UK Atomic Energy Authority and the Road Construction Unit respectively. Such concentration of expertise reinforces the power and influence of these organizations. J. Tyme has argued consequently that the civil servants are in a position to control the flow of information but because of the road lobby's influence it is they who are in a position to limit Parliamentary scrutiny: 'with the closest co-operation of their friends in the Department, these agents, clearly with very substantial budgets, are able to decide precisely what information MPs receive, to distribute information apparently having the imprimatur of the Department, and to give outright mis-information which might prove an "administrative difficulty" for the lobby' (*Express and News*, 17 September 1975).

In America the situation is not quite as serious with respect to the nuclear power debate as M. Flood and R. Grove-White point out: 'some prominent critics of the US nuclear power programme, such as T. Taylor, J. Goffman, and A. Tamplin, are former employees of the Automic Energy Commission, the US equivalent of the AEA. In their public statements they appear to rely greatly on details acquired during their service with the commission. Such candour seems to have contributed greatly to opening up nuclear debate in the US. In the UK, however, it would render an individual liable to penal sanctions' (1976:39).

The environmental lobby has recognized the implications for civil liberties of continuing the nuclear power programme so as to incorporate fast-breeder reactors (Flood and Grove-White, 1976), Anarchists and Marxists have also emphasized the possibilities of alternative technologies furthering the possibilities of workers' control, as well as being less dangerous to the physical and social environment (more about this in later chapters).

On the whole, however, environmental groups have reacted against the symptoms of recent technological developments. H. Nowotny, for example, claims that the social movement against nuclear power derives its strength from a reaction against big technology and the concentration of power associated with the centralization of decision-making:

By focusing on the long-term effects of nuclear energy and by opposing it they express the strain they experience in the present: that social change in the form of large-scale further industrial developments, with its accompanying concentration of power and decision-making, holds little if any benefit out for them and threatens to further undermine their present position, both economically and in terms of their capacity to influence social and political developments. They feel at best marginal to the ongoing technological developments calling for further centralization. Their demands are therefore directed towards de-centralization in decision-making, 'small' technologies, rather than 'large' ones; and protection of the environment as a resource preventing its falling into the hands of those who will only use it for their own benefits and at the expense of others (1976:19).

What Nowotny and the environmental lobby have failed to grasp is the way that capitalism encourages the centralized concentration of power and decision-making so as to increase its influence on policy outcome. Transport, water and energy have more and more become resources of state concern, but in doing so the state has increasingly become the servant of private enterprise. The environmental lobby has been deceived into the belief that the state is an impartial mediator in a pluralist society, but the state responds to power that different interests are able to mobilize. The environmental lobby has succeeded in extracting annual White Papers on transport, but has failed to redirect transport policy away from the interests of private enterprise. The first objective of transport policy, according to the White Paper in 1977, was 'to contribute to economic growth and higher national prosperity, particularly through providing an efficient service to industry, commerce and agriculture' (*Guardian*, 28 June 1977).

Motorway and nuclear power projects will not be opposed successfully by mere technical debate behind closed doors or in public forums. The way to effective opposition lies in demonstrating how these projects fail to be in the objective interests of the mass of people in Britain and elsewhere. Collective mobilization of power and a broad protest campaign through the Labour movement could then decrease the power of capitalist interests. Opposition to the nuclear power and motorway lobbies has not been mobilized but dissipated in ideological mystification in large part conveyed by pluralistic academics but supported in the interests of capital. The power of capital is not invincible. It is more like the Chinese notion of the paper tiger which can be easily defeated by collective resistance. Nuclear power and motorway lobbies remain tigers which threaten to destroy the environment, but only so long as protest remains divided and divorced from the majority of people who are the losers.

It has already been suggested that what the pluralist perspective fails to deal with is the fact that policy-making tends to serve the interests of the ruling class and that there is unequal opportunity of mobilizing power (and the so-called power resources of money, information, media support, etc.). By focusing on government and overt decision-making, pluralism fails to grasp the significance of class differences in mobilizing power. As Parenti observes:

Studies of policy struggles involving lower-strata groups are a rarity in the literature of American political science, partly because the poor seldom embark upon such ventures, but also because our modes of analysis have defined the scope of our research so as to exclude the less visible activities of the underprivileged (1970:115–16).

Parenti challenges the pluralist assertion that the political system is equally responsive to the interests of all groups, and argues that the deprived strata suffer liabilities. He looked at the activities of the Newark Community Union Project which was set up in 1964 with the help of thirteen members of the students for a Democratic Society. This protest group lasted for three years. During this time various demands for improved housing and traffic improvements were made. Parenti documented how Newark's officials were less favourably disposed and discriminated against the demands made by lower-class groups.

M. Castells has analysed various struggles against urban renewal and property speculation in the Cité du Peuple, Paris. In a comparative study, he argued that success was considerably dependent upon socio-economic characteristics of the different protest groups. Lower-status groups tended to make less progress, but in one quarter a handsome building was successfully protected against property speculation by tenants who were mainly office workers and middle management. These tenants were able to alert the press, councillors and administration and were able to create the right conditions for successful protest:

Having thus alerted public opinion as to the purely speculative character of an operation concerning buildings whose condition was well above average, the committee obtained full satisfaction. The property company, which was no longer interested in the matter from the moment the demolition was set aside, resold the buildings to another company, which itself resold to the tenants at very advantageous prices, and all the lower because their attitude had been tough during the protest period. Certain tenants, who were unable to buy, had to move, but they were given very high compensation. The buildings were not touched (1977:331).

P. Lowe (1977) has argued that although the amenity movement regards itself as non-political its membership betrays a class or sectional interest. The majority of groups, he claims, are predominantly represented by middle-class owner occupiers, living in privileged districts. The activities of these groups are likely to have profound distributional consequences. Although many organizations take the name of a geographical locality such as the Council for the Protection of Rural England's various County Branches, the Dartmoor Preservation Association, the Faversham Society and so on, it can hardly be claimed that they represent all local interests. Certainly one of the weaknesses of the pluralistic perspective is the striking fact that certain occupational and class interests are much better represented than others.

Where less privileged groups have become successfully mobilized it has often been at the initiation of outside community workers or protest groups. One example is that of the West Harlem Coalition for Morningside Park (WHCMP) which developed out of a community sit-in and student protest in 1968 against the proposed plan for the Columbia University Gymnasium to be sited in Morningside Park. The project had already been approved by the State and City Government, but the protests were successful in blocking these plans. The WHCMP, with the assistance of the City College of New York and the Architects Renewal Committee of Harlem, put forward alternative proposals in February 1972. These included: a child-care facility for about 55 children; a play environment for children; an outdoor exhibition area; an amphitheatre; a swimming pool/skating rink and landscape restoration. Later that year the coalition of groups supporting these proposals had succeeded in obtaining the city's approval for $125,000 design funds and $1,375,000 construction funds (Collins, 1972).

The case of the Port Tennant Anti-Pollution Association is a much rarer example of a working-class and largely female-organized protest group. It was formed in 1970 to further a campaign against the pollution from a United Carbon Black factory. I. Hall has studied this seemingly isolated working-class anti-pollution campaign, and although its exceptional character is hard to explain she does suggest a few possible reasons. The particularly annoying form of pollution, which affected furnishing and laundry through the deposition of a fine black oily dust, and the public opinion favouring anti-pollution measures were clearly important. The study, however, emphasized the community structure of the Port Tennant area which was '"predisposed" towards community action – there was a potential action base for a socially closely-knit population with similar occupational and class backgrounds and with similar attitudes towards the area' (1976, 109). The Anti-Pollution Association adopted militant tactics, mounting a twenty-four day blockade of United Carbon Black in February 1971. Hall suggests that this action was the result of twenty years of frustrated attempts to effect pollution control through petitions to the Guildhall and the local MP. By adopting blockade tactics the Association was able to redefine the rules of the game and so bring about meetings with the Alkali Inspectorate, of whose existence they had no prior knowledge.

The importance Hall attaches to community structure is supported by N. Dennis's study of a residents' action group in Sunderland in which he suggested: 'the homogenity, solidarity and lack of social geographical mobility of the inhabitants facilitates community action. If the action is militant, the strength of personal loyalties once formed means stable support' (1972:4). Despite this and further examples of working-class community action, it is probably a safe generalization to say that environmental groups representing the working class in deprived areas will be less able to draw on the political resources which are considered to be equally available by pluralists. While success in opposing the interests of capital is clearly possible, the power that the capitalist class is able to mobilize results in considerable structural constraint.

The different capabilities of occupational groups in mobilizing power can be illustrated by examples where there is an overt clash of interests over land use changes and objectives. J. Ferris's (1972) study of Barnsbury, for example, gave support to the view that working-class community groups are less positive and aggressive than their middle-class amenity group counterparts.

The Barnsbury study is based upon a clash of interests in the London Borough of Islington during the mid-1960s. The Barnsbury Association (newly arrived middle-class owner occupiers) was formed in August 1964 specifically to oppose a housing redevelopment scheme proposed by the local council. This scheme was seen as a threat to the amenity values of the area, and the Barnsbury Association produced their own plan involving the exclusion of through-traffic and improvement of older houses in the area. In the first instance, the Barnsbury Association's activities met with a great deal of suspicion from the council, but over a period of six years it succeeded in persuading the council to accept its view of Barnsbury's problems. It succeeded despite a majority of the population's opposing its alternative proposals. The Barnsbury Association attempted to exclude opposition by institutionalizing it in a Housing Action Group. It also put pressure on the local authority through various measures including the election in 1968 of three Barnsbury Association members as Independents on the council.

The success of a minority interest must, however, be seen in the context of its ability to exploit a favourable attitude towards planning at central government level. The Barnsbury Association argued that the area should be treated along the lines outlined in the Buchanan Report, *Traffic in Towns* (1963) which had much influence on central government attitudes to planning at this time. Departmental policy was aimed at changing local authority attitudes towards large redevelopment projects because of high cost, and at encouraging them to upgrade existing districts instead by improving housing and applying traffic management schemes. Public participation was also encouraged by central government both by the Skeffington Report in 1968 and in town and country planning legislation.

The Barnsbury Action Group (more working-class support) was formed in March 1970 after a belated recognition of the need to defend interests that were threatened by the Association's activities. The Action Group argued against what they saw as a misallocation of resources on environmental 'tarting up', and aimed to get the traffic scheme reconsidered, and the housing stress of the area recognized by the Council. The Action Group's proposals for housing redevelopment were a response to schemes already in an advanced stage of formulation and had not been actively pursued in the critical early stages of planning.

One can see in this particular case how the pluralist demand for increased public participation strengthens the position of organized groups, because it creates a lever for the implementation of policies that are to their advantage. Possibilities for participation and influence are by themselves of little help to the unorganized and to those lacking insight into the working of bureaucratic professionalism, who have little chance of influencing policy. Indeed, one may go so far as to claim that public participation, as opposed to stronger forms of public control, tends to help the powerful to consolidate their power.

Another example that demonstrates the differences in opportunity for various groups to resist adverse development projects is the case of the expansion of Turnhouse, Edinburgh's airport (see Mutch, 1977). The proposed expansion threatened two communities, one at Cramond and the other at Newbridge. Cramond was a highly articulate community of owner-occupiers. There was a wealth of expertise and resources that could be mobilized against the plans to develop the airport. Even before the proposal became public knowledge Cramond had formed an association in 1960 'to promote the amenity of the community of Cramond and to safeguard its heritage'. Plans for a new runway were made by the British Airports Authority (BAA) in the early 1960s.

The Cramond Association made several attempts between 1967 and 1971 to find out what the proposals involved. They were not successful in finding this out until April 1971, by which time the plans were well developed. The Cramond Association, in conjunction with other local bodies, set up the Runway Joint Committee to fight the proposed plan. They were able to raise £20,000 to support the campaign and were successful in persuading the inquiry inspector to recommend that the government should reject the plan. The main reason behind this recommendation was the risk to the public at Newbridge, who lived below the flight path at the other end of the runway. The effect of aircraft noise at Newbridge and Cramond were other but less important grounds for rejecting the application.

Two interesting lessons can be drawn from this case. The first is that despite the more serious implications for those living in Newbridge, no effective opposition developed from this community. Unlike the people of Cramond almost all the residents of Newbridge rented their homes from the council. There was high unemployment, an old primary school sited at an accident black-spot at the junction of the M8 and M9 motorways, and in 1969 to 1970 there was a threat of a motorway interchange at the edge of the village. The community showed all the characteristics of deprivation, and the lack of capacity to mobilize resources when their amenities were threatened.

In this respect the Edinburgh airport study illustrates the fact that professional groups, higher income groups and the better educated are more able to make use of the planning system and are consequently more able to exploit the geographical space. Many other examples of this phenomenon exist, for example, urban motorways in the 1960s tended to destroy more homes of the poor than the rich, and yet it was the rich who could make better use of this change in land use (see Hall *et al.*, 1974; Harvey, 1971; Simmie, 1974). R. Pahl (1971) has argued that the distribution of urban resources is controlled by 'social gatekeepers' that is to say the most powerful groups such as landowners, planners, developers, estate agents, local authorities and all kinds of pressure groups.

There is, however, another interesting lesson that may be learnt from the Edinburgh airport study. Despite the success of the middle- and upper-middle class residents of Cramond in getting the support of the planning inquiry inspector, it was in the final event the Secretary of State for Scotland who ignored the inspector's advice and allowed BAA to proceed with the construction of the runway. One may conclude from this that although middle-class pressure groups have been more able to influence planning in their favour than have lower-class groups, the really decisive factor is the interests of financial and industrial development. In this particular example BAA had prior access to the planning system and was able to ensure that its commitments to the development of a new runway were such that government was given no option but to proceed, despite environmental hazards, because of the economic consequence of not doing so. Our focus on pressure groups should not therefore merely be on the differences between the lower and middle classes' ability to mobilize resources but between the dominant capitalist classes and the rest of the community.

H. Molotch's (1971) study of the Santa Barbara oil spill caused by the eruption of a well owned by Union Oil in 1968 demonstrates the ability of major corporations to define and manipulate issues. The upper-middle class Santa Barbarans sought concessions from the oil industry through a community organization called GOO (Get Oil Out). Typically its activities were confined to pluralistic courses of action such as petitions, raffles, court action and legislative lobbying. However, the whole problem of pollution and the damage to the environment became considerably distorted in favour of Union Oil. Molotch argues that a cover-up operation took place in which the mass media, scientific evidence, and other information played down the significance of the oil spill. The academic community's arms were tied, he claims, by oil grants which, if withdrawn, would have had considerable adverse consequences for California universities.

When President Nixon made a personal visit to inspect the damage to the beaches, he was reputedly taken to a beach that had been specially cleaned up. Estimates of bird deaths were released only from two special bird-cleaning centres set up to help injured birds. Those that died at sea or on the beach were not recorded. Such were the mechanisms and forms of deception legitimated in large part by the participation of scientists and local state officials, but supported and influenced in the main by the oil industry. Molotch claims that such events as the Santa Barbara oil spill and the behaviour of corporations in 'managing' the development of the issue completely undermine pluralist theories of decision-making. He concludes:

What the citizens of Santa Barbara learned through their experience was that the parties competing to shape decision-making on oil in Santa Barbara do not have equal access to the means of 'mobilizing bias'. The oil/government combine had, from the start, an extraordinary number of advantages. Lacking ready access to media, the ability to stage events at will, and a well-integrated system of arrangements for achieving their goals (at least in comparison to their adversaries), Santa Barbara's citizens have met with repeated frustrations (1971:194).

The power that commercial interests can muster need not necessarily involve the overt mobilization of resources as in the Santa Barbara oil spill example, although it is more likely that this will be necessary in situations where events threaten their power. Many more routine developments occur without overt conflict, but nevertheless reflect differences in power according to capital. Where industry is smaller and fragmented one can expect less power and ability to mobilize and control decision-making.

M. A. Crenson's study of the *Un-politics of Air Pollution* (1971) demonstrates how power is more often associated with industrial concentration and how pollution control issues can be suppressed without overtly mobilizing the so-called power resources. His research was aimed directly at the question of why many American cities failed to develop air pollution control as a political issue. He chooses for comparison East Chicago which began to take action in 1949, and Gary which took no action until 1962. Crenson's thesis is that in Gary industrial sources of pollution come principally from the 'powerful' US Steel Corporation. The concentration of power within one company, he argues, was implicitly recognized so that no action was needed to suppress the pollution issue. In Crenson's words: 'where industrial corporations are thought to be powerful in the matter of anti-pollution policy either the emergence or growth of the dirty air issue is likely to be hindered' (1971:122). In East Chicago, on the other hand, industry was more disparate and had less reputation for influence. Hence there was not the same political opposition.

Crenson's argument rests on the idea that development of issues is dependent in part upon the power reputations of different organizations. Anticipated reactions of others is sufficient to prevent an issue from arising just as anticipated reactions act as a constraint on immoral or deviant actions. When Gary did eventually raise the air pollution issue largely as a threat of federal or state action Crenson argues that 'US Steel . . . influenced the content of the pollution ordinance without taking any action on it, and thus defied the pluralist dictum that political power belongs to political actors' (1971:69–70). Crenson supports his argument by empirical studies aimed at elucidating political leaders' perception of industry's reputation for power. From interviews covering fifty-one cities his conclusions confirm the distinctions already referred to, namely that 'the air pollution issue tends not to flourish in cities where industry enjoys a reputation for power' (1971:145).

H. E. Bracey (1963) has suggested a similar process of pressure group behaviour according to anticipated success when discussing the activities of the CPRE: he argues that the CPRE is a realistic body and so does not oppose all objectionable development. It recognizes that a national group which has to persuade Ministers and others of the strength of its case must know when and when not to fight. Some development is reckoned to be unavoidable and the Council only acts when it thinks success is possible or when a proposal is monstrous.

This brings us back to the concept of power itself which was earlier defined as the ability of a class or group to realize its own specific objectives. It is not inevitable that a group will fail to gain concessions from the capitalist, but merely that constraints exist which make it very hard for objectors to realize their own interests when they would seriously undermine the position of commercial interests. Environmental groups have often not been afraid to take on powerful companies. For example, the Friends of the Earth challenged Schweppes' policy on non-returnable bottles, Rio Tinto Zinc's prospective mining operations in Snowdonia and more recently British Nuclear Fuels' application to extend its reprocessing operations at Windscale. It is doubtful though if any of these campaigns were sufficiently broadly based to have seriously threatened the power that major corporations are able to wield, nor their sources of profit which are often the root cause of environmental problems.

When community organizations and pressure groups fight to defend decent human rights for a clean environment or for the preservation of housing against new roads and property speculators, decision-making invariably becomes constrained by commercial interests. The dialectic between power and structure is illustrated by N. Wates's study, *The Battle for Tolmers Square* (1976).

The struggle to save Tolmers Square, in the London Borough of Camden, involved tenants' groups, the Tolmers Village Association, student architects and squatters, as well as both local and national political parties. Tolmers Square was a twelve-acre site of largely working-class population. In 1961 only 4 per cent of houses were owner occupied and 87 per cent of the housing was rented from private landlords. The population had declined from 5,200 in 1871 to 1,040 in 1961. A sizeable proportion of the community were Asian in origin, some light industry, commerce and offices had developed in the area, and there had been some improvement in health standards. The Tolmers Square Tenants' Association began the fight for the future of Tolmers Square in 1957 when members of the community were galvanized into action over a threat of eviction. The Tenants' Association successfully countered the first attempt by a property developer to develop a twenty-four storey office block in 1959.

The Stock Conversion Company became the main property developer to try and claim Tolmers Square for commercial development. From 1962 properties were bought up in speculation and left to decay, causing blight and the necessary conditions for redevelopment. The various community groups campaigned against the activities of Stock Conversion and were even able in 1972 to prevent a planning deal between the company and local authority (the 'Leavy deal') which would have involved the building of 250,000 square feet of office space and 120,000 square feet of mixed commercial property, while 8.5 acres (600 dwellings) were to be transferred to the council at a concessionary rate of £200,000 per acre. Wates describes the interconnections between local and national campaigns which led to the breakdown of the 'Leavy deal':

For the Left generally, the Tolmers Square campaign was secondary to the campaign against the government's Housing Finance legislation.
... The national campaign created a climate for the Tolmers Square issue, and indeed Tolmers Square became one of the foci of the national campaign. In general the left helped to create the right political climate for a change in Council policy on Tolmers Square. The strategy was to delay decision, and to publicize the issue so as to prevent a deal from being pushed through the Council quickly and secretly. In this they were totally successful (1976:116).

Property speculation at Tolmers Square, Centre Point, the Euston Centre, and elsewhere helped to focus Labour party attention on the office development scandal. When it became clear that a Community Land Bill was to be introduced in 1974 which would enable local authorities compulsorily to purchase development land the Stock Conversion Company decided to sell its property to the council. So in 1975 Camden Council were able to purchase six acres of land formerly owned by Stock Conversion for £4 million. Property speculation had increased the 'value' of the land to such an extent that even under the Community Land Act, which allowed councils to purchase land at use value rather than development value, an enormous sum could be exacted from the council.

The cost to the council of the six acres meant that huge interest repayments had to be paid on the necessary loans. In 1976/77 these amounted to over £500,000. When the transaction took place revenue from rents amounted to about £60,000 which left an enormous amount of revenue to be found. These financial pressures consequently meant that the council had to consider redevelopment of the site on a more profitable basis. Financial pressures were forcing the council into the same sort of policy proposals that had originally been made by Stock Conversion.

The Tolmers Square protest campaigners illustrate how the power of community organization is constrained by political and economic structures that are deeply rooted within the capitalist state. It also shows how the power of capital can be decreased by co-operative community action.

In the next three chapters we will analyse the extent to which technology reflects and reinforces the social and economic order. The issue of technological alternatives was of central importance to the anti-nuclear power campaigns and was touched upon earlier in this chapter. This issue now deserves much closer scrutiny.

5 Technology and Capitalism

Introduction

During the last three decades, the role of technology in development has been of central importance to economists and other social scientists, as well as the public at large. Much of the environmental debate has also been concerned about the role of technology in development. The 1960s began with a burst of technological optimism. It was the period of the 'white hot' technological revolution and Anthony Wedgewood Benn's Ministry of Technology. Major technological projects were heralded annually with great enthusiasm, but within a few years technological optimism had grown sour as a result of the Vietnam war, the escalating costs of Concorde, and the pollution concomitant with a modern industrial society. By the mid-1970s, nuclear power policy had become the subject of widespread concern (see Nelkin, 1977(b)). Mass demonstrations, often resulting in violent clashes, became common, especially in France and Germany.

A variety of views have been expressed about the relationship between technology and society (for a review see Elliott and Elliott, 1976). A broad distinction can be made between three positions: those that hold essentially technological determinist assumptions; those that see technological choice as a product of economic and political factors; and those who see technology and social change as a dialectical process of mutual interaction. In a Marxist perspective the forces of production (technology and economic organization) are influenced and constrained by the social relations of production (ownership and class relations).

TECHNOLOGICAL DETERMINISM

In recent years there has been a good deal of support for the view that the development of technology has become an independent and autonomous force (see Winner, 1977). T. Roszak, J. Ellul, C. Reich and others have portrayed technological development as malevolent and anarchic. Irrespective of political ideology and economic structure, they argue, man is gradually becoming a slave to science and technology. This view is a particular example of a more general perspective of technological determinism. That is to say, social, environmental and economic changes are considered to be a consequence of technological development.

In contrast to the 'technology-out-of-control' view, there is a common technological determinist view which claims that technology can be freely manipulated by decision-makers in the public interest so as to enhance economic and environmental conditions. Pollution and resource problems, like any other economic or social problem, can be dealt with by technological innovation – a technical fix.

Case studies of technological developments and undesirable consequences associated with them have been the staple diet in the environmental literature. Typically, the proceedings of symposia, such as those on ecology and international development, bring together many examples of unwanted environmental effects (see Farvar and Milton, 1972). One project that received such attention was the Aswan Dam, which had an enormous number of environmental and social consequences. The aims of the project were principally to create Lake Nasser, which would help to irrigate the upper parts of the Nile region, and at the same time produce some ten billion watts of hydro-electric power, while preventing thirty billion silt-laden tons of water from flowing unused into the Mediterranean. Some of the unplanned consequences of this major technological project made it much less desirable than had been intended. Lake Nasser did not fill up as expected because evaporation was much greater than anticipated. Water hyacinths on the surface increased the rate of evaporation and prevented the use of boats on the lake. The Rule moved faster after the dam was built because of the silt loss; this resulted in the undercutting of bridges further down the river. Consequently ten new barrier dams costing a quarter as much as the Aswan Dam were considered necessary in addition to new bridges. There was not enough industry to utilize all the electricity capable of being produced. Millions of tons of fertilizer are now needed to replenish natural resources that were deposited during the annual Nile floods. The crustacea and fish that depended upon the sediments were reported to have been wiped out, causing the collapse of major fishing industries. As a result of the decreased water flow at the delta, there has been an increase in salt accumulation from the sea into the soil. The extended irrigation and concentration of settlements have been responsible for an increase in diseases such as schistosomiasis (bilharzia) (see Heyneman, 1971; Farvar and Milton, 1972; Van Der Schalie, 1974).

The answer to projects such as the Aswan Dam and similar technological developments is for greater analysis of the potential environmental and social consequences – technology assessment, as it is called. Technology assessment has generally been adopted under the assumption that it will help policy-makers to choose the most appropriate technology. The constraints on policy-making are considered to be technical rather than political.

ECONOMIC AND POLITICAL DETERMINISM

The second view about the relationship between technology and society is one of economic and political determinism. Economists have generally considered the determinants of technology to be a product of supply and demand. According to H. Singer, those factors on the supply side consist of:

(a) existing technologies: the 'technology shelf', from which technologies are selected, transferred and disseminated;
(b) a country's ability to adapt existing technology to its own special or changing conditions;
(c) a country's capacity to create national or indigenous technology suitable for and specifically geared to a country's objectives and circumstances;

and on the demand side:

(d) the state of factor prices and other incentives facing decision-makers;
(e) income distribution, which determines the effective market demand for various products and sectors;
(f) the nature and situation of those who make decisions about technology to be used in concrete projects (1977:11).

The pluralist position reinforces the liberal economic perspective. Political influence, like economic influence, results from the competitive market of individual and group interests, and leads to the promotion of technology that satisfies political demand. Both the liberal economic and the political theorists assume a model of technological determinism, but because they claim that knowledge of technological implications can be obtained, then the choice of technology reflects the political and economic culture. The 'technology-out-of-control' view, on the other hand, emphasizes the difficulties of technology assessment and the unintended consequences which have led to failure in harnessing technology for desirable social goals.

THE MARXIST PERSPECTIVE

In Marx's account of history there was a dialectical interaction between technology and the social relations of production. This can be summarized best in Marx's own words when replying to Proudhon in 1846–47 (*Poverty of Philosophy*): 'In acquiring new productive forces' Marx writes, 'men change their mode of production, and in changing their mode of production, in changing the way of earning their living, they change all their social relations. The hand-mill gives you society with the feudal lord; the steam-mill a society with the industrial capitalist' (Bottomore and Rubel, 1963:198). Although Marx here refers to the social character of technology, he also makes it clear that social relations influence the choice of technology. Technology can help transform social relations, but only if those relations are in the process of being changed.

For a Marxist, innovation and choice of technology in capitalist societies are influenced by two major considerations. The first consideration is the role technology plays in reinforcing the control of the capitalist over his workforce whose freedom and exercise of influence on the organization of work would otherwise threaten to depress profits (see Marglin, 1976). The second and related consideration is the role technology plays in preventing the falling rate of profit (see Gorz, 1976(a)). To ensure the maintenance of profit, an essential condition for the survival of capitalism, the capitalist needs to do one of three things: firstly, labour (working capital) can be replaced by technology (fixed capital); secondly, the market for goods can be expanded through economic imperialism, for example, and thirdly, new demand can be created through product innovation.

During early industrialization the development of the factory system and various technological innovations helped to reinforce the power of the capitalist over his workforce. Other innovations involving mechanization had the main function of reducing the costs of products. This substitution of technology for labour began in the textile industry but was gradually adopted in other areas of manufacturing. After the 1870s, when this first stage of development had become well advanced, expansion of markets through economic imperialism became important. However, it was not until stagnation of the world economy in the 1930s and particularly since the Second World War that product innovation became a major source of profit-making and a stimulus to economic growth.

Innovation and technological choice, according to a Marxist interpretation, are closely influenced by the requirements of capital accumulation. The deleterious consequences of technology to health and safety at work, and the external environment, tend consequently to be of secondary importance. This is all the more true if consideration of them reduces the rate of profit. Process innovations such as oxygen bleaching rather than chlorine bleaching in paper-making help to reduce pollution and lead to cost savings (Council on Environmental Quality, 1975). Naturally enough such technological change is in the interest of the capitalist and the public at large. In many other cases, however, pollution control, risk avoidance, and the general enhancement of the quality of life conflicts with the interest of capital accumulation. While capitalists are willing to suffer some loss of profits from state-imposed constraints on technological choice, such constraints will nevertheless be strongly resisted.

Early Marxists stressed that alienation as well as undesirable social and environmental problems arose primarily from the social relations of production rather than from a particular mode of production. Technology was usually considered to be intrinsically without political consequences and only resulted in harm when under the wrong ownership and control. Indeed, for many Marxists technology *per se* was an unalloyed good. The forces of production, it was claimed, had a largely independent pattern of growth, but were held back by the development of contradictions within the social relations of production. Ensuing economic crises, resulting in technology becoming idle or even destroyed, would then help to bring about revolutionary changes and so break the shackles preventing the speedier development of technology. Partly as a result of a failure of this prediction, Marxists today are more inclined to emphasize the role technology plays in reinforcing power. Thus in H. Braverman's (1974) classic work, *Labour and Monopoly Capital*, technology and the form of industrial organization reflect the requirements of capitalist domination as well as the requirements of technical efficiency. It is arguable whether the mutual integration of forces of production and social relations of production has become more complete since Marx's time. There is now a well-developed military and industrial economic base to society which reflects and reinforces advanced capitalism.

Public and private research and development expenditure on military weaponry far exceed that in any other sector and dominate the direction of technological innovation in the United States, Britain, behind the Iron Curtain, and elsewhere. Military activities in the world engage approximately 25 per cent of all scientific talent and use 40 per cent of all public and private expenditure for research and development (Pavitt and Worboys, 1977). Development of military technology and defence expenditure plays an important 'stabilizing' role in capitalist economies. In a Keynesian management of the economy, such expenditure can be used as a buffer against changes in other areas of economic activity. If there is a depression, public expenditure may be increased to protect the economic system (see Baran and Sweezy, 1968). Military research and space research have been encouraged in an attempt to stimulate the economy and promote technological advance which spill over into other areas of the economy – the miniaturization of electronics, for example. Never before in history have science and technology been elevated so effectively in the interests of capitalism as in the period since the Second World War. But at the same time, the potential for human and environmental destruction is beyond description. It is certainly naïve to believe that the military and industrial base to society is amenable to the so-called objective techniques of technology assessment when the destructive potential of many modern technologies is so apparent.

Within a Marxist account, a change from the development of undesirable technologies is dependent upon a struggle against capitalism. Within a market economy the interests of capital demand technologies that lead to capital accumulation. If profit remains the most important criterion in technological choice then undesirable environmental and social consequences are inevitable. However, although technological choice and its consequences are influenced by capital ownership and class, it is also true to say that they are affected by interests such as those of labour and environmental activists. The Lucas Aerospace workers are a prime example of a well-organized group who have been campaigning for their firm to produce socially useful products (see Cooley, 1977/78).

The Lucas Aerospace Combine Shop Stewards Committee produced a corporate plan for a number of environmentally sound products, such as a more efficient petrol engine. It also made proposals for work reorganization that would help create employment, and bring a halt to the increase in unskilled and de-humanizing work. The plan was produced between 1974 and 1976 in the face of rationalization and redundancy. The total number of people working in the aerospace industry had fallen from 283,000 in 1960 to 195,000 in 1975. In the Lucas Aerospace firm itself, there had been a cut in the labour force from 19,000 to 14,000 workers in the five years preceding 1974. In 1978 there were fears that the labour force would be cut again to 10,000.

To date, the plan has been almost totally ignored by the management, which claims that it is not a business plan. According to Lucas Aerospace, the plan is merely a technical feasibility study, and lacks detailed marketing requirements, manufacturing considerations, and potential for profit. Management has avoided taking action initiated by the workers by claiming that the shop stewards' combines are unrepresentative and that this sort of plan should be dealt with through the democratically elected trade unions. Nevertheless, the Lucas Aerospace shop stewards' plan represents a decisive step forward for the labour movement. It represents a hotly debated campaign for the right to work on socially useful projects.

Campaigns similar to the Lucas one have taken place elsewhere with some success. Building workers in Australia have refused to work on environmentally undesirable projects such as office blocks. Glass bottle workers in the SURTE factory in southern Sweden campaigned for diversification of production when their factory was threatened with closure as a result of its dependence upon the production of environmentally damaging non-returnable bottles (Elliott, 1977).

It will be argued in this section of the book that the first two views of technology and society, which emphasize technology assessment, are inadequate because the liberal economic and pluralistic assumptions about the mechanisms of technological choice are unsatisfactory. Technology instead plays a significant and dynamic political and economic role in supporting or diminishing the interests of different classes. Technological innovation may be influenced by class relations, but it may also facilitate changes in class relations. In this chapter, the techniques and limitations of technology assessment will be evaluated by looking at the process of technological innovation and the transfer of technology to less developed countries. Finally, the nuclear power debate will be used as a case study.

Technology assessment

As a response to the undesirable consequences of the Aswan Dam and similar projects in the less developed countries, the World Bank made recommendations for careful analysis of the environmental, health and human ecological considerations in economic development projects before implementation (see World Bank, 1973). In the United States, a similar concern over technological consequences led to the establishment in October 1972 of an Office of Technological Assessment. Public law 92–484 defined its objectives as being to provide 'early indications of the beneficial and adverse impacts of the application of technology and to develop other coordinate information which may assist Congress' (Holt, 1977:283). The duties of the Office of Technological Assessment were to:

1 identify existing or probable impacts of technology or technological programmes;
2 where possible, ascertain cause-and-effect relationships;
3 identify alternative technological methods of implementing specific programmes;
4 identify alternative programmes for achieving requisite goals;
5 make estimates and comparisons of the impacts of alternative methods and programmes;
6 present findings of completed analyses to the appropriate legislative authorities;

7   identify areas where additional research or data collection is required to provide
adequate support for the assessments and estimates described in paragraphs
(1) through (5) . . . (Public Law 92–484 92nd Congress, 13 October 1972; Holt,
1977:284).

The scientific and political objectivity of technology assessment is
typified by the following definition from the Congressional Research
Service of the American Library of Congress:

Technology assessment is the process of taking a purposeful look at the consequences of technological change. It includes the primary cost/benefit balance of
short-term localized market place economics, but particularly goes beyond these
to identify affected parties and unanticipated impacts in as broad and long range a
fashion as is possible. It is neutral and objective, seeking to enrich the information
for management decisions. Both 'good' and 'bad' side-effects are investigated
since a missed opportunity for benefit may be detrimental to society just as is an
unexpected hazard (Braun and Collingridge, 1977:64).

Generally speaking, the complexity of technology assessment requires
investigation by multi-disciplinary teams of experts. The main distinction
between technology assessment and related techniques such as
cost–benefit analysis and environmental impact analysis is that it is
usually applied to technology innovation rather than to one particular
planning application. It also adopts a much broader content of analysis so
as to include all kinds of possible impacts.

   Although technology assessment has not been institutionalized as such
in Britain, there are a number of organizations which carry out somewhat
similar functions as the Office of Technology Assessment in the United
States. The social and environmental consequences of nuclear power
technology, for example, have been subject to investigation by the
Parliamentary Select Committee on Science and Technology, and by the
Royal Commission on Environmental Pollution. Energy accounting has
also become an established and specialized form of technology assessment, but is carried out in terms of energy consequences alone (see
Chapman, 1975).

   One example of technology assessment is that by J. W. Dickey *et al.*
(1973) on various solid waste management programmes in a community
in Fairfax County, Virginia. Assessment was made in terms of effects on
solid waste production, collection, processing, re-use, transportation and
disposal. Various groups affected by the different programmes were also
identified and an assessment of effects upon them was undertaken. These
groups included the local solid waste management agency, waste pro-
ducers, public solid waste employees, private collection and disposal
firms, equipment manufacturers, neighbours, environmentalists, low-
income or minority groups and end-product consumers.

The effects of technology can be numerous, and one way of exploring them is to identify them on what is called a 'relevance tree' (Cross, 1978). Like cost–benefit analysis and environmental impact analysis, technology assessment comes up against the problem of adequately managing all the consequences of development. In the study by Dickey *et al.*, only first-order effects were considered over a ten-year period.

Some critics of technology assessment have argued that the impossibility of predicting all the consequences of technology mean that its use is extremely limited. R. Holt (1977), for example, claims that it would have been impossible to predict the 'benefits' and 'adverse' effects of the automobile had such a technological assessment study been conducted at any time between 1895 and 1925, crucial years in the growth of the automobile industry. Just how far-reaching the impact of the car has been is illustrated in table 5.1. This particular argument, as in the case of opposition to cost–benefit analysis, is particularly misleading as it presupposes that choice between different technologies is impossible. One may not know, for example, all the likely consequences of nuclear power or solar power, but nevertheless a choice must be made, and it should not go by default. Elucidation of possible consequences can only aid decision-making.

Table 5.1   *How the automobile has altered our lives (1895 to present)*

Values

Geographic mobility
Expansion of personal freedom
Prestige and material status derived from automobile ownership
Over-evaluation of automobile as an extension of the self – an identity machine
Privacy – insulation from both environment and human contact
Consideration of automobile ownership as an essential part of normal living (household goods)
Development of automobile cultists (group identification symbolized by type of automobile owned)

Environment

Noise pollution
Automobile junkyards
Roadside litter

Social

Change in patterns of courtship, socialization and training of children, work habits, use of leisure time, and family patterns
Created broad American middle class, and reduced class differences

Table 5.1—*continued*

Created new class of semi-skilled industrial workers
Substitution of automobile for mass transit
Ready conversion of the heavy industrial capability of automobile factories during Second World War to make weapons
Many impacts on crime
Increased tourism
Changes in education through bussing (consolidated school versus 'one-room country schoolhouse')
Medical care and other emergency services more rapidly available
Traffic congestion
Annual loss of life from automobile accidents about 60,000
Increased incidence of respiratory ailments, heart disease, and cancer
Older, poorer neighbourhood displacement through urban freeway construction

Institutional

Automotive labour union activity set many precedents
Decentralized, multi-divisional structure of the modern industrial corporation evident throughout the auto industry
Modern management techniques
Consumer instalment credit
Unparalleled standard of living
Emergence of US as foremost commercial and military power in world
Expansion of field of insurance
Rise of entrepreneurship
Basis for an oligopolistic model for other sectors of the economy
Land usage for highways – takes away from recreation, housing, etc.
Land erosion from highway construction
Water pollution (oil in streams from road run-off)
Unsightly billboards
Airpollution – lead, asbestos, hydrocarbons, carbon monoxide, nitrous and sulphurous oxides

Demography

Population movement to suburbs
Shifts in geographic sites of principle US manufacturers
Displacement of agricultural workers from rural to urban areas
Movement of business and industry to suburbs
Increased geographic mobility

Economic

Mainstay and prime mover of American economy in the twentieth century
Large number of jobs directly related to automobile industry (one out of every six)
Automobile industry the lifeblood of many other industries
Rise of small businesses such as service stations and tourist accommodations
Suburban real estate boom

Table 5.1—*continued*

Drastic decline of horse, carriage, and wagon businesses
Depletion of fuel reserves
Stimulus to exploration for drilling of new oil fields and development of new
  refining techniques, resulting in cheaper and more sophisticated methods
Increased expenditure for road expansion and improvement
Increased federal, state, and local revenues through automobile and gasoline sales
  taxes
Decline of railroads (both passengers and freight)
Federal regulation of interstate highways and commerce as a pattern for other
  fields
Highway lobby – its powerful influence

(*Source:* Gibbons and Voyer, 1973:469)

On the other hand, it may be more relevant to argue that technology
assessment of the large-scale technologies of modern society necessarily
implies technocratic élitism, but if this is the case then it is reliance upon
large-scale technology which is the problem and not necessarily technology assessment itself. D. Elliott and T. Emerson argue against the rule by
technocratic élites, but instead of blaming the techniques of assessment,
they ask the question: 'Is direct participation possible in the large,
complex, modern socio-economic organization? Is it possible to involve
everyone in this higher-level decision-making process and to keep them
informed of the crucial issues and data, thus enabling them to formulate
priorities, criteria and policies decentrally?' (1976:120). The solution they
suggest is not more technocratic élitism and computer-based assessment
techniques, but much smaller-scale technologies which allow greater
opportunities for workers' control.

Holt gives a second and more relevant reason for doubting the value of
technology assessment which is carried out exogenously, that is to say
without reference to the 'inducement mechanisms'. Technology, he
argues, is induced under various economic and social pressures and
cannot simply be modified by an arbitrary and external assessment of its
effects. In other words, the same criticisms that can be levelled against the
corporate planners' notion of planning without constraint can be applied
to technology assessment. Some of the basic forces acting on technological
innovation and diffusion are illustrated by the work of Y. Hayani and V.
Ruttan (1971) on the comparative development of agriculture in Japan and
the United States from 1880 to 1960.

During the early part of this period, Japan was primarily short of land
but not of labour, whereas America was short of labour but not of land. In
Japan, innovations occurred primarily in biological and chemical techno-

logy which increased the productivity of the land. In America, on the other hand, it was innovations in mechanical technology that increased the productivity of labour, allowing more land to be worked by the same workforce. During the last thirty years, as land has become scarcer in the United States, attention has been increasingly focused upon biological and chemical technology such as hybrid grains, fertilizers and pesticides. In Japan, an increasing labour constraint has induced the development of new mechanical technology.

Technology may be induced by pressures of demand, as above, but may also be induced in response to the relations of production. Dickson (1974) cites several examples such as scientific management techniques associated with Taylor, and the introduction of containerization to counteract the militancy of dockers and control wage demands. Many innovations during the early stages of the industrial revolution were aimed at transforming the worker from his rural craft tradition to the discipline of an industrial 'hand' or appendage to the machine. To make this transformation innovations were necessary to strengthen the capitalists' control over the workforce, to strengthen the social relations of production, and hence to secure the foundation of greater profits for the ruling class. Thus, mechanical innovations in the textile industry were induced not only in response to bottlenecks in demand for spinning and weaving, but also as a means of controlling a restless and belligerent workforce. Dickson describes some of these examples which are to be found in A. Ure's *The Philosophy of Manufacture* (1967, first published 1835):

A typical example was increasing the length of the spinning mules. By decreasing the overall number of mules required, this displaced adult spinners and increased the number of their assistants, thereby weakening the factory apprentice system and reducing the spinners' authority. 'This necessity of enlarging the spinning frame has recently given an extraordinary stimulus to mechanical science', writes Ure. 'In doubling the size of his mule, the owner is able to get rid of indifferent or restive spinners, and to become once more master of his mill, which is no small advantage.' This was despite the fact that such modifications were often costly, and that the larger machines meant that the lay-out of factories often had to be replanned at considerable expense (Dickson, 1974:80).

The transfer of technology to less developed countries

Development of new technologies may of course serve to reinforce social relations of production and at the same time be more efficient at serving the interests of the ruling class. This is often the case when technology is transferred to developing countries. In this situation, technology may be adopted which is quite inappropriate to the general needs of the mass population. For example, much of modern technology has been designed to meet the needs of large stable markets, availability of skilled management, trained experts, well-developed distributional channels, economies of scale, shortage of manpower, availability of capital, and so on. The situation in most less developed countries is not similar: there are often small and season markets, undeveloped distributional channels, lack of suitably skilled management and an abundance of underemployed labour. Moreover, customs and beliefs are often alien to the discipline demanded by advanced technology (Schumacher and McRobie, 1969).

The adoption of the snowmobile by the Skolt Lapps, who live in the north-eastern part of Finland, illustrates the destructive consequences of technological transfer which is both efficient and serves the interests of the ruling class. The first snowmobile was introduced by a teacher in early 1962, and by 1967 the use of sled reindeer was considered to be an anachronism. The main advantage of the machine was in saving time. One of the disadvantages was that it caused the reindeer herds a certain amount of stress. According to some Lapps, this stress caused the scattering of herds upon which they depend for their livelihood. The snowmobile has, it seems, rapidly transformed a stable pastoral relationship from a symbiotic to a parasitic form, which is dependent upon fossil fuels from elsewhere. It was an emerging capital-owning élite that benefited most, and the introduction of the snowmobile was accompanied by increasing social stratification (see Pelto, 1973, and Ingold, 1976).

An interesting example of the influence of forces of production and social relations of production on the transfer of technology is provided by the European missionaries' introduction of steel axes to the aborigines. This particular study was made by American anthropologists in the 1930s when the traditional stone axe was fast disappearing (Sharp, 1952). It looked at the impact of the steel axe on the Yir Yorant, a hunter-gathering group of aborigines living in the region around the mouth of the Coleman River in the west coast of the tropical Cape York peninsula in Australia.

Before coming into contact with European settlers in the late nineteenth century, the Yir Yorant depended principally upon a stone axe for a variety of tasks essential to their survival. This stone axe had important social significance as well as the obvious practical function. The stone used for the axes came from quarries 400 miles to the south. The Yir Yorant made spears which they traded with other tribes for stone axe-heads. While the use of the axe required little skill, its ownership was the exclusive preserve of the tribesmen. Women and young children had to ask a male for the use of an axe, a necessary request for domestic and other activities. If one of the Yir Yorant, whether male or female, adult or child, wanted to borrow an axe, there was a hierarchy of male status that determined which adult male should be sought out. For example, the eldest brother was always superordinate to the younger. In religious ritual and the gathering of wild honey, the use of the axe was strictly confined to men. Hence the axe helped to reinforce the social relationships, and the axe was an important symbol of masculinity among the Yir Yorant. In the case of religious ritual, the axe symbolized the connection between man and the environment. The axe also played an important part in mythology; it was their ancestors who had discovered the axe and its value to the tribe.

When European missionaries came, they distributed steel axes which were somewhat more efficient than the stone axes. The steel axes were given freely to women and children. Some of the men were reluctant to accept these gifts and then found themselves on occasion asking their wives to borrow the sharper implement. As a result of the wider distribution of the axes there was, according to L. Sharp, 'a revolutionary confusion of sex, age, and kinship roles, with a major gain in independence and loss of subordination on the part of those able now to acquire steel axes when they had been unable to possess stone axes before' (1952:84).

The steel axes rapidly came to symbolize the authoritarian position of the European missionaries. As the Yir Yorant became dependent upon the missionaries, they also lost the reciprocal relationship with their neighbouring tribe with whom they used to exchange axe-heads for spears. Again Sharp comments, 'with trading partnerships weakened, there was less reason to attend the fiestas, and less fun for those who did. A decline in one of the important social activities which had symbolized these great gatherings created a lessening of interest in the other social aspects of these events' (1952:84). As ownership of axes became less well defined, stealing and trespassing became more frequent. Moreover, the superior steel axe undermined the mythological tradition. All in all, the stability of Yir Yorant culture was lost through the destruction of the symbolic and social function of the stone axe.

Not all technological innovations involving greater technical efficiency are so pacifically accepted. The introduction of hybrid corn to Spanish American farmers in New Mexico is an example. Attempts were made to introduce a hybrid corn with three times the yield of traditionally cultivated corn. In 1947 in one village sixty farmers planted the hybrid. The following year only thirty farmers replanted the hybrid, and in 1949 only three farmers persisted with it. The reason for the failure was, according to A. Apodaca, not technical or economic but simply that 'all the wives had complained. Some did not like its texture; it did not hang together well for tortillas; the tortillas were not the colour of nixtamal (the corn-flour dough to which they were accustomed). Few cared for the flavour, but the farmers who persisted in planting it after the first year hoped that they would get used to it. It made abundant food for the stock and they were reluctant to drop it for that reason. However, after three years they had not become accustomed to the flavour or texture, and their wives were up in arms' (1952:38).

New hybrid grains with much greater yields have, however, been successfully introduced in many countries. In the 1940s, rapid increases in yields had taken place in some of the advanced countries such as the UK, US and Australia. Thus for the UK, yields of barley that were approximately 700–800 kg/acre in the pre-Second World War period rose to 900 kg/acre in 1942, to 1,000 kg/acre in 1949, and to 1,400 kg/acre in 1963. The technological 'package' associated with these yield increases included: energy inputs in the form of mechanized power which applied seed and spray more efficiently, and made for better harvesting; greater use of fertilizers, irrigation and pesticides; plant genetics and selection of seeds which are more responsive to fertilizers, give rise to shorter plant stems that can bear the weight of a heavier head of grain, have different photo-period sensitivity and shorter growing periods (allowing multi-cropping), and are more suitable for harsher climates.

Since the Second World War, the Rockefeller Foundation and Ford Foundation have supported work on developing high yield varieties (HYV) of wheat in Mexico and rice in the Philippines. These programmes, at least in the first instance, proved to be very successful, especially in the case of wheat. Whereas the old long-stalked wheat varieties were only able to take up some 40 lb of nitrogenous fertilizer per acre, the new varieties produced much higher yields by taking up to 120 lb/acre of nitrogenous fertilizer. During the 1960s, the rapid spread of wheat and rice hybrids in the less developed countries became known as the Green Revolution (see table 5.2.).

Table 5.2   *Total area of high-yielding varieties of grain in developing countries (excluding countries with centrally-planned economies)*

Crop year	Wheat	Rice	Total
1965/66	9,300	49,400	58,700
1966/67	651,100	1,034,300	1,685,400
1967/68	4,123,400	2,605,000	6,728,000
1968/69	8,012,700	4,706,000	12,718,700
1969/70	8,845,100	7,848,800	16,693,900
1970/71	11,344,100	10,201,100	21,545,200
1971/72	14,083,600	13,443,400	27,537,000
1972/73 (prelim)	16,815,500*	15,658,600	32,474,100

* Includes Turkey at 1971–72 level
(*Source:* Dalrymple, 1974(a))

The most rapid increase in area under HYVs occurred in the period 1966–71. Overall food production in India, for example, increased during this period from 72 million tons to 108 million tons, and imports declined from 10 million tons to 2 million tons (Dasgupta, 1977). The diffusion of the Green Revolution depended upon the following factors listed by A. Pearse:

1 a technological 'package' or recipe produced in scientific research centres and designed to fit the environmental conditions of the region in which it is to be applied;
2 arrangements whereby knowledge of this technology could be communicated to cultivators;
3 measures to ensure the availability of physical inputs, that is, HYV seeds, fertilizers, pesticides, machinery and fuel;
4 measures to favour the prospect of profitable sale sufficiently attractive to compensate for the greatly increased production costs and risks involved;
5 indispensably, some system of credit so that the payment for inputs and additional cultivation expenses could be financed, pending the receipt of income from the sale of the product after harvest (1977:130).

The yield ratios of the new hybrids relative to traditional seeds have declined (see table 5.3). The declining yield ratios in the period after 1970/71 can be attributed to several factors including unfavourable weather, the spread of the Green Revolution to less favourable soils, and failure to comply with some of the conditions necessary for successful

Table 5.3 *High-yielding varieties yields in India as multiples of yields of traditional varieties*

Crop year	High-yielding varieties yields	
	Wheat	Rice
1966/67	2.87	2.58
1967/68	3.70	2.18
1968/69	3.49	2.05
1969/70	3.68	2.26
1970/71	3.44	2.27
1971/72	2.50	2.03
1972/73	2.35	1.76
1973/74	2.59	1.71

(*Source:* Dalrymple, 1974(b))

application of the Green Revolution technology. The energy crisis of 1973 and spiralling fertilizer costs discouraged demand and led to a deteriorating quality of farm inputs such as seeds; some farmers failed to renew the stock of hybrid seeds, not being accustomed to do so with traditional grains. The rapid turnover of hybrid varieties made it difficult for poorly educated farmers to organize the crop calendar accordingly (Dasgupta, 1977).

The impact of the Green Revolution has been much debated. Among the environmental consequences were increased vulnerability to pest problems, loss of genetic diversity through monocropping and neglect of local varieties, fertilizer-induced increase of weeds, the threat of fertilizer pollution in fragile soils, and erosion accelerated by multiple cropping. Resulting social problems included consumer resistance to the rice hybrid IR8, which became soggy on cooking, and the destruction of harvest rituals where multicropping meant that another crop had to be sown immediately after harvesting (see Palmer, 1972; Wade, 1974(b)).

It has been argued by many development economists that the Green Revolution is scale neutral and inherently equitable. As long as credit and support services are available, it is argued, the Green Revolution technology will work as well on small farms as on larger ones; although it is conceded that on plots smaller than ten acres it may be uneconomical for the farmer to invest in his own tube wells and it would be too risky to grow HYVs without reliable irrigation. In reality, however, the large farmers have continued and are bound to continue to make better use of the technology. They are generally better equipped (in terms of financial resources, education, expertise, and social position) to make better use of the technology (Wade, 1974(a)). Rich farmers in relatively prosperous agricultural areas such as the Punjab were more able to exploit the Green Revolution. The advantages have not percolated down to the smaller and poorer farmers, while there has been a growing proletarianization of the peasantry and a concentration of land and assets in fewer hands.

India has been unable to extend its food production through a policy of more egalitarian distribution of land, despite the large number of empirical studies in the mid-1960s which showed that small holdings were on the whole more productive. Fertilizer and energy demands have also created greater dependence upon overseas supplies. B. Dasgupta describes the market orientation of the Green Revolution:

Unlike the traditional cultivation, where the farmer largely uses the last year's seed, manure produced by farm animals, home-made tools, family-owned bullocks, and family labour as the major inputs, the new technology makes him dependent on the market for the supply of new seeds, chemical fertilizers, pesticides and herbicides, hired labour and hired agricultural machinery (1977:241).

The Green Revolution is a not uncommon example of technology transfer which benefits an indigenous ruling élite as well as the exporters of the technology who provide the inputs and the know-how. This kind of technology transfer, however, can lead to technological dependence which has serious disadvantages for the developing country as a whole. Increased costs, dependence upon the vagaries of a world market, the loss of control over decisions, and failure to develop indigenous scientific and innovative capacity are typical consequences of technological dependence (see Stewart, 1977). E. Feder summarizes the results of the Green Revolution in terms of 'sharply increased land ownership, massive dispossession of small-holders, proliferation of landless workers, rural unemployment, poverty, hunger and increase in the domination of the multinationals over production and distribution of agricultural products and inputs' (1976:532).

It would be a mistake to regard all the results of the Green Revolution as a simple consequence of the technological package. Of much greater importance has been the way the Green Revolution was introduced. Indeed, one can make a fairly strong case that the Green Revolution technology is scale neutral and its consequences are almost entirely due to the political and social order. In China, for example, new hybrids have been introduced without the same consequences, despite the fact that yields of wheat and rice per acre are approximately twice those in India. The lack of rich peasants and landlords, the commune organization, local construction of irrigation projects and indigenous development of local chemical fertilizer plants have enabled the Chinese to avoid the problems often attributed to the Green Revolution technology alone (Caldwell, 1977). Nevertheless, in non-socialist countries, the Green Revolution has been very amenable to manipulation in the interests of owners and operators of the technology. The technological package, in conjunction with the institutional framework, has ensured that the rich gain at the expense of the poor. Credit facilities, for example, reduced the risks for the rich farmers, but were insufficient to help the poorer farmer.

It has been shown in these examples how diffusion of technology is closely tied to social relations and the distribution of power. Technology assessment is generally only concerned with social and environmental consequences or the impact of technology without investigating why technological choice and undesirable effects take place. The controversy over nuclear power is a classic example of the inadequacy of technology assessment as a means by itself of countering undesirable technological choice.

Nuclear power

The development of nuclear power has been a principal target of the environmental movement throughout the 1970s. While general environmental issues have been of declining importance, the nuclear power issue has attracted mounting debate (see figure 5.1). It is the consequences of

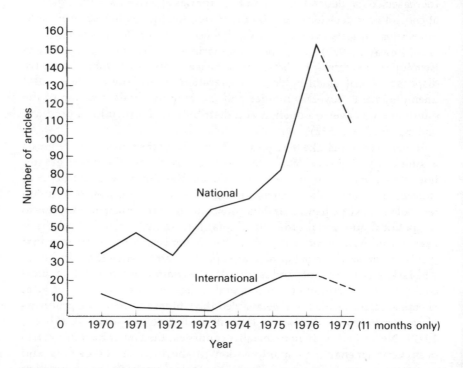

Figure 5.1   United States articles on atomic power listed in the Readers'
Guide 1970–77*

*With the exception of the 1977 data, the articles for each year are taken from the annual cumulative index issued by the Readers' Guide to Periodical Literature. The *Guide* indexes periodicals of 'general interest' and includes several environmental magazines (such as *Audubon* and *National Wildlife*) as well as other periodicals ranging from the *Readers' Digest* to *Science*. The annual indexes are dated March-February but virtually all the listings are for the year indicated (for example the 1976 listings only included one article published in early January 1977).

All articles listed under the following headings were counted: 'Atomic Power', 'Atomic Power Industry' and 'Atomic Power Plants'. Discussions of and replies to articles were counted as separate articles when they appeared in subsequent issues of the magazine. The 1977 data are partial and are taken from the several partial compilations issued for that year. They reflect roughly eleven months of articles.

(*Source:* Mitchell, 1978:25)

nuclear power that have captured the arena of public debate. This debate has been conducted, as is so often the case, as if policy-makers and governments were in a perfectly free position to weigh up the pros and cons of alternative energy policy strategies and make the appropriate decisions accordingly. In the context of this discussion, the lengthy and largely unresolved issues surrounding nuclear power will be mentioned here, but not elaborated in any detail. The personal conviction of the author is that the risks of nuclear power in the real world of political instability, makes a future catastrophe almost certain. However, any such assertions based upon technology assessment are inadequate by themselves, because however well-founded in fact and logic, they ignore the social and economic interests that seek to benefit from a nuclear future. It is this aspect of the nuclear power controversy which still remains a latent but none the less crucial issue for resolution.

The nuclear power issues are numerous and diverse. They include pollution, safety, economic viability, civil liberties, and energy policy in general. The pollution consequences can be divided into two categories. The first is the thermal effects from the production of electricity on acquatic life. This is probably the least important issue as no doubt some valuable use could be made of the cooling water, whether it be for aqua-culture or district heating. The second form of pollution is caused by radiation. It is this problem which involves the unresolved questions of risk. Low-level radiation leakage from nuclear installations has been a common phenomenon. Much debate has occurred on the question of whether or not low levels of radiation will significantly increase the incidence of cancer and genetic mutations.

Higher level risks are also an important feature of nuclear power. These include first the safety of reactors and the possibility of a major release of radiation due to malfunction. Secondly, there is a radiation risk in storing nuclear wastes as they need to be stored for thousands of years before becoming harmless. Wastes can be reprocessed and fission material, including plutonium, recovered for further use in nuclear reactors and fast-breeder reactors. However, if the reprocessed waste is returned to the countries of origin, there are the further risks of terrorist activity and nuclear proliferation. To help avert such risks, fuel rods made from reprocessed wastes can be 'spiked' so that they become highly irradiated and less easy to use as a material for nuclear weapons. However, even this would not give a hundred per cent protection against terrorists or rogue governments, and it makes reprocessing a doubtful economic prospect (Bugler, 1978(a)).

Terrorist activity is a real possibility. Terrorists could foreseeably construct a bomb from fissile material or could disperse the material so as to cause radiation damage. Terrorists might also be able to sabotage a nuclear installation. While there has been some debate about the harm terrorists could inflict, little attention has been paid to the possible consequences of a conventional war. In a nuclear economy dependent in the main on centralized electricity production, nuclear plants would be a prime target. Dependence upon large-scale nuclear installations would increase the vulnerability of a country against military attack. With the proliferation of nuclear power in a world that is continually racked by wars, it would seem almost inevitable that a radiation disaster will occur in the future.

The risks of terrorism necessarily require increased security for nuclear plants and for the transportation of fissile material. In Britain, for example, the UK Atomic Energy Authority promoted the Special Constable Act 1976 which allows its police to be armed in case of attack. Rigorous surveillance and possible interrogation of all employees of the nuclear power industry and others posing a potential threat to security are necessary in order to cut down risks of sabotage. Justice and the National Council for Civil Liberties have been particularly concerned about the consequent erosion of freedom of information and civil liberties (see Flood and Grove-White, 1976).

The economic arguments for nuclear power are also debatable, but much complicated by the enormous subsidies from governments in both Britain and the United states. In America, for example, the government has spent tens of billions of dollars on subsidizing uranium exploration and mining, uranium enrichment and reprocessing, research and development of nuclear reactor technology, and the transportation and storage of wastes (Brown *et al.*, 1976).

Finally, debate has broadened considerably in recent years over the whole question of energy policy and energy alternatives to nuclear power. The critics of nuclear power claim that an alternative 'soft energy path' (see Lovins, 1976 and 1977) exists which is feasible, economic and less risky. The questions of whether or not such economic alternatives exist and the extent of the risks for either path have been the subject of thoughtful and rational debate, especially in Britain where the anti-nuclear lobby has fought its case along traditional lines through lobbying at public inquiries and in Parliament. In other countries, opposition has on occasion been less peaceful. 'The nuclear power debate', commented Leo Abse, 'has brought down a Swedish government; it has provoked extensive riots in France; it has racked the West German government and activated fierce debates within the German Social Democratic Party' (House of Commons debate, 2 December 1977). In 1977, between fifty and sixty thousand demonstrators gathered at Malville, France, on the site of the world's first commercial fast-breeder reactor. After five hours of clashes with the police involving tear-gas and percussion grenades, nineteen people had been arrested and six of these received prison sentences of between three and six months (*Undercurrents*, October–November 1977). The actual achievements of the anti-nuclear lobby have been few, although in Austria in a referendum on 5 November 1978, the electorate narrowly voted against nuclear power.

The nuclear power controversy has thus raised serious issues and even led to violent opposition. Nevertheless, both sides have generally confined the controversy to technical considerations of social and environmental consequences without considering the role that nuclear power plays in furthering ruling class interests. One may demonstrate the point by references to A. Lovins' writings on soft energy paths.

Lovins, like so many other writers on this subject, confines his discussion to the rational case for and against nuclear power. He makes a comparative technology assessment of what he calls a hard energy path and a soft energy path. The hard energy path is based upon nuclear power and other large technologies principally geared to a centralized supply of electricity. Nuclear power technology has, he claims, the following consequences:

... it is the most complex and slowest kind of technology to deploy, is remotely administered by a highly bureaucratized technical élite with little personal commitment to its clients, is vulnerable to large-scale and extremely expensive mistakes and failures, and is entirely at the mercy of a few people. (A handful of power engineers can turn off a country, and a single rifleman can black out most cities.) Finally, very few end-uses of energy in modern societies actually require electricity, and they require little of it at that (1975:xxviii).

Lovins offers an alternative soft energy path which can be brought about by social changes in life-style, such as 'value changes in work, leisure, agriculture and industry' (1977:37). Energy would be conserved through changes in habits – through car pooling, mass transport, cycling, etc. The soft path also requires technical fixes which involve less social change. Thermal insulation, heat pumps and more efficient engines would help conserve energy, while renewable sources of energy, such as solar power, would be substitutes for electricity.

Very few end-use energy requirements need to be met by electricity. Space heating, for example, is a major source of demand for energy but need not be met by electricity which wastes a major proportion of primary energy as heat when it is generated. The few absolutely necessary demands upon electricity could be met in the United States by the current hydro-electric capacity. Lovins claims that soft technologies, unlike the high technologies of the hard path, are already known to work well. The small soft technologies make for easier planning to meet demand because the lead time for construction is much smaller than for high technologies which must be planned ten to twenty years before they come into use. The nasty consequences of the high energy future are contrasted with the advantages of the soft energy path:

Solar technology is reliable, not easy to disrupt, sufficient for our needs, simple, low technology, transferrable, flexible with respect to cultural and settlement patterns, safe, with minimal environmental and climatic impacts, has free fuel, tends to resist commercial monopoly . . . reduces international tension arising from uneven distribution of fuels and of high technologies, is a spur to decentralization and local self-sufficiency, and helps to redress the severe energy imbalance between temperate and tropical regions (1975:xxx).

Lovins (1977) believes that the hard and soft paths are incompatible. Further progression along the hard path would, he claims, inhibit development along a soft path for three reasons. First, it would starve the soft path of material components. Secondly, it would bring about changes in social values and concepts that would tend to inhibit soft technology innovations. Thirdly, it would create political, institutional and policy barriers to the development of soft technologies. Lovins believes that the two paths are diverging and one path must be chosen to the exclusion of the other.

There are three initial steps which Lovins believes are necessary in order to ensure that the soft energy path is taken. The first is to correct institutional barriers which hinder the development of conservation and low energy technical fixes. The second is to remove the subsidies favouring conventional fuels. These subsidies in the United States alone are estimated to be well over $10 billion per annum. The third is gradually to increase energy prices to a level consistent with long-term costs when cheap fuels have been used up. If these three steps are taken, then 'ordinary market and social processes' will ensure that the soft energy path is taken (1977:19).

There are several weaknesses in Lovins' argument. The mutually exclusive argument and the distinctions between the hard and soft paths are certainly debatable. There seems, for example, to be no reason why certain so-called soft technologies such as solar power, could not be monopolized by a few large enterprises under central control. Soft technologies are already being manufactured by large multinational firms. B. Martin (1978) argues that soft technologies, such as solar power, can be introduced in such a way as to preserve private financial control and central planning, and at the same time maintain economic inequality and alienation resulting from lack of local control. Conversely, some of the high technologies such as techniques of automation could be indispensible to a more satisfying and ecologically sound society. Bookchin (1971(b)) argues that highly advanced and complex automated techniques can reduce working time, unnecessary toil and drudgery, and help to do away with much of the need for specialization. In recent years, for example, mechanization and technological advances in the do-it-yourself field have enabled large numbers of people to become good carpenters and plumbers with little or no training.

Lovins also argues that soft technologies are economically feasible and would be profitable for private enterprise. So why should the two paths be mutually exclusive? Lovins offers no convincing reasons. However, the limitations of his analysis are not in the main what he believes are the social consequences of nuclear power and solar power, although he does adopt a crude technological determinist perspective. The main weakness of his analysis is the lack of understanding of the pressures for nuclear power and the way that it is legitimated.

Every effort by the anti-nuclear lobby to paint a picture of the disastrous consequences of nuclear power is swamped by the legitimating exercises of the nuclear power industry. In recent years, developers have relied heavily upon technical expertise to legitimate their plans (see Nelkin, 1975). In the nuclear power controversy, the nuclear industry is able to monopolize this expertise and hence is in a powerful position to influence committees, inquiries and other political institutions.

An interesting example of legitimating activity on the part of the nuclear power industry has been the publication of estimates of risks from different energy sources. The Atomic Energy Control Board (AECB) of Canada studied the risks of alternative fuels and their estimates were very favourable to nuclear power (see table 5.4). The AECB makes a distinction

Table 5.4   *Risk in man-days lost per unit energy output*

	Occupational	Public
Coal	73	2,010
Oil	18	1,920
Nuclear	8.7	1.4
Natural gas	5.9	–
Ocean thermal	30	1.4
Wind	282	539
Solar		
space heating	103	9.5
thermal	101	510
photovoltaic	188	511
Methanol	1,270	0.4

(*Source:* Inhaber, *New Scientist*, 1978:446)

between occupational and public risks. The former applies to the activities necessary in producing an operating energy system. The latter applies to health risks associated with the operation of the energy system. Coal and oil involve more risk than nuclear power, largely because of air pollution. The production of methanol from wood involves high occupational risk due to the dangerous activity of logging. The high risks from the alternative technologies, solar and wind, are largely due to their material and labour demands for both production and storage of the energy (Inhaber, 1978).

This type of analysis may be countered by referring to the high risk but low probability of serious accidents from nuclear power, to the techniques of accounting, to the overestimation of the material requirement for wind generated electricity by a factor of about 100 (*The Times*, 27 November 1978) and so on. The difficulty is, however, that the whole process of legitimation is facilitated by the wealth and backing of nuclear power interests. Moreover, the opinion of nuclear scientists within the nuclear power industry is more likely to carry authority than that of less 'experienced' opponents from outside the industry. This was clearly demonstrated at the Windscale inquiry into THORP which was conducted in a semi-judicial manner with Justice Parker acting as judge over the emperical debate (see Wynne, 1978). In this type of policy-making forum, the advice of Lovins and others of the same genre is likely to fall on deaf ears.

In the United States, the Atomic Industrial Forum (AIF) is an industry trade group and is a 'primary source of information to policy-makers, the national media and special interest groups of the public' (Mitchell, 1978:6). This public relations arm of the nuclear power industry is the main legitimator of nuclear power and is supported by the major and most influential capitalist interests in America. The board of directors of AIF includes top management, vice-presidents and presidents of the countries' largest bankers, utility services, nuclear industries and oil companies. There is, in other words, a strong industrial–oil–coal–nuclear interest behind the development of nuclear power. The oil multinationals have considerably diversified their interests and the seven main companies control 30 per cent of the coal reserves and between 50 per cent and 80 per cent of the uranium reserves in America (Brown *et al.*, 1976).

So the main weakness of Lovins' attack on nuclear power and similar protests is that they ignore the power and interests that promote this form of energy. There is a lack of any insight into the power struggle necessary if a soft energy path is to be taken. B. Martin (1978) has produced a very clear critique of Lovins' writings along these lines. Nuclear power, unlike the soft energy technologies, he argues, is favoured by advanced industrial capitalism because it furthers centralized control over investment and production, keeps decisions in the hands of employers and their hired experts, and maintains passive consumerism. For Lovins, promotion of a soft technology future is a matter of technological assessment, debate and appropriate policy-making. For Martin, choice of technology is more strongly influenced by the social relations of production which favour nuclear power. The only way to ensure the introduction of the soft energy path for Martin is through fundamental changes in the social order, especially in production relations. Rather than just seeking rational debate in an open forum, Martin argues that nuclear power should be countered by organized opposition within the workplace, unions, schools, community groups and neighbourhoods.

Much of the debate about the consequences of nuclear power and the technical fix of an alternative energy policy can be seen as largely ideological, for it obscures the real influences on technological choice. Technology assessment, like cost–benefit analysis, assumes that environmental and social problems can be dealt with by technical assessment rather than political resolution. Technology assessment can therefore be used as a means of legitimation by those interests most able to wield power and resources. History has all too often shown how the most atrocious distortions of humanity can be made to appear benign. It is naïve to assume that a few concerned environmentalists stating some of the dangers of nuclear power are going to disturb the nuclear–industrial free market economies. In the next chapter, this discussion will be extended by looking in more detail at proposals for so-called 'appropriate technologies'.

6 Utopian and Alternative Technologies

Economic, social, moral and environmental problems have, it was indicated in the last chapter, frequently been attributed to the development of advanced capital-intensive technology. Utopian thinkers have reacted against poverty, alienation and pollution by suggesting remedies based upon 'alternative' technologies. The soft energy path advocated by Lovins has been just one of many recent policy proposals involving so-called 'alternative', 'intermediate', 'low-cost', 'inequality-reduction', 'radical' or just plain 'appropriate' technologies. In this chapter the limitations of this strategy, based as it is upon technology assessment and a pluralistic notion of technological choice, will be explored further.

The study of alternative technologies has been roughly split institutionally into those concerned primarily with economic development problems in less developed countries and those concerned with the economic development problems of the advanced industrial countries. The issues that will be raised are in many ways similar for both developed and less developed countries, but for convenience will be dealt with in separate sections.

Alternative technology in less developed countries

During the last twenty-five years transfer of capital-intensive technology to the less developed countries has failed to prevent mass migration to the cities, large-scale urban and rural underemployment and slow economic growth. At the same time it has involved many disastrous social and environmental changes. In India the urban population increased by 38 per cent between 1961 and 1971 (Sigurdson, 1976). At the end of this period some 60 per cent of the population still had a *per capita* expenditure of less than one rupee per day and about 20 million were underemployed. A. Reddy believes that the transfer of capital-intensive technology has intensified the social problems:

The result is a sharpening of the contrast in living standards, opportunities and outlook between the urban rich and the rural poor. It is Western technology, therefore, which has buttressed the polarization of Indian society into a dual society with a small, comparatively rich, acquisitive, conspicuously consuming, politically powerful, city-centred élite drawing its ideas and values from the West, and a large mass of poor people left out of the circle of production and consumption by the lack of employment and purchasing power (1975:332).

From the mid-1960s there was a revival of views earlier expressed by Gandhi. 'Men go on saving labour', Gandhi proclaimed in 1940, 'till thousands are without work and thrown on the open streets to die of starvation. I want to save time and labour not for a fraction of mankind but for all; I want the concentration of wealth, not in the hands of a few, but in the hands of all. Today machinery merely helps a few to ride on the back of millions. The impetus behind it all is not the philanthropy to save labour but greed. It is the constitution of things that I am fighting with all my might' (Hoda, 1973:284). After independence in 1947 Gandhi set up numerous village industry complexes in an attempt to improve small industries in the rural areas. He also tried to get the villages to become self-sufficient in their basic needs for cloths, oil, shoes, etc (Hoda, 1976). In 1963 E. F. Schumacher visited India and became much influenced by the Gandhian ideas of industrialization.

In 1965 Schumacher founded the Intermediate Technology Development Group (ITDG) to promote what he called an intermediate technology, or a technology intermediate between traditional tools and highly sophisticated Western technology. Thus an ox-driven plough, which has recently been introduced into several tropical African countries, is intermediate between hand-operated tools and the tractor. Schumacher formulated four features which characterized his concept of intermediate technology:

First, that these workplaces have to be recreated in the areas where the people are living now, and not primarily in metropolitan areas into which they tend to migrate.
Second, that these workplaces must be, on average, cheap enough so that they can be created in large numbers without this calling for an unattainable level of capital formation and imports.
Third, that the production methods employed must be relatively simple, so that the demands for high skills are minimized, not only in the production process itself but also in matters of organization, raw material supply, financing, marketing and so forth.

Fourth, that production should be mainly from local materials and mainly for local use (1973:163).

By providing workplaces at lower cost more employment would be created. This might mean lower productivity per worker, but nevertheless ought to be acceptable if it resulted in the same or greater output and capital return per unit of investment. One example of a successful project resulting from ITDG innovation has been the construction of brickworks in Ghana. The first of these was built at Asokwa, a small village near Kumasi. It cost about $20,000 and employs twenty-six men, which represents an investment of under $800 per workplace. This is about one-fiftieth of the capital per workplace of a conventional brickworks. The Kumasi brickworks produced about 10,000 bricks a week, or thirty times fewer than the conventional brickworks.

Only 10 per cent of the capital costs of building the Kumasi brickworks involved imports. The rest of the materials were obtained locally. Had a conventional brickworks been built some 70 per cent of the materials would have had to be imported. The Kumasi brickworks also involved fewer complex skills, maintenance could be carried out by local mechanics. The kilns burned local firewood and the only fuels that had to be brought in were required for a 10 hp diesel engine which was used to mix the clay. Labour was involved in hand-moulding, stacking the bricks in the kiln, and operating the simple mixer. Apart from employment benefits the brickworks avoided as much as possible dependence upon imports and expatriot labour. The success of the Kumsai brickworks led to the Ghanaian government ordering three more brickworks (Parry, 1975).

This brickworks example is a case of what Schumacher and G. McRobie called scaling down and redesigning high-cost technologies. Two other categories of intermediate technology have been promoted by ITDG; they are the upgrading of traditional methods and new product designs. Improved weaving looms and traditional rice mills are examples of the former. New agricultural equipment such as the snail (a winch-operating plough which substitutes for a tractor) and ferro-cement boats are examples of the latter (Schumacher and McRobie, 1969). One other category has been added to this list by Hoda (1976) and that is of reviving old technologies. For example, watermills and windmills played an important part in providing energy for industry before the industrial revolution. These earlier techniques of energy production are now important intermediate technology tools.

In 1974, the ITDG Board agreed that the group's aims should be:

1 to compile inventories of existing technologies which can be used within the concept of low-cost, labour-intensive production;

2 to identify gaps in the range of existing technologies;
3 to research into and develop by invention or modification new or more appropriate processes;
4 to test and demonstrate in the field the results of its investigations;
5 to publish and make known the results of its work as widely as possible, so as to facilitate the transfer and use of appropriate technology.

One of the first tasks in communicating the possibilities of alternative technologies for development was to publish a directory called *Tools for Progress*. By publicizing the range of technological options that existed Schumacher believed that better choice of technologies would follow: 'In India', he argued, 'some splendid solutions have been found of an intermediate technology kind, but in Peru or, say, Tanzania, nobody knows about them – and *vice versa*. It is tragic to see people struggling to find solutions to quite straighforward problems, which have been solved long ago somewhere else (*The Listener*, 14 November 1974).

The concept of intermediate technology has been considered by some to stress the economic aspects of technology – the labour-intensive/capital-intensive angle – without sufficient regard to social and environmental aspects. The term 'appropriate technology' has been used for this wider definition. Thus the development of technology for building small concrete houses in tropical countries meets the requirements of intermediate technology but is most inappropriate when one considers the effect it has on overheating. According to one definition: 'Appropriate technology is neither intermediate technology nor miniaturization of production processes: it is a radically new approach in which production technique becomes subordinate to social needs. Solutions of unresolved problems in the realm of appropriate technology must be inspired with this basic concern for the masses' (Hanlon, 1977:467).

Reddy has listed the following preferences which should determine the choice of appropriate technologies:

1 a preference for capital-saving and employment-generating, rather than capital-intensive and labour-saving, technologies;
2 a preference for cottage-scale and small-scale, rather than large-scale, technologies;
3 a preference for the technologies of goods and services appropriate for mass consumption, rather than for individual luxuries;
4 a preference for technologies requiring little skill, or small modifications in the skills of traditional craftsmen like potters, weavers, blacksmiths, carpenters, cobblers, tanners, oil millers, midwives and medicine men;
5 a preference for technologies using local materials, rather than materials which have to be imported from abroad or transported from distant parts of the country;

6 a preference for energy-saving, rather than energy-intensive, technologies;

7 a preference for locally available sources of energy such as the sun, wind and bio-gas;

8 a preference, in the machine-building and machine-tool sector, for the technology of mass-producing scaled-down, dispersable, miniaturized factories, rather than the technology of mass-producing consumer goods in gigantic city-based enterprises;

9 a preference for technologies which promote a symbiotic and mutually reinforcing, rather than parasitic and destructive, dependence of metropolitan industry upon the rural population;

10 a preference for technologies based on rational use, rather than indiscriminate rapid devastation, of the environment (1975:333-34).

Similarly, when considering the choice between water supply and sanitation technologies, J. Pickford (1977) argues that the most appropriate method must improve health, be of low cost, be most beneficial to local users, be constructed from locally available materials, be easily maintained and operated. The ideas behind intermediate technology or appropriate technology are consequently forms of technological assessment.

The success of ITDG is hard to measure. In terms of its objectives there has clearly only been a partial success, and ITDG have recognized a failure to get intermediate technology concepts accepted in practice. On the other hand there has been a growing interest in the ideas. By October 1977, twenty-six countries had formed centres concerned with appropriate technologies. Eight of these were established in industrialized countries; the rest were in the Third World. In 1974 ITDG employed only twenty-five people, but by early 1978 it employed a total staff of fifty-five and was engaged in recruiting twenty-five to thirty new staff. Aid agencies have been particularly keen on intermediate technology. In 1977 the Overseas Development Ministry accepted the recommendations of a working party that various new activities in the field of intermediate technology be supported out of the aid programme initially by at least £500,000 a year for three years. In the United States a bill in 1977 earmarked a sum of just over $3 million to form a National Centre for Appropriate Technology in Butte, Montana.

The activities of these different appropriate technology centres vary enormously (see Singer, 1977). In the developed countries, apart from ITDG, the better-known organizations include the Brace Research Institute in Canada, the Tool Foundation in the Netherlands, and Volunteers in Technical Assistance in the United States. The Brace Research Institute is particularly concerned with energy supply in rural areas. It has undertaken Research and Development (R and D) work on sun and wind power for agricultural and private use, on desalination, and on implements for agriculture and processing industries. Like ITDG, it has published material, notably its *Handbook on Appropriate Technology* in 1974, on the principles of appropriate technology, on the available tools, and on several case studies.

Volunteers in Technical Assistance, on the other hand, is an association of some 6,000 volunteer businessmen, scientists and engineers. It has been involved in designing intermediate technologies but also promotes small businesses. In common with ITDG and the Brace Research Institute it has published its own source book on available tools – the *Village Technology Handbook*. Like the other organizations it runs an inquiry service and acts as an information centre.

In the less developed countries, India would probably claim to have the greatest government and non-government interest in appropriate technology. The Appropriate Technology Cell, in the Ministry of Industrial Development, was set up in 1971. It helps to disseminate information on available technologies for potential users, but concentrates its work particularly on scaling down plant size for cement; sugar and paper; road construction; building construction; and bio-gas, or methane, plants.

The Programme on the Application of Science and Technology to Rural Areas, was created in 1974 at the Indian Institute of Science at Bangalore. It is also involved in bio-gas and has been working on the design of a community-size plant. It has done work on establishing the most crucial problems of the rural poor. Its main object is to develop village-orientated technologies on the campus and then transfer them to the rural areas. Projects include windmills, handpumps, and cement plants.

Other organizations, such as the National Research Development Corporation and the Planning Research and Action Institute, are also involved in promoting appropriate technologies in the rural areas. The Appropriate Technology Development Unit of the Gandhian Institute of Studies, Varonasi, acts as an information centre on technologies relevant to the urban and rural poor. There are also organizations that promote small-scale industries such as the National Small Industries Corporation, the Small Industry Service Institutes, and the Small Industry Extension Training Institute.

There has been some generalized criticism of intermediate technology on the grounds that it is often an inferior technology because it produces a lower output and savings from the same investment. Hence, if this assertion is correct, intermediate technology is less likely to bring about economic growth. The question of whether labour-intensive technology can be substituted for capital-intensive technology without loss of efficiency has been investigated in a series of neo-classical micro-economic case studies. Most of these studies have considered factors such as machinery (capital investment) and labour necessary to make a particular product. An estimate is then made of the most efficient techniques available. Some studies have been more sophisticated in considering multi-factor substitution of inputs such as labour for material inputs, or for working capital, skilled or unskilled labour, etc. (Bhalla, 1975). The choice of technology within this type of analysis depends upon what factors a country is endowed with: that is, labour, skills, capital, land, and natural resources. It also depends upon the efficiency of different technologies.

H. Pack (1974) has attempted to show that efficient intermediate technolgies do exist by comparing labour/output and capital/output ratios for industries in different countries. These ratios were calculated from UNIDO data and plotted on a graph giving a scatter of points. The continuous line joining up those observations closest to the origin is called the efficiency frontier. Movement along this line from top left to bottom right indicates the possibility of labour-capital substition without loss of output. Thus in figure 6.1, which plots grain-milling possibilities of substitution, plants 4 and 5 (Israeli) are efficient capital-intensive plants while 6 and 7 (Japanese) are efficient labour-intensive plants. Japanese plants used $280 to Israeli's $6410 capital per man-year of labour in direct production; other points on the graph indicate firms suffering from inefficient equipment.

There are two main problems with Pack's study. First, it compared industries rather than products. A true comparison is often impossible because the products may vary in quality and design. S. Langdon (1975), for example, found that soap produced by multinational companies in Kenya was more highly packaged than the products from labour-intensive techniques used by local firms. Technological advance, often involving greater proportions of capital to labour, may produce new products which make old products less attractive or obsolete. Thus in a comparison of can-making techniques in different countries C. Cooper *et al.* noticed that 'the very labour-intensively produced open-top cans in Thailand (and also in East Africa) are of poor quality by comparison with those that are made on automated lines. The same is true in the case of shoe-polish tins, though not for kerosene tins' (1975:106).

The second problem with Pack's study is that it fails to consider the cultural and economic infrastructure which influences the efficiency of different techniques. Consideration of technology choice only in terms of different factor prices is far too simplified. The size and organization of the market, the organization of the labour force, the availability of skilled labour and supervision, and differences in wage rates will clearly affect the efficiency of technology in different countries and even within one country. Moreover, some multinationals may prefer to use more or less standardized plant everywhere in order to save administrative and servic-

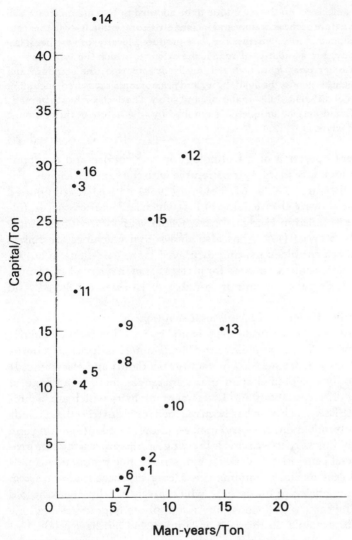

Figure 6.1 Substitution possibilities in grain-milling

(*Source:* Pack, 1974:392)

ing expenses (Cooper *et al.*, 1975). F. Stewart points out that the efficiency of a technology is dependent upon other technologies and consequently cannot be truly assessed without reference to the infrastructure in which the choice of technique is made:

For example, a decision on the technique to be adopted in tyre manufacture will depend on the nature of the economy and income structure within it – whether cars are being consumed locally, whether they are produced locally, or whether it is a bicycle economy, the standards of roads, the extent to which the tyres have to compete with other tyres manufactured locally or imported, the standard and prices of competitive goods, the availability and price of inputs required, including energy, labour of different skills, materials and so on. The decision has to be made in the light of, and may be uniquely determined by, the nature of the economic structures as a whole (1977:23).

The efficient operation of a technology in one culture and economic context does not imply that it is transferable with the same efficiency. For example, in the early 1920s, M. Polanyi (1964) noticed that imported machinery for blowing electric lamp bulbs, which had worked successfully in Germany, failed in Hungary for a whole year to produce a single flawless bulb. Stewart (1977) has also shown that machines for maize-grinding and cement block making displayed large variations in output per hour. Variations are accounted for in terms of management efficiency, workers' skill, demand for output, number of workers employed, and repair facilities.

The economic efficiency of technological options has now been investigated in a large number of studies sponsored by the International Labour Office (ILO) as well as in studies at the Livingstone Institute on 'Appropriate Technology' (Strathclyde University, Scotland) and elsewhere. It is now generally accepted that in many instances there is a range of techniques of different labour and investment intensity which are technically efficient. This conclusion has been reached for industries that include salt and sugar production, rice- and maize-milling, textiles (spinning and weaving, including carpet-weaving), brewing, grain-processing, the production of metal cans, metal-working industries, shoe production, road-building and cement block manufacture. However, these findings are in part due to the choice of industries, which are generally speaking old industries. The same conclusions may not apply to middle-aged or new industries. For example, in the case of canning and fertilizer production the relatively investment-intensive techniques are favoured in terms of efficiency.

A study of fertilizer production in India by R. Disney and H. Aragaw (1977) illustrates the point. Urea, which is used as a fertilizer, can be manufactured from ammonia by at least twelve different techniques. Those techniques with the highest capital/labour ratios tend to be most efficient. Disney (1977) has also compared fertilizer production costs, using conventional manufacture of urea and production of manure and methane gas from cow dung using the gobar-gas plant. Conventional methods are, in most circumstances, more efficient than the gobar-gas plants. Rich farmers, if deprived of fertilizer, will only buy a gobar-gas plant as a second-best policy, while for the smaller farmer the capital costs, despite a 25 per cent government subsidy, are too great.

Technological progress has then usually resulted in innovations which are more capital-intensive than older ones. The new industries have thus responded in part to the availability of labour and capital in advanced capitalist countries. Given a change in product resulting from an innovation, there is often in effect only one way of making it. Choice of technology with different labour and investment requirements may therefore mean a choice of products – the rubber sandal made from discarded tyres versus the leather fashion shoe, for example. As Stewart (1977) has shown, there are probably many more differences between labour- and investment-intensity methods of producing cement blocks, mud-bricks, and stones, which can all be used for housing, than between different methods of producing cement blocks alone.

Micro-economic studies of different techniques are in themselves an inadequate tool for promoting more 'appropriate' technological development. Most of them fail to take account of the external costs and benefits of different techniques, for example risks to health and safety or pollution. However, the main shortcoming of the neo-classical approach is that it takes the economic and social organization of production as given. It assesses efficiency in a static fashion and ignores the political and social influences which favour the development of certain techniques at the expense of others. While micro-economic studies may help to fill a gap in information about available technologies, they do not in themselves offer an explanation of the apparent failure of less developed countries to adopt 'appropriate' technologies. There are several influences which strongly discourage the adoption of 'appropriate' technologies.

Firstly, about 98 per cent of the World's research and development expenditure is undertaken in developed countries where the trend has been towards capital-intensive rather than labour-intensive technology. These technological products are often more efficient than those that are labour-intensive. The total amount of money spent on a world-wide basis by organizations directly concerned with promoting 'appropriate technology' was in the order of $10 million for the year 1975. Less than half this was spent on research and development whereas about $80 billion are spent annually on developing new modern technologies (Jéquier, 1976).

Secondly, the use of techniques is often linked to many other techniques so that once they are established in the modern sector (F. Sector) alternative products are at a disavantage. Stewart stresses the importance of the historic situation: 'In a society which has already adopted inappropriate technology, alternative techniques tend to appear inefficient, and even where apparently efficient they are often rejected in favour of the further use of inappropriate techniques (as shown in the empirical evidence) because of the links between different parts of the system' (1977:110).

Thirdly, demand for products will be influenced more by income distribution than by basic needs. Hence there is often a demand for consumer durables in the modern urban sector while large numbers go starving. The choice of technology and product will be geared to effective market demand.

Fourthly, the absence of evaluative expertise in many less developed countries, especially in Africa, explains why entrepreneurs will sometimes favour expensive but dependable Western technology rather than cheaper and less well-known technology from another less developed country (Uhlig and Bhat, 1977).

Fifthly, labour costs are often different from those predicted by aggregate supply and demand. C. Cooper (1973), for example, argues that a unionized modern-sector working class has inhibited the growth of employment opportunities. Capital-intensive techniques may also be chosen to avoid labour unrest.

Sixthly, developing country élites have often been educated in the more technologically advanced countries and have experienced their consumption patterns. Consequently they are more likely to import technologies especially if they have a brand name with proven commercial value (N. Clarke, 1972). ILO studies in Columbia and Kenya have demonstrated that a small number of high-income élites have been extremely influential in creating a demand for consumer goods with a brand name. In Kenya highly refined maize promoted by large companies, despite its greater cost and lower nutritional value, has been displacing unrefined maize (Cooper, 1973).

Finally, technological choice is influenced by those with power and capital – the multinationals and big business in particular. It is these interests that are in a position to influence choice in the private sector and have also gained a large measure of control over the government machine which determines technological choice in the public sector. The multinationals are in a particularly strong position to influence consumer taste and hence demand for 'inappropriate' products. For example, the powerful tobacco industry has been able to stimulate demand for cigarettes in less developed countries by vigorous advertising campaigns which include sponsoring sporting activities. In 1976, the two major tobacco companies spent nearly £1 per adult male on advertising in Malaysia alone, a country whose GNP stood at only £400 per capita (Muller, 1978). Encouragement of more appropriate technologies will only occur through the exercise of political power aimed at controlling these minority élites whose vested interests may not coincide with the technological choice which in the long run would favour the majority of the population. Cooper argues:

It is not enough to rely on a massive programme of small-scale rural industrialization to achieve a redistribution of income. Usually some measure of income redistribution is a prerequisite for such a programme anyway. At the very least, a programme of this kind requires more or less direct control over the consumption patterns of the rich and over the promotional activities of the large-scale modern sector enterprises. Luxury consumption will have to be curtailed and there would have to be more stringent and effective measures to prevent the erstwhile luxury consumers from expatriating the resources that are released from consumption. The role of the foreign enterprises – and of many local enterprises using foreign brand-names – would have to be controlled and changed. The trouble is that these policies often run counter to the interests of the most powerful sections of the community (1973:300).

Appropriate technology enthusiasts have focused attention on technologically-determined consequences and have paid insufficient attention to the social and political changes necessary for the development of appropriate technology. Without such changes, J. Hanlon argues, 'the power and profits remain with those who have been able to exploit the new technologies as they did the old. In the present economic system, appropriate technologies exist and survive only by the grace and favour of the multinationals and big business houses. The issues are not technical, but social and political – about who controls the means of production and distribution' (1977:469).

Even in countries such as India, that profess to encourage the development of small-scale industries in the rural areas, there are grave doubts about the success of this unless supported by radical changes in ownership and social control of industry. In 1977 the Indian Janata Government formulated a policy which on the face of it favoured the rural areas. The plan contained the following points: new licences were to be refused on all new industrial units within urban areas of over 500,000 people; assistance was to be given to industries locating themselves in approved backward areas, industrial centres were to be established to help village entrepreneurs; 'appropriate technology' was to be encouraged, and plans were begun to develop a chain of mini-cement plants in the countryside as had already been done in China. However, despite the attempt to deal with the problems of poverty and unemployment in the rural areas, there have been strong criticisms that the proposals do not go far enough.

Small industries in rural areas will not be able to call upon local skilled manpower, nor will they be able to sell their products where they are needed because of the lack of demand caused by poverty. The rich landlords, on the other hand, will continue to buy from the towns which meet their consumer needs. India's industrial policy, unlike China's, is not closely integrated with the development of rural co-operatives and communes. It is land reform and changes in social organization that would enable rural areas to exert control over small industries and convert need into demand (see Agarwal, 1978 (b)).

D. Dickson (1974) sees the promotion of intermediate technology as a politically naïve technological fix. For Dickson, the technology chosen embodies the social relations of production, and the professed benefits of intermediate technology will only be possible after a class struggle which removes the 'economic and political shackles of a dominant class'. It is only after such changes, he argues, that intermediate technology will become widespread rather than just Utopian. Despite these criticisms of the intermediate technology concept the proposals do help to draw attention to the contradictions which prevent the realization of more appropriate development. Moreover, a Utopian vision of an alternative society based upon appropriate technologies is perhaps necessary to bring about a realization of the fruits possible if people are willing to press for social change.

Alternative technology in developed countries

The debate concerning intermediate technology in the less developed countries has been very similar to that concerning alternative technologies in the technologically developed countries. Schumacher's attention to small-scale technology was aimed at the developed as well as the less developed countries. He argued that much of the large-scale technology, urbanization and centralized planning was encouraged in an era of plentiful and cheap energy. Small-scale technology, on the other hand, would be more easily designed to conserve energy and at the same time introduce skills which make employment more satisfying. With the energy crisis in the early 1970s (in 1970 Britain's monthly crude oil inputs of 8.3 million tons cost the country £40 million. In March 1974, the crude oil imports of 9.6 million tons cost £278 million) the time was ripe to encourage small-scale energy conserving technologies (Schumacher, 1974 and 1976).

To illustrate his argument, Schumacher referred to the brick industry, currently dominated in the UK by the London Brick Company which makes use of huge acres of Bedfordshire clay. Because energy costs have been low it has paid London Brick to make bricks on a large scale, automating most of the processes with the aid of energy-consuming machinery. Energy costs involved in trasporting bricks long distances are compensated for by economies of scale. In the process, vast areas of Bedfordshire are despoiled and job satisfaction is low. In contrast Schumacher recommended the development of a model brick industry devised by J. Parry. Brickworks would not use non-renewable oil or coal but instead operate using three sources of renewable energy: the methane produced by a local community sewage plant, wood grown locally (which would also help to camouflage the plant), and wind power. Those employed at the brickworks would be involved in all of the work, including felling timber, excavating clay, driving battery-powered trucks and stocking the kiln (*The Listener*, 14 November 1974).

Schumacher recognized the need for social change if a more appropriate technology was to be developed. What he advocated was co-operative ownership of the means of production along the same lines as the Scott Bader Commonwealth which was owned and worked by about four hundred people. Given co-operative ownership there would be less chance that boring thankless tasks would be adopted, as these would be self-imposed. Schumacher was not alone in calling for such changes. M. Bookchin (1971 (a) and (b)) has long advanced similar demands for small-scale technology designed to meet social needs rather than techno-cratic ends. Indeed Bookchin's emphasis upon integrating libertarian values and ecological ideas, and his proposals for small-scale decentral-ized technology, have had a profound effect on the American ecological movement since the publication of *Post-Scarcity Anarchism* in 1971.

Those concerned with promoting alternative technologies tend to be idealists in the sense of recommending techniques and blueprints which support a Utopian vision of a new society. The need for changes in social values, and the need to design technologies so as to satisfy various criteria derived from the Utopian vision, have been much emphasized. Although there is obviously no consensus amongst the protagonists on the absolute characteristics of the Utopia, a dominant form is that portrayed in *A Blueprint for Survival* which was written in 1972 by the editors of *The Ecologist*.

In *A Blueprint for Survival*, the ideal envisaged is a society of decentral-ized self-sufficient communities with small-scale and simple technologies that can be controlled by the community. Production is geared to meeting the 'needs' of the community. The social structure would enable a close and harmonious relationship with nature. Consequently there would be a minimum of disruption to the ecological system. Boring, monotonous and aimless work would be replaced by diverse and stimulating work.

In many respects this vision of decentralized harmonious communities producing goods from small workshops can be traced back within the romantic and idealist tradition that has reacted against the abuses of industrialization. Indeed many of the current supporters of alternative technology find that their views are similar to those of Robert Owen, William Morris and Prince Kropotkin. In many respects the syndicalist movement and Guild Socialists in the nineteenth and early twentieth centuries supported a similar Utopian vision. One of the dominant features of today's manifestation of this movement is the emphasis upon alternative technologies or the soft technological path instead of the hard technological path which dominates the forces of production. This distinction was made by Lovins in his criticism of nuclear power, but is a common distinction amongst the promoters of alternative technology. Perhaps the clearest exposition of the alternative paths of development has been made by R. Clarke (1972) – see table 6.1.

Various centres have been set up to promote alternative technologies.

Table 6.1   *Characteristics of 'hard' and 'soft' technology communities*

Hard technology society	Soft technology community
1. ecologically unsound	ecologically sound
2. large energy input	small energy input
3. high pollution rate	low or no pollution rate
4. 'one-way' use of materials and energy sources	reversible materials and renewable energy sources only
5. functional for limited time only	functional for all time
6. mass production	craft industry
7. high specialization	low specialization
8. nuclear family	communal units
9. city emphasis	village emphasis
10. alienation from nature	integration with nature
11. consensus politics	democratic politics
12. technical boundaries set by wealth	technical boundaries set by nature
13. world-wide trade	local bartering
14. destructive of local culture	compatible with local culture
15. technology liable to misuse	safeguards against misuse
16. highly destructive to other species	dependent on well-being of other species
17. innovation regulated by profit and war	innovation regulated by need
18. growth-orientated economy	steady-state economy
19. capital intensive	labour intensive
20. alienates young and old	integrates young and old
21. centralist	decentralist
22. general efficiency increases with size	general efficiency increases with smallness
23. operating modes too complicated for general comprehension	operating modes understandable by all
24. technological accidents frequent and serious	technological accidents few and unimportant
25. singular solutions to technical and social problems	diverse solutions to technical and social problems
26. agricultural emphasis on monoculture	agricultural emphasis on diversity
27. quantity criteria highly valued	quality criteria highly valued
28. food production specialized industry	food production shared by all
29. work undertaken primarily for income	work undertaken primarily for satisfaction
30. small units totally dependent on others	small units self-sufficient
31. science and technology alienated from culture	science and technology integrated with culture
32. science and technology performed by specialist élites	science and technology performed by all
33. science and technology divorced from other forms of knowledge	science and technology integrated with other forms of knowledge
34. strong work/leisure distinction	weak or non-existent work/leisure distinction
35. high unemployment	(concept not valid)

(*Source:* Clarke, 1972)

These include the New Alchemy Institute and the Kurt Foundation in the United States, the Minimum Cost Housing Groups Ecological Operation and Zoneworks Corporation in Canada, and the Centre for Alternative Technology in Wales (Gerrand, 1975). The aims of these centres are similar in many respects to those promoting intermediate and appropriate technologies. That is to say they are involved in promoting technological innovation, acting as a resource centre and creating publicity. J. Todd (1976), founder of the New Alchemy Institute, expresses their aim as one of inventing new technologies based upon the following criteria: the technology should be available to individuals and small groups; it should be cheap; it should be designed according to ecological and social considerations rather than in terms of economic efficiency.

Those favouring alternative technologies see them as an answer to the failures associated with modern industrialized society. P. Harper (1973) believes that the radical followers of alternative technology want socialism but get technocracy; want equality but get hierarchies; want self-determination but get bureaucracy; want community, but get suburbia; want good working conditions, but get automation; and want cleanliness, but get pollution. The causes of this situation are, however, in dispute. Some adopt a technical solution but nevertheless alternative response while others adopt a more radical political stance (see table 6.2). Harper, a more critical advocate of alternative technology, believes that 'organizing within the production system, although vital, is insufficient. Revolutionary alternatives are needed which simultaneously (a) reveal the contradictions and absurdities of the *status quo*; (b) erode the prerogatives of the established institutions and economy; and (c) create visible alternative institutions which express post-revolutionary life styles, relationships and economy' (1973:292).

Harper (1976) is also suspicious of the professed environmental benefits of some of the so-called alternative technologies such as windmills. The environmental costs, he argues, of building two million one kilowatt windmills may be as great as or greater than those of building one power station producing the same amount of energy. Likewise the capital costs and the alienation resulting from producing such alternatives may outweigh the lower running costs and supposed satisfaction derived from the alternative technology.

Economic arguments of inefficiency, as in the case of intermediate technology, may be explained in part by the lack of research and development involved. The amount spent on solar and wind power is miniscule in comparison to that devoted to nuclear power and more traditional forms of energy supply. There are some writers, such as Dickson, who believe that alternative technology cannot be introduced without a change from the current capitalist social and economic order. This view has been forcefully

Table 6.2   *Technical problems and some social responses*

Technical problem	Alternative response	Radical political response
1. Pollution	Invent non-polluting technologies	Pollution is a symptom of capitalism not of poor technology
2. Capital dependence	Invent labour-intensive technologies	Capital is a problem only in capitalist society
3. Exploitation of resources	Invent technologies that use only renewable resources	Wrong problem: exploitation of man by man is the real issue
4. Liability to misuse	Invent technologies that cannot be misused	Misuse is a socio-political problem, not a technical one
5. Incompatible with local cultures	Design new technologies which are compatible	Local culture will be disrupted by revolutionary change in any case
6. Requires specialist technical élite	Invent and use technologies that are understandable and controllable by all	Provide equal chance for everyone to become a technical specialist
7. Dependent on centralization	Concentrate on decentralized technologies	Centralization an advantage in just social systems
8. Divorce from tradition	Evolve technologies from existing ones	Traditions stand in the way of true progress
9. Alienation	Decentralize; retain mass production only in exceptional cases	Alienation has social, not technical, causes

(*Source:* adapted from Clarke, 1973:262–63)

expressed by C. Garman and K. Alper in an article in *Science for the People*:

The ruling class now owns or controls most of the resources of the country and certainly is not willing to let them or the power associated with them go without a fight. For instance suppose everyone tried to participate in food co-ops, would they have more control or better food? No! If co-ops significantly increased their size they would become more and more dependent on agribusiness which could then increase their prices if they wanted, forcing people back to supermarkets to pay higher prices. . . . Another example would be alternative power sources. But again who would produce them? (Assuming they were cheap enough for people to buy, which they aren't.) Does one think that the steel, oil, gas, and electric companies would sit by and let people break up their power monopoly? The prices for raw materials would be made too high or the materials would become unavailable. Again only the few would be able to invest in alternative technology (1976:16).

This type of argument tends to paint too extreme a picture of the differences between dominant forms of technology and alternative technologies. It fails to recognize the increasing commercial interests in much of the alternative technology which had been advocated on the whole by minority groups in the period prior to the 'energy crisis' precipitated in 1973 by OPEC.

B. Martin distinguishes between alternative technologies that could be adopted without any threat to existing political and economic structures and those technologies which are more likely to be developed under local control. With the latter and radical form of alternative technologies 'people might be encouraged to take control over their lives in many ways: working conditions, education, health, and perhaps eventually choice of goods produced and control of production itself' (1978:11). To illustrate the argument he refers to the development of solar power. While solar technology could be produced in small units on a widespread small-scale basis it is also amenable to mass production and central control. Furthermore, certain research innovations, especially in the solar technology-electricity production sphere, and large-scale storage would enable solar power to be introduced with little threat to the social and economic order.

Commercial development of alternative technologies may indeed be a welcome stimulus to market economies. A study by the US Office of Technology Assessment claimed that by the mid-1980s, given the right support, solar energy could be made competitive in markets dealing with over 40 per cent of US energy demand. Many new jobs would be created, especially in construction trades, metals and chemicals (*New Scientist*, 29 June 1978). During the late 1970s the costs of solar energy began to fall rapidly. The US Energy Research and Development Administration (ERDA), now absorbed into the US Department of Energy, estimated that the cost of solar cells would come down from $11 per peak watt to $1 to $2 per watt (in 1975 dollars) by 1982 and to 50 cents by 1986. Solar-powered irrigation pumps, for example, will probably be competitive with diesel pumps by the mid-1980s (Agarwal, 1978(a)).

In the transport field, mass transport systems which are environmentally superior to private automobile transport systems may also be introduced out of necessity for energy conservation but need not necessarily threaten political and economic structures. A centralized public transport system run by planning 'experts', reliant upon private enterprise to provide the resources and equipment and designed to meet the needs of business, would probably enhance the efficiency of market economies. Drastic social changes would only be necessary if transportation became more dependent upon bicycles and vehicles which were multi-purpose in use, resource-efficient and were produced and used on a local basis (Martin, 1978).

We have seen in this chapter how alternative technologies have been advocated like medical palliatives to the symptoms of a disease. While many aims of alternative technology enthusiasts are undeniably valid in terms of humanistic and environmental objectives, technology proposals by themselves ignore the realities of technological choice. What good is it to recommend a cure (alternative technology) when the problem (adoption of 'inappropriate technology') is a product of the social order itself? Dickson (1974) would seem to be correct when he suggests that alternative non-alienating and ecologically sound technologies can only be developed to any substantial extent after a change in the social order. Without such changes supporters of alternative technology will remain like Robert Owen and his followers in the early nineteenth century – Utopian thinkers with only isolated community experiments as a product of their action. To establish alternative technologies political campaigns must become part of the main labour movement's struggle to reduce the influence of the capital-owning ruling class. In the next chapter the development of technology and its environmental consequences in socialist countries will be explored with particular attention to the changes that have taken place in China.

7 Technology and Environment under Socialism: the Case of China

Environmental problems in socialist countries tend to be related to the system of public ownership and control of technology. While serious problems undoubtedly exist, they are not rooted in production based principally on private ownership and profit. Different types of socialist organization have had varying success in ensuring that industrial advance is compatible with conservation and environmental protection. At one extreme there is the centralist model of rapid heavy industrialization as in Russia. At the other extreme is the decentralized development policy of China which has relied to a much greater extent on local initiative and small-scale technology.

In Russia the development of heavy industry became of paramount importance, especially after the first Five Year Plan from 1928 to 1929. Obsession with economic growth *per se* led in many respects to a neglect of environmental conditions. Pollution control agencies have had a low standing in the Ministerial hierarchy, and strong control of a legalistic and bureaucratic character has tended to inhibit local initiative in tackling pollution control and conservation projects. As a consequence pollution and waste of resources have been similar in many respects to those found in Western capitalist states. D. R. Kelly *et al.* record some of the water pollution problems:

Fires blazed on the Iset and Volga Rivers in the late 1960s, forcing the Volga steamers to carry signs warning the passengers against throwing lighted cigarettes overboard. Near the town of Vitebsk, residents watched the Dvina River hourly change colour depending on the volume of dye discharged by a local factory. Fish kills also became common on major waterways, forcing the fishing industry to turn increasingly to the now threatened fisheries of the Pacific and North Atlantic. Oil spills were common place, with 65,000 tons of crude oil – twice the capacity of the *Torrey Canyon* – seeping annually into the Caspian Sea near the oil production centre of Baku. In recent years, Soviet naturalists have also noted spreading algae growths on stagnant rivers and reservoirs (1976:78).

Some writers, such as H. L. Parsons (1977) and W. M. Mandel (1972), have argued that public opinion and mass-based ecological movements have had some success in preventing undesirable projects, in controlling pollution, and conserving resources in Russia. However, these measures have been much less impressive than those adopted in socialist countries that have emphasized rural development, decentralization and local self-reliance. In this respect North Korea, Vietnam and above all China have demonstrated a more positive approach towards the enhancement of the quality of life.

One of the key features of China's development since the 1949 Revolution has been the integral relationship between health, agriculture and environmental policy on the one hand and industrial and economic policy in general on the other. It seems to the outside observer at least that development has been more closely geared to improving the quality of life for the mass population than to any artificial indicator such as growth in GNP. As an article on environmental protection in the *Kuang Ming Daily* stated, China does not 'just promote industry without taking agriculture into consideration, promote production without taking living conditions into consideration, or promote economic development without considering the protection of the environment' (*The Times*, 7 November 1973).

What one understands by economic policy in China is certainly not to be regarded as efficient in market economy terms. Economic policy instead has been strongly influenced by political demands such as self-sufficiency in rural areas, worker management of factories, and the priorities of developing the agricultural base to the economy and of creating an overall economic balance in keeping with Chinese socialist politics. The politics of socialism have been in command of economic development as opposed to the politics of capitalism in the West.

It is probably true to say that China did not have a specifically defined environmental policy before 1970, when she became involved in the mounting international concern for environmental problems. Before 1970 environmental policy was very much a secondary consideration to the problems of economic development (Orleans, 1975/76). Fortunately economic development incorporated many policies, such as intermediate technology and land reclamation, that were to have a direct and beneficial effect on conservation of environmental resources and pollution control.

Economic and political development: the role of intermediate technology

China's economic record since liberation has been impressive by any standard. She has had an average overall compound growth rate in food grains during the years 1949–75 of something over 3 per cent. Between 1952 and 1957, during a period when priority was given to heavy industry, the growth rate was 2.3 per cent. There was a slump between 1958 and 1960, but a rapid recovery from the early 1960s as China developed a policy favouring rural development. The growth rate was 5.4 per cent between 1963 and 1967, 3.9 per cent between 1963 and 1970, and 3.1 per cent between 1963 and 1975. In comparison to India there has been much less output instability. In the fifteen years since 1960 output fell in only two years (1968 and 1972) whereas in India output slumped back below the preceding year on six occasions. By 1965–66 China had become a net exporter of food, and by the early 1970s she had become self-sufficient in foodgrains (Paine, 1976).

China's industrial record has been equally impressive, with an average annual compound growth rate of between 12.3 per cent and 13.1 per cent between 1949 and 1975. When industry received the greatest priority in the 1950s the annual growth rate was in the order of 20 per cent. There was a two-fifths decline in industrial production during the economic crisis of 1960–61 when Russia withdrew her technical aid and blueprints for industrial development. There was then a rapid recovery although this was followed by a slight decline in 1966 at the beginning of the Cultural Revolution. China's record can again be compared with that of India. Between 1950 and 1975 there was a 5.7 per cent average annual compound growth rate of industrial production in India which was approximately half the rate of growth in China (Paine, 1976).

While China's record of economic growth has been impressive, so too has its development towards greater equality, health and general quality of life. The main factors in this improvement have been the decentralist development of the rural areas, the organization and control of production, and the provision of social services.

In the early period, 1949–57, China made her first attempts at breaking away from her imperial post – she turned to the USSR for aid and concentrated upon urban development through heavy industry. During this period only about 6.2 per cent of the state budget was spent on agriculture (Wheelwright and McFarlane, 1973). Nevertheless there were important agricultural changes and land reform had a marked effect on the distribution of rural incomes. Prior to land reform, 3 per cent of the population received 25 per cent of all rural income. In the 1930s the top 10 per cent of the rural population earned ten times as much as the poorest.

By the mid-1950s this ratio had dropped to 4:1 (Perkins, 1978). Land reform was accompanied by changes in organization of work and in the division of labour. The rural population were mobilized to undertake farmland and waste-control projects. Improved seeds were introduced and 'night soil' was collected as a fertilizer (Paine, 1978).

During the first Five Year Plan, 1953–57, China had clung to the orthodox communist obsession with large-scale enterprises for two reasons. First it was widely believed throughout the communist block and elsewhere that heavy industry would positively stimulate all other areas of the economy. Secondly, it was thought that heavy industry would provide sufficient employment for the rural labour surplus. The Chinese discovered that both these assumptions were wrong (Gray, 1978(a)).

Long-term Maoist industrial policy was influenced by this experience. It was also influenced by the experience of the Communist Party before liberation in the border regions. The communists resisted the Japanese invasion and the Kuomintang repression which increased during the Second World War with the advent of United States aid. It was then that communist activity relied upon the development of labour-intensive construction, intermediate technology, land reform and community development. Industry could more easily be immobilized in the large cities, but the small-scale mobile machinery in the hinterland suited the guerilla tactics of the communists.

So it was before the communist seizure of power in 1949 that the achievements of industrial co-operatives and local reform first appeared. This experience clearly distinguishes the origins of Maoist policy from the policy developed in Soviet Russia in the 1920s. In China the basic revolutionary force had been the peasantry rather than the industrial proletariat, whereas in Russia the Bolshevik party had been largely isolated from the rural peasantry. Self-sufficiency in the rural areas had been a strategy of defence, and continues to be so especially since the termination of international relations with Russia.

In contrast to the centralized model of development the Maoist line emphasized a strategy of planning from below and a minimum of state interference. It recognized that widescale differences still existed and balanced economic development was necessary. Maoist strategy became clearly formulated in two speeches in 1956. In the 'Ten Great Relationships' speech Mao put the case for a balance between the productive forces and productive relations. A balanced development strategy required an integration of industrial and agricultural policy which could be facilitated by decentralization of planning, participatory economic management and greater self-reliance in the rural areas. Modern and small-scale intermediate technologies would serve the majority of the population living in the rural areas and would help reduce the gap between the 'Three Great Differences': agricultural and industrial, rural and urban, and manual and mental. S. Paine (1976) suggests that during the anti-Confuscius campaign in the early 1970s another great difference was added to the list, namely male and female.

The Maoist line on technological development was in many respects similar to that more recently advocated by supporters of alternative technology. Mao's three great differences were to be reduced by development of technologies in the rural areas with workers, rather than experts alone, encouraged to participate in the process of innovation. Specialism and work demarcation such as that between mental and manual work was discouraged. Mao's technology policy, unlike proposals for alternative technology in the West, was however firmly integrated in the overall strategy of economic and political development.

Intermediate technology in the rural areas was therefore to be a key element of Maoist industrial policy. This was also stressed in the other great speech of 1956 – 'On the correct handling of contradictions among the people'. It was therefore realized that in a predominantly rural-based economy balanced development could best be achieved by increasing the peasants' purchasing power through rural development. It was the rural market which could stimulate mechanization and demand for goods from heavy industry. Industrialization and mechanization in the rural areas would make better use of available manpower, and would lead to rational development of the country's resources. J. Gray describes the Maoist rural policy:

The route to peasant community development is through simple small-scale local industrialization. First, local processing of agricultural products and local manufacture of farm tools, then the gradual mechanization of handicraft production of consumer goods, then the creation round each country town (as far as resources allow) of a mini-base of heavy industries – iron and steel, fuel and power, machine tools, chemical fertilizers. In this way, peasant incomes will gradually be raised to urban levels, and peasant consciousness be modernized (1978(b):657).

Before this rural industrial policy could be put into practice it was necessary to develop local co-operatives and communes. Most of the re-organization took place very quickly – the co-operatives were created largely in 1955–56 and the communes in 1958. However, there had been earlier movements in this direction which predate the Communist Revolution, and Mao Tse-Tung had made several previous appeals to form co-operative organizations and mutual aid teams. In many cases there was a gradual development of collectivization. For example, at Hsin Fa it took six years to develop from labour-exchange and mutual aid teams to a co-operative organization, another four years to develop into a socialist co-operative and then two years to form a commune (Burchett and Alley, 1976).

The development of co-operatives and communes facilitated a wide range of labour mobilization for both agriculture and industry. There was a pyramidal organization from the team (200–800 people) to the brigade (2,000 to 5,000), which roughly corresponds to the former co-operative, to the commune itself (15,000 to 30,000) and then up through to the county, provincial, and state level. The team is run by the 'leading body', while the brigade and commune activities are administered by the 'revolutionary committees'.

Present-day economic activity is based upon collectivization that took place in the 1950s. The basic unit of co-operation is the production team, which undertakes fundamental and routine activities in agriculture and machine maintenance. It owns the land, animals, farm tools and small equipment such as irrigation pumps, 'walking tractors', small harvesting equipment, etc. It may also run some spare-time sidelines such as handicrafts.

The brigade co-ordinates the production plans of its constituent teams. It takes on tasks such as small irrigation, flood-control work, and minor overhaul of machinery, which are beyond the capacity of the individual teams. It owns some of the larger agricultural machinery such as tractors. It also runs full-time industries typically associated with agriculture such as food processing, production of simple tools like pressure sprays for insecticides, and machine maintenance stations. The brigade is responsible for primary schools and small health clinics.

The commune revolutionary committee takes on tasks that are beyond the capability of the brigade, such as major overhauls of machinery. It is also responsible for technologies and social services that are at a level intermediate between those of the brigade and the county. Typically these will include small fertilizer plants, hydro-electric plants, military affairs, secondary and technical schools, and larger health clinics capable of handling basic surgery.

These institutional developments enabled sufficient labour mobilization at the commune level to undertake large public works, and so off-season unemployment has been largely eliminated. It also facilitated a more effective delivery of social services to the rural areas. Communes' farm tools and equipment could be shared, as could certain consumer goods such as radios and washing machines, which helped to ensure better use of a limited technology.

So the development of the communes paved the way for the first phase of Maoist industrial policy between 1958 and 1969 called the Great Leap

Forward. This involved the strategy of 'walking on two legs' – the use of small-scale technology and modern large-scale technology. Heavy technologies were necessary for certain key products such as oil but small technologies were encouraged so as to develop the rural areas and make them self-sufficient. At the same time mass campaigns were encouraged and bureaucracy criticized.

The policy of walking on two legs led to the development of backyard blast furnaces. Other small-scale industries included plants for producing sulphuric acid, petroleum products, ball bearings, nails and so on. J. Sigurdson (1973) suggests that the rural small-scale industries were intended to serve four different objectives. Firstly, they were to supply the necessary agricultural inputs such as fertilizer and machinery. Secondly, they were to provide necessary consumer goods such as clothing. Thirdly, they were to support the larger industrial complexes through subcontracting. Fourthly, they were to provide some export products.

Development of intermediate technology was encouraged because it made better use of the growing rural population. It encouraged the development of self-reliant enterprises that could be run by the masses rather than by technocrats and bureaucrats. The masses could be encouraged to innovate and make modifications to existing primitive and indigenous technologies. Intermediate technologies could also be modified to meet the particular needs of the commune and the geographical characteristics of the area. Small-scale industries could make better use of resources such as iron ore which are widely dispersed geographically. In a country with a poor transportation infrastructure intermediate technologies and self-reliance made economic sense as well as saving scarce energy resources.

Finally, intermediate technologies became part of the Maoist policy of reducing the differences and inequalities between urban and rural areas. This difference and the other two great differences described by Mao Tse-Tung were further reduced by transferring 20 million people from the urban to the rural areas between 1959 and 1963. (A further 30 million were also transferred during the Cultural Revolution.)

By 1960 there were approximately 60,000 small industrial units run by the Hsien (county) and 200,000 units run by the rural communes as well as the numerous small workshops run by the brigades. But after the withdrawal of Russian aid which caused a major economic setback and a period of bad harvests there was a swing back towards more centralist planning and a resurgence of bureaucratization. This revisionist line of development became associated with Liu Shao-Chi. It was based upon the assumption that the class struggle had finished, and that economic growth had become a matter for the experts. The skills necessary to bring about faster growth ought, it was argued, to be encouraged by pay incentives. Planning ought also to be from the top downwards with commune activities under the strict control of the state. Many of the small-scale factories and workshops were shut down in 1961 and 1962, partly as a response to the political changes and the direction of Liu Shao-Chi, but partly also as a result of the economic crisis.

There was another upsurge of intermediate technology during the Cultural Revolution of 1966 which once more more brought the radicals back into power with a Mao-inspired attack on élitism. Further emphasis was placed upon rural areas, criticisms were made of Western science and technology, universities were closed and a reinterpretation of education and innovation by the masses was encouraged.

In recent years, small heavy industries such as nitrogen chemical fertilizers, cement, and pig-iron plants have been most outstanding. The plants involved serve the needs of a county or even smaller area. J. Sigurdson (1976) observes that the production of cement in small-scale plants has increased from 5 million tons in 1965 to 19 million tons in 1973. During this time the average size of the plants has decreased as they rapidly adopted a new vertical shaft kiln technology. The number of small plants, mostly in rural areas, has increased from about 200 in 1965 to 2,800 in 1973. Small plants employ roughly ten times as many people as large plants in order to produce the same quantity of cement. However, the economies of scale are more than offset by transport costs from large plants to consumers. Small plants can also use scrap material in their construction with little opportunity cost.

In comparison with cement plants, the size of fertilizer plants has increased considerably since 1965. The reason for the differences are, firstly, that there are more economies of scale with fertilizer plants. Secondly, it is easier to control the quality of cement in small plants. Thirdly, it is not so easy to use scrap metal for small fertilizer plants. Fourthly, there has been more state direction over the construction of fertilizer plants. S. Paine describes the progress of the chemical fertilizer industry:

Between 1964 and 1974, total chemical fertilizer output (of which that of nitrogenous fertilizers was about 60 per cent) rose more quickly (by a compound growth rate of 15.7 per cent p.a.) then in any other branch of industry except petroleum (at 22.3 per cent p.a.) and tractors (at 20 per cent p.a.). And in 1975 output was 2.5 times that of 1971. This was achieved partly by expanding the number and capacity of larger scale factories – indeed in 1973, China ordered 13 best practice urea-ammonia plants from abroad; primarily, however, it was done by establishing – at only a fraction of the fixed investment cost of large plants – small-scale fertilizer plants based on modern technology, either under collective ownership or under state ownership and county leadership (1976: 1,372).

By 1972 rural industries were producing about three-fifths of the national chemical fertilizer output, half the cement output, and the bulk of farm machinery and equipment (Riskin, 1978(a)). Although there has been a considerable emphasis on devolution of industrial development to the communes in the rural areas, and upon initiative from the bottom up rather than centralist planning, the state is still the major employer and producer of industrial products (see table 7.1).

Table 7.1   *Total industrial employment and production value (1973)*

	Employment		Production value	
	million	percentage	billion	percentage
State sector	32	63	315	86
Urban collective	6	12	30	8
Rural collective	12	24.2	20–25	6
Private	0.4	0.8	–	–
Total	50	100	365–370	100

(*Source:* Sigurdson, 1978:670)

In the early 1970s there was rather less political enthusiasm for small-scale rural technologies. C. Riskin suggests the following reasons:

First, the perceived threat of military attack from abroad receded, and with it the strategic reasons, for dispersed small industries. Secondly, China gained much greater access to the world market, and thus to the means of eliminating bottle-necks in the modern, urban-based sector. Thirdly, technological changes in famring, partly due to the output of the rural industries themselves, made possible the productive absorption of much greater quantities of labour in agriculture, leaving small surpluses available for non-farm employment (1978(b):97–98).

Since Mao's death, the priorities of agriculture, light industry and heavy industry have been maintained. By 1977 the earlier primitive production of simple agricultural tools such as sickles had been developed into a much more comprehensive industrial system. In Wusih County more than 90 per cent of the 4,355 tractors and 70,000 other farm machines were locally made. The county, communes and brigades produced their own steel, chemical fertilizer and cement plants while other small plants served agriculture or provided accessories for the big state plants (see table 7.2).

Table 7.2   *Industry in Wusih County (1976 figures)*

	Number of plants	Number of workers and staff
County-run plants	119	19,033
Commune-run plants	266	30,148
Brigade-run workshops	1,511	45,206

(*Source:* Chi-Chu, 1977:34)

Sigurdson (1978) has estimated that in the mid-1970s there were some 800,000 small enterprises in rural areas: 750,000 under the control of production brigades and 50,000 run by the communes. It seems likely that the productivity of the 'intermediate', small-scale and local technological projects is still relatively low. In a market economy few would be regarded as profitable. Yet as G. Dean points out, 'they use resources of equipment, labour and raw materials which would otherwise be discarded, under-utilized or neglected, to produce light consumer manufactures, agricultural equipment, and even components for the larger enterprises' (1972:372).

With the rise of Chairman Hua Kuo-Feng there have been certain political changes most notably a strengthening of the party's power and the banishment of potential opposition such as the Gang of Four – Chiang Ching (Mao's widow), Chang Chun-chiao, Wang Hung-wen, and Yuo Wen-yuan. J. Gray, (1978(b)) suggests that the intolerant attitude to-wards party criticism may evoke stronger centralist policies and inhibit autonomous local development, but as yet there are few signs of this happening. There is, moreover, great pressure to mechanize agricultural work, for despite population growth massive irrigation projects, fertilizer production and seed improvement developments have put a strain on the labour force. Small industries are playing an important part in this road to mechanization (Riskin, 1978(b)).

To sum up the Maoist industrial and rural policy in terms of environmental objectives, it has had the following advantages: firstly, the rational development of rural resources; secondly, the co-operative and communal sharing of productive agricultural equipment and consumer durables, and hence the rational use of scarce resources; thirdly, prevention of the massive urbanization and disruption that has occurred in most less developed countries. Large-scale industrial urban sprawl has been pre-vented. Today more than 80 per cent of China's population still lives in the countryside and the population in the cities has been decreasing in relative terms. Fourthly, massive concentration of pollution in one place has been avoided; fifthly, local technologies have been adapted to meet local agricultural requirements and environmental conditions; sixthly, there has been an avoidance of the massive energy-consuming transport systems which would have been necessary had there not been as great an emphasis upon local self-sufficiency.

Environmental policy as an integral feature of agricultural policy

One of the most important tasks the Chinese have encountered has been the problem of expanding agriculture to feed their enormous and expanding population. Before the 1949 revolution over 70 per cent of the farming land was controlled by the landlords and rich peasantry. The population, which was probably less than 300 million people, suffered from frequent famines and a high mortality rate. Agricultural experts often attributed the problems of poverty and starvation to over-population (see Mallory, 1926). However, land reform, land reclamation, irrigation, improvements in seeds and fertilization of the soil have transformed the quality of life for the rural population. In 1973, after the population had grown to about 800 million, there were no problems of recurrent famines or starvation despite the smallest cultivatable plots of land per person in the world (Power and Holenstein, 1976).

China hopes to reclaim 13 million hectares of wasteland in the period 1976–85, which is approximately two-thirds of the land reclaimed between 1949 and 1976. In 1970 alone, 2.26 million hectares of waste land were brought into cultivation. Most of the wasteland that is to be reclaimed is in the frontier regions, in the coastal or hilly areas, and on the shores of lakes (*Peking Review*, 30 June 1978). Reclamation has in some parts been helped by reafforestation to prevent desertification and to improve the climate. Between 1949 and 1960 an area twice the size of Britain was put under trees (Caldwell, 1977).

For the Chinese people, perhaps the most important model of waste reclamation has been the achievement of Tachai, a small production brigade of only 83 households and a population of about 450. They made a superhuman effort to build terraces and irrigation schemes in the poor and badly eroded mountainous slopes in the Shasi Province. They were successful despite major setbacks such as the catastrophic flood disasters in 1963 when 97 per cent of the houses and farm buildings were lost. The Tachai brigade refused to accept state aid at the time of the disaster.

In 1974 the grain production at Tachai was nearly ten times the highest pre-liberation level. The average *per capita* income distributed to brigade members had increased 2.7 times between 1955 and 1974. The proportion of public savings, for agricultural expansion, mechanization and welfare, was much greater than this (Chi-Chu, 1975). All in all the achievements of Tachai have been a model of self-reliance, and since 1964 Mao Tse-Tung's slogan of 'in agriculture learn from Tachai' has been adopted as a major rallying call to other agricultural workers. Typically Maoist quotations of this kind, military analogies, such as massing the people against the enemy so that they appear as paper tigers, and stories such as the 'foolish old man who moved a mountain' help to inspire mass campaigns and public works which require great labour over long periods of time.

The industrial equivalent of 'learn from Tachai', has been the Maoist line of 'self-reliance, hard work and learn from Taching'. Mao praised the development of the Taching oilfield during the Cultural Revolution as a supreme example of industry overcoming seemingly impossible obstacles by self-reliance and hard work. The first oil had been discovered in 1959 and China became self-sufficient in oil within four years. In the early days all the ditch digging for pipes was done by hand as there was no available mechanical equipment. Success through co-operative effort of workers, cadres and specialists was achieved despite the withdrawal of Soviet experts and the two-line struggle between Mao and Liu Shao-Chi. Taching was developed without the corruption and night-life entertainment that accompany oil development elsewhere in the world. While the old oil refinery was built with machinery from fourteen different countries (none of it was Chinese), the later Yumen refinery and petrochemical plants were made entirely by Chinese machinery – such was the emphasis upon self-reliance (Burchett and Alley, 1976).

Irrigation projects have played a crucial part in the development of agriculture. One of the more impressive projects has been the Red Flag Canal which was constructed in the mountainous Linhsien County in the Hanan Province. It was built in an area that regularly suffered from drought. Indeed the county was known as a place of 'four poors': poor mountains, poor water, poor fields and poor people. The canal project was begun in 1960 and completed nine years later in 1969. It made use of water from the Changho River which was damned north-west of Linhsien in Pingshun County in the neighbouring Shansi Province. The canal, 1,500 kilometres in length, transformed the country-side and was able to irrigate two-thirds of the arable land of Linhsien.

Huge irrigation and water control projects have also been developed to harness the Yangtse and Yellow Rivers. Central government undertakes the planning and organization of the large-scale projects, including reservoirs, dams and flood-diversion projects. The communes supervise and construct the numerous small wells and irrigation canals. Hydro-electric projects have been rapidly developed to utilize the available water power. Hydro-electricity increased threefold between 1950/51 and 1970/71. By the late 1970s China had 100 big and medium sized stations and, in addition, over 60,000 small hydro-electric power stations. The smaller plants are justified on the grounds that they may be built quickly and yield much greater returns. Usually the materials for building them can be found locally, and any prefecture, county, commune or production brigade can carry out the construction (Cheng-ying, 1978).

Agricultural development was closely integrated with health policy. Mass campaigns to conserve water, clean up pollution, and kill pests were aimed at improving the health and hence productivity of the workforce and at the same time providing valuable resources for agriculture. One of the early campaigns that received much attention was that aimed at the four pests: flies, mosquitoes, rats and sparrows. Later, sparrows were replaced by bed-bugs and other vermin, depending upon local considerations. Apparently sparrows were taken off the list because they were found to perform the useful job of eating injurious insects which threatened the grain harvests.

Careful control of household sewage in rural areas was encouraged to prevent the spread of parasitic diseases, and to provide a much needed fertilizer (see Sandbach, 1977(b)). The first attempt to irrigate extensively with urban sewage was made in 1956 around Chuchow in Hunan Province. During the Great Leap Forward period such projects were encouraged under the slogan of turning something harmful into something useful. To begin with there were problems of flies and pollution of wells, but by 1966 forty-three cities were satisfactorily employing sewage irrigation and were claiming substantial improvements in farm yields (Orleans, 1975/76). Mass campaigns were often directed to cleaning up rivers and irrigation channels, partly for health reasons and partly to supply fertilizer. The New China News Agency made this not atypical report of one such operation:

90,000 persons were mobilized on the industrial and agricultural fronts in Shanghai to form muck-dredging and muck-transporting teams, waging a vehement people's war to dredge muck from the Suchow River. After 100 days of turbulent fighting, more than 403,600 tons of malodorous organic mire had been dug out (Orleans and Sultmeier, 1970:1,176).

Environmental policy as an integral feature of industrial policy

While the main health problems in rural and urban areas have been a consequence of organic rather than inorganic pollution, industrial pollution has given rise to health problems in some of the major cities. Control of industrial pollution became part of health policy in the first Five Year

Plan. Those responsible for the location of new industries were encouraged to consider various environmental factors such as the direction of the prevailing wind. It was not until the mid-1960s that pollution control became an integral part of production policy. Utilization of resources that were previously being wasted became justified on economic grounds as well as on grounds of health.

Scarcity of resources for industry and agriculture encouraged recycling, or multi-purpose use as the Chinese preferred to call it (see Schnell, 1973; Sigurdson, 1972; Kapp, 1974(a) and (b); *China Reconstructs*, 21 June 1972). The most important principle governing the policy of multi-purpose use, as in other areas of health and environmental policy, is to 'put prevention first'. Prevention provides better protection to the environment and health, and can also lead to greater economic advantages: harmful waste products are turned into useful resources. For example, cinder and slag from iron and steel works are used in cement, brick and phosphate fertilizer manufacturing, while yarn has been made from the pulp of sugar-cane waste. In schools children are taught that waste has a use and that it should be turned into treasure. Industrial workers are encouraged to suggest measures for dealing with wastes. Through multi-purpose use economic development was considered to be compatible with environmental protection as explained in an article in the *People's Daily* on 16 June 1973 (which marked the first anniversary of the UN Conference on the Human Environment in Stockholm):

What is 'waste' in one situation, under other conditions can become something useful: that which is 'harmful' under certain conditions can be changed to something 'beneficial' in other circumstances. The extensive experience of industrial development in our country proves that, through multi-purpose use, waste can be turned into value and harm into benefit, the environment can be protected and wealth created (Hsin, 1973).

Recycling became part of a mass campaign in 1970 when people were urged to make the maximum use of the 'three wastes' – waste materials, waste water and waste gas (waste heat was sometimes added to the list as the fourth waste). The Chinese state that as a result of this policy pollution is reduced and valuable resources reclaimed. For example, it is claimed that over a hundred chemical materials can be recovered from coke oven gas (Orleans, 1976). Between 1971 and 1973 the North-East General Pharmaceutical Factory found more than three hundred kinds of usable materials that could be recovered from its waste materials, and that from a hundred of these 4,000 tons of chemical raw materials were recovered (*China Reconstructs*, 22 February 1973).

In Peking 60 per cent of raw material needs for paper-making is met by using recovered waste paper, hemp, cotton and rags (*Peking Review*, 14 July 1978). In the rural areas there are thousands of small plants that make use of local wastes. Alcohol, glucose, antibiotics, and other products are manufactured from organic wastes such as cotton-seed hulls and sugar-cane residue (Caldwell, 1977).

It is worth stressing that many such cases of resource recovery and environmental improvement would not appear economic if the systems of accounting within market economies were applied. However, campaigns are conducted during slack periods of the agricultural season, and the Chinese emphasis is upon the use of resources rather than profit or technical production for its own sake. Resource recovery can also improve environional health and working conditions. Resource recovery at the Shenyang chemical plant in north-east China has meant that gas-masks are now no longer necessary in the production of trichlorobenzene, and black smoke no longer pours out of the chimneys (Cheng-Ko, 1977). Mass campaigns to utilize waste also serve an important political function in that they emphasize what can be achieved through co-operative action. Examples of success stories abound. One such case is recounted by L. A. Orleans:

One success story that received considerable publicity in China is the Nun-Chiang, a river in Heilungkiang on which Tsitsihar – an industrial city with more than a million inhabitants – is situated. With the construction of numerous industries in the city, some 250,000 tons of water [industrial waste water] were being dumped daily into the once clean river, killing off most of the fish and reducing the catch in 1969 to about one-fifth of what it had been in 1960. After identifying the problem and discussing possible solutions with the masses, a program was approved requiring individual enterprises to recover the harmful substances in their industry's waste water, to make comprehensive use of these substances and then to divert waste water to a reservoir for eventual use in irrigating fields. Between June and November 1970, more than 5,000 workers, peasants, Liberation Army soldiers, Red Guards and city inhabitants took part daily in the projects. It was a big undertaking and apparently produced big results. Among the materials recovered from the waste water were cadmium, oils, acids, alkali, paper pulp, and silver; the oxygen content of the water was raised and fish returned to the Nun-Chiang; and fields irrigated by waste water produced greater yields than ever before. Since Tsitsihar is the only large city along the banks of the Nun-Chiang, the fairy-tale success story described above is very believable (1976:30).

Waste organic materials have been widely used in the production of bio-gas (methane), especially in those areas that are not readily serviced by the abundant resources of oil and coal. The first attempt to popularize bio-gas production occurred during the Great Leap Forward, but this was largely unsuccessful. The first main production of bio-gas occurred between 1970 and 1972 in the north-east regions of China, which lacked sufficient wood for fuel or alternative sources of energy. In Spring 1974 there were 30,000 bio-gas digesters in the Szechwan Basin Province, but by the end of the year there were 209,000 digesters, of which 169,000 were used to produce gas and the remainder to produce manure alone. In India, by comparison, there were only 8,500 bio-gas digesters built for the whole period from 1962 to 1973. In May 1977 there were an estimated 4.3 million bio-gas digesters operating in China.

The capacity of bio-gas digesters ranged from a few cubic meters to communal tanks of around 100 cubic meters. They reputedly produce a superior organic manure with increased concentration of ammonia and quick acting phosphate. Use of bio-gas saves labour in supplying coal and firewood, it saves fuel supplies, it eliminates many insect pests and vectors of disease, it helps conserve forestry, and it helps to narrow the standard of living gap between town and country (Smil, 1977).

Chinese environmental policy can best be summarized by reference to the first six of the ten principles which Chinese delegates advocated for international approval at the United Nations Conference on the Human Environment at Stockholm in 1972 (Peking Review, 23 June 1972). The first principle was that economic development and social progress can and ought to be made compatible with environmental conservation. The second principle claimed that population growth was not a major cause of resource depletion and pollution. People, after all, were the creators of social wealth and could transform the environment for good or ill. The third and fourth principles outlined the causes of environmental abuse. These causes were first the wanton destruction by imperialist countries through the use of bio-chemical weapons. Further destruction was threatened by the nuclear arms race. Secondly, profits from monopoly capitalism encouraged anarchy of production and pollution with scant regard for the people affected. The fifth and sixth principles dealt with the struggle necessary to protect natural resources and to fight against pollution. The final four principles dealt with matters of international relations.

The Chinese road to socialism, then, has rested upon an economic strategy aimed at improving the quality of life rather than being governed by the market and the requirements of maximizing profits. The planned economy, at local and state levels, has reacted against the contradictions of production and consumption, and of urban and rural development which had come about in feudal and capitalist China. The Chinese 'model' of development has consequently been very different from that in many of the less developed countries and indeed the advanced countries during their path to industrialization.

No doubt many lessons may be learnt from the Chinese case study, not least how technological choice and environmental problems are related to the economic and social order. Technology policy in China has been one of fluctuating development. Shifts in emphasis between large-scale and small-scale technology were in part a consequence of political struggles between the two lines of Mao Tse-Tung and Liu Shao-Chu. They were also a product of economic circumstances, defence strategies and a reaction to the consequences of technological change itself.

8 Environmental Futures

The question of whether or not there will be substantial physical and social limits to economic growth cannot be answered with any degree of certainty. While one can be certain that spring will follow winter, and autumn will follow summer, the same kind of certainty does not exist when forecasting the state of the environment in the future. The type of demands upon the environment will depend as today upon the form and extent of social activity. It is necessary to state the obvious, namely that different societies both today and in the past have made different demands and impacts upon the environment. If, for example, present-day energy consumption in different countries is compared, one tends to find that high levels of consumption occur in countries with high levels of economic activity. Nonetheless, there is a good deal of variation between countries with similar levels of economic activity. G. Foley comments:

Although Swedes and Canadians have roughly the same *per capita* GDP, Canadians consume on average twice as much energy. West Germany and the UK, on the other hand, have almost identical average energy consumption but the *per capita* GDP in West Germany is over 70 per cent higher than in the UK (1976:89).

Energy demands in the future will depend to a considerable extent upon the form of economic development. Using energy-accounting techniques, P. Chapman, G. Leach and others have demonstrated vast differences in energy consumption for different ways of producing similar objectives in transport, agriculture, heating houses, packaging of goods, etc. (see Chapman, 1975; Leach, 1976). For example, changes in transport policy could have significant effects on energy demand. This may be illustrated by the different energy consumption of various systems of freight transport. Estimates by the OECD in 1974 indicate energy consumption of 0.11–0.12 kWh per tonne-km for rail (depending upon the weight of load), 0.18–0.30 kWh per tonne-km for a 20-tonne lorry (depending upon the type of road – urban or motorway), 3.73 kWh per tonne-km for air freight, and 0.16 kWh per tonne-km for waterway transport (Foley, 1976). In Chapters 5–7, it was noted that environmental effects depend not only upon the choice of technology, but upon how it is organized. Hence, the policy of decentralization and local self-sufficiency in China has reduced the need for freight transport in general.

Changes in technology policy and forms of social organization could have marked influences on future demands upon the environment without necessarily affecting the level of economic activity, as conventionally measured in terms of GDP or GNP. Although it is stating the obvious to say that the future predicament of man is dependent upon the type of economic activity and planning that arises, it is nonetheless important to do so. There has been a stubborn belief that the future can be predicted by projecting, with little modification, trends from the past. Commercial interests no doubt have something to gain from intervention by a government committed to the view that the rate of growth in energy demand or automobiles will continue as fast in the coming decades as it did in the 1960s and 1970s. Building more power stations and better roads creates a greater commitment to centralized electricity production and private transport. The question of whether such projections along the same path are desirable is seldom asked.

Those concerned with promoting alternative technology have, with some success, despite the limitations of political strategy, emphasized the possibility of alternative futures. There need not, for example, be an energy gap between demand for and supply of energy in the year 2000 if no nuclear power development takes place. Development of alternative technologies and conservation of energy could enable a better future to exist. It makes sense to consider various possible courses of action. These courses of action must, however, be grounded in political reality rather than Utopian blueprints. Alternative policies cannot be divorced from the social commitment necessary for their fruition. In the second part of this chapter, various policies will be considered in terms of their plausibility.

An assessment of future possibilities clearly depends upon an understanding of the real and imagined physical and social constraints upon economic development. So before discussing the merits of different policies, it is necessary to establish the scientific and ideological aspects of the varying opinions on the physical and social limits to growth. The 'limits to growth' debate is not of recent origin; many of its intellectual roots can be traced back to some of the principal economists and writers of the eighteenth and nineteenth centuries. The views of Thomas Malthus, David Ricardo, John Stuart Mill, W. Stanley Jevons, Karl Marx and Friedrich Engels were all concerned at one time or another with essentially the same issues. The ideas are not new, nor indeed are many of their shortcomings.

The limits to growth debate

Scientific and ideological views on the limits to growth debate can be broadly divided into three categories. In political terms they correspond to conservative, liberal and radical views, but they are couched in theoretical language. The first standpoint holds that there are physical and social limits of immediate concern. Physical limits are supported by the neo-Malthusian argument about exponential growth in a finite world, and the 'diminishing returns' hypothesis of Ricardo and Jevons. Social limits are supported by arguments concerning the social strain caused by growth and the depletion of positional goods, a view which can also be traced back to the writings of Ricardo, but which have been popularized recently in the work of F. Hirsch.

The second and more optimistic outlook is the economic/technological fix position of liberal economists. This stresses the mechanistic and economic responses to resource scarcity and pollution in a market economy. The third and more neutral view is the Marxist political economy position. This stresses the inter-dependence of, on the one hand, the social organization of production and consumption and, on the other, the institutional superstructure that develops to control resource flow through the economy and to bring instruments of pollution control into action. According to this view, resource scarcity and pollution depend upon underlying principles of economic and social organization.

THE NEO-MALTHUSIAN POSITION

In *An Essay on the Principle of Population*, Malthus argued for the existence of a universal law governing the relations between population and resource scarcity. Given that food is necessary to the existence of man, as also is passion between the sexes, then Malthus argued that unless there are checks on population growth, the problems of subsistence itself will constrain population – the reason being that 'population, when unchecked, increases in a geometrical ratio. Subsistence increases only in an arithmetical ratio' (1970:71).

Malthus used historical data of population growth in the United States and Europe to give empirical justification to the geometrical increase in population. Without checks from lack of food or 'peculiar causes of premature mortality', Malthus argues that the natural rate of population increases involved a doubling of the population every twenty-five years. Malthus might possibly be excused for assuming a cast-iron law of exponential growth, as demographic sources of data have been notoriously weak until much more recent times. Today, of course, it is known that improved standards of living and health, resulting in the main from economic growth, have been responsible for a decline in population growth rates in the world's developed nations. However, Malthus gave much less satisfactory evidence for the mere arithmetic growth in subsistence. It was this part of his theory that was attacked most strongly by nineteenth-century critics. Owenites refuted the assumption on the basis that if the soil was properly managed, vast populations could be supported. For example, H. McCormac (1830), a Belfast Owenite, argued:

To be sure in the year eighteen thousand and thirty, when the earth is crammed with human beings, the ocean with junks, and men grope in diving-bells over the beds of the sea for submarine food, or chase the birds in their native elements, some new Malthus of the then Church of England, may usefully employ his time and talents in devising means to check the prolific tendency of mankind, but not till then (quoted from Kingston, 1976:245).

Engels (1844) also took issue with Malthus, claiming that he had offered no proof that the productivity of the land could only increase arithmetically. Engels argued that, on the contrary, if population grew exponentially so too would the labour power employed to produce food. Furthermore, he went on:

If we assume that the increase of output associated with this increase of labour is not always proportionate to the latter, there still remains a third element – which the economists, however, never consider as important – namely science, the progress of which is just as limitless and at least as rapid as that of population (quoted from Meek, 1971:63).

In successive editions of his *Essay*, Malthus came to rely increasingly upon the law of diminishing returns more usually associated with Ricardo. Ricardo's argument with respect to agriculture was that, as population grew, inferior land would have to be used and hence a lowering of productivity would follow. Then 'the exchangeable value of raw produce will rise, because more labour is required to produce it' (Ricardo, 1962:37). Jevons, in *The Coal Question* (first published 1865), extended the argument to the debate on coal resources. His Malthusian contemporaries argued that with the rate of coal consumption doubling every twenty years, coal reserves of an estimated 83,000 million tons would be depleted by the year 2034. Jevons, following the diminishing returns argument, claimed that long before this the cost of fuel would rise as it became harder to mine and as demand outstripped supply. As Jevons thought that replacement by wind, geothermal or oil power was totally improbable, it was clear to him that progress was unlikely to be sustained.

This refined pessimistic view deserves close attention, especially with respect to physical resources, for many experts now appear to agree that there are not likely to be any constraints of an absolute type for many years to come. The amount of most resources in the first mile of the earth's crust probably exceeds presently known reserves by multiples ranging from thousands to millions (see Connelly and Perlman, 1975). And, contrary to the view that resources would become harder to extract, there is every indication that the opposite has occurred. Systematic studies by H. J. Barnett and C. Morse (1965) of the trends of extraction costs over the period 1870–1957 indicated, almost without exception (apart from forestry and possibly copper), that the costs of exploitation had fallen significantly.

Engels had been correct to assume the importance of science, for these changes in exploitation costs can be accounted for by technical change and substitution. To give some specific examples: in the United States, the amount of energy needed to generate a kilowatt hour of electricity fell by just over 35 per cent between 1948 and 1968; and in Great Britain, the energy demand to produce a ton of steel decreased by 74 per cent between 1962 and 1972, chiefly as a consequence of the introduction of the basic oxygen process. For particular plants, the changes are even more impressive. At the Luckawanna plant of the Bethlehem Steel Corporation in the US, energy needed for steel production was reduced from 22 gallons (US) of oil to 6.4 gallons of oil per ton (Maddox, 1975). Or take the example of the pint milk bottle. In the 1950s, a pint milk bottle weighed eighteen ounces (510 g); today bottles of eight ounces (227 g) are on trial. In twenty years, the energy required to melt the glass for a milk bottle has more than halved, and the furnace efficiency has been improving at a rate of 3.5 to 4.0 per cent per annum (Glass Manufacturers Federation, 1975). Some mineral resources that were in the past unprofitable to mine have, as a result of new techniques, become reclassified as valuable raw materials. For example, copper ores containing as little as 0.4 per cent copper ore are worked today whereas ores containing less than 4 per cent would have been considered useless in the nineteenth century. The mineral nemeline (about 20 per cent aluminium) was until recently considered to be of little value, but is now considered to be of great value (Kahn *et al.*, 1977).

In the 1960s, the Malthusian view of population pressure on limited resources regained its popularity. According to P. R. and A. H. Ehrlich (1970), if the population were to remain at 3.3 billion, then at current levels of demand lead would run out in 1983, platinum in 1984, uranium in 1990, oil in 2000, iron in 2375, coal in 2800, and so on. In *The Limits to Growth* study by D. H. Meadows *et al.* (1972), Malthusian assumptions lie behind the results of computer predictions. Data from 1900 to 1950 on the exponential growth of materials use, population, pollution, and the like are projected into a future which can only provide at best arithmetical growth in solving the problems of physical constraints. It needed no computer to follow the implications of the assumptions. As with earlier Malthusian predictions, the argument breaks down on empirical grounds because of the failure to allow for the expansion of resources to meet demand. The postulate concerning the fixity of exploitable resources has been proved wrong by scientific and technological developments as well as by increased exploration of surface minerals using currently known techniques. Moreover, as H. Kahn, W. Brown and L. Martel (1976) argue, there is little incentive to search for more reserves than would meet a few decades of demand. There would be little return on such investment and it might even be counter-productive as more known reserves could put pressure on current prices.

A few examples will help to illustrate how known exploitable reserves have increased in pace with industrial demand. For instance, in 1944 the United States prepared a study of its own known reserves of forty-one commodities. Had the predicted reserves remained static, then twenty-one of these commodities would now be exhausted (see Pehrson, 1945; and Page, 1973). Or take the example of aluminium: between 1941 and 1953 the known world bauxite reserves increased by an average of 50 million tons a year, and between 1950 and 1958 the average annual increase was about 250 million tons (Page, 1973). Or if one were to take the current concern for oil reserves: in 1938 the known reserves were sufficient for fifteen years' use at contemporary rates of consumption; in the early 1950s, after a doubling of consumption rates, the known reserves were sufficient for twenty-five years; in 1972, after a further trebling of consumption, the known reserves were sufficient for thirty-five years. Tables 8.1 and 8.2 indicate how between 1950 and 1970 most known reserves increased, and how between 1900 and 1970 the price of minerals relative to the average cost of labour decreased.

A useful distinction may be made between absolute resources in the earth's crust, exploitable resources, and currently known commercial reserves. Various estimates for eleven resources are given in Table 8.3. According to this distinction, Zambia is rich in copper ores, but these are uneconomical to work under present conditions. Hence, Zambia has no copper reserves but plenty of copper resources (see Roberts, 1978). The weakness of neo-Malthusian arguments, as in *The Limits to Growth*, is that they often talk about reserves as if they were total resources.

A. Shenfield, former economic director of the Confederation of British Industry, dismisses the energy doom-mongers on three grounds. First, resources are assumed to be fixed; secondly, technological innovation is disregarded; and finally, predictions of doom in this field have so far proved to be false:

Table 8.1   *How 'known reserves' alter world reserves*

Ore	Known reserves in 1950 000 tonnes	Cumulative production 1950–70 000 tonnes	Known reserves in 1970 000 tonnes	Percentage increase in known reserves 1950–70
Iron	19,000,000	9,355,000	251,000,000	1,221
Manganese	500,000	194,000	635,000	27
Chromite	100,000	82,000	755,000	675
Tungsten	1,903	630	1,328	−30
Copper	100,000	80,000	279,000	179
Lead	40,000	48,000	86,000	115
Zinc	70,000	70,000	113,000	61
Tin	6,000	3,800	6,600	10
Bauxite	1,400,000	505,000	5,300,000	279
Potash	5,000,000	216,000	118,000,000	2,360
Phosphates	26,000,000	1,011,000	1,178,000,000	4,430
Oil[a]	75,000,000	180,727,000	455,000,000	507

[a] = thousand barrels
(Data from National Commission on Supplies and Shortages, 1978:16)
(*Source:* Williams, 1978:166)

Table 8.2   *Relative price of important minerals to labour*
1970 = 100

	1900	1920	1940	1950	1960	1970
Coal	459	451	189	208	111	100
Copper	785	226	121	99	82	100
Iron	620	287	144	112	120	100
Phosphorus	–	–	–	130	120	100
Molybdenum	–	–	–	142	108	100
Lead	788	388	204	228	114	100
Zinc	794	400	272	256	126	100
Sulphur	–	–	–	215	145	100
Aluminium	3,150	859	287	166	134	100
Gold	–	–	595	258	143	100
Crude petroleum	1,034	726	198	213	135	100

Values are the price per ton of the mineral divided by the hourly wage rate in manufacturing. Data are from *Historical Statistics, Long-Term Economic Growth, Statistical Abstract*.
(*Source:* Nordhaus, 1974:24)

Table 8.3   *Resource availability of important minerals assessed in three ways*

	Known reserves annual consumption (R/C)	Ultimate recoverable resource annual consumption (URR/C)	Crustal abundance annual consumption (CA/C)
Coal	2,736	5,119	na
Copper	45	340	242,000,000
Iron	117	2,657	1,815,000,000
Phosphorus	481	1,601	870,000,000
Molybdenum	65	630	422,000,000
Lead	10	162	85,000,000
Zinc	21	618	409,000,000
Sulphur	30	6,897	na
Uranium	50	8,455	1,855,000,000
Aluminium	23	68,066	38,500,000,000
Gold	9	102	57,000,000

Data from *Geological Survey*, pp. 22–23, 613–14,140. *Statistical Abstract*, p. 651.
(*Source:* Nordhaus, 1974:23)

Thus in 1866 the United States Revenue Commission urged the development of synthetic fuels against the day in the 1890s when petroleum would be played out. In 1891 the United States Geological Survey declared that there was little or no oil in Texas. In 1914 the United States Bureau of Mines estimated that output would be six billion barrels in the whole remaining history of the country. This is now produced about every eighteen months (1977:16).

Neo-Malthusian arguments also pervaded the debate over pollution control. P. R. and A. H. Ehrlichs' (1970) equation $I = PF$ (where I = total impact, P = population size, F = the impact *per capita*) was a manifestation of this. According to this formula, 80 million users of disposable plastic bottles would create much worse problems than 60 million users. *The Limits to Growth* claimed that 'virtually every pollutant that has been measured as a function of time appears to be increasing exponentially' (Meadows *et al.*, 1972:135). However, the dangers of projecting present growth rates exponentially into the future are well known. For example, it has been suggested that projection of the trends of the 1880s might have shown cities of the 1970s buried under horse manure (Du Boff, 1974).

In *The Limits to Growth*, empirical justification for exponential growth in pollution is suggested from studies indicating rising levels of carbon dioxide, waste heat generation in the Los Angeles basin, nuclear wastes, oxygen content of the Baltic Sea, lead in the Greenland ice cap, and so on. The evidence is, however, selectively chosen and covers only those areas of pollution where little attention has been paid to control programmes. A different picture is painted if one turns to those successful areas of legislation involving often only small amounts of public expenditure. There have, for example, been several areas of noticeable improvements in the oil-refining and the pulp, paper and chlorine industries: progress in the oil-refining industry has involved significant reductions in overall discharge of effluents per unit of output, in many cases to about one per cent of earlier levels; while in the case of pulp and paper mills in Sweden, output increased by 70 per cent in the ten years up to 1973 and yet, in the total discharge, Biochemical Oxygen Demand (BOD) was reduced by 65 per cent (see Beckerman, 1974). Legislation, such as the Clean Air Act 1956 in Britain, has helped to effect pollution control. Despite a ten per cent increase in population and a seventeen per cent increase in energy consumption in the fifteen years following the Clean Air Act, there has been a steady reduction in smoke and sulphur dioxide emissions into the air over Britian. In many large towns this has provided the added bonus of increased winter sunshine. In Central London there has been a 50 per cent improvement in mean sunshine hours per day, the differential between previously less polluted areas such as Kew having narrowed considerably (Royal Commission on Environmental Pollution, 1971).

There have been, of course, more recent problems arising from pesticides, lead smelters, mercury poisoning and nuclear wastes. However, successful pollution control in the past makes it plausible that such problems are just as amenable to control as were the older forms of abuse. It might be argued that if chemical pesticides do become a real threat to economic growth through the pollution they cause, then alternative biological pest control (or even changes in the use of agricultural land) could offer substitute means of pest control without the same costs. Even without such dramatic changes, W. Beckerman (1974) claims that satisfactory pollution control programmes are well within the grasp of advanced industrial economies.

Simplistic Malthusian arguments have been countered in the main by historical reference to technological improvements and substitution. However, faith in technology as a saviour may well be unwise, for past experience (or at least this kind of interpretation of the past) is not necessarily a good guide to the future. The fact that the efficiency for generating electricity in the UK was about eight per cent in 1900 and is twenty-five per cent today is no guarantee of ever-increasing efficiency: indeed, the best possible practical efficiency is predicted to be around forty per cent. Furthermore, improvements in mining efficiency cannot be guaranteed to offset decreasing average grades of ores. For example, copper ores contained about 2.5 per cent copper at the turn of the century, whereas today the average grade is about one per cent in South America and as little as 0.6 per cent in the United States. Increasing efficiency of extraction processes, which offset the decline in ore grades in the first half of the twentieth century, cannot be expected to improve indefinitely, and there is evidence that the fuel used per unit of output has started to rise steeply (see Chapman, 1975). The UK Atomic Energy Authority's case for the large scale use of nuclear fast reactors also rests in part upon the view that:

Because of limits inherent in the technologies concerned, there is now only modest scope for continuing further improvements in the efficiency of energy conversion which, from the turn of the century to the beginning of the Second World War, permitted economic growth with little growth in energy consumption (Gosling and Montefiore, 1977:32–33).

Energy analysis of food production demonstrates even more dramatically diminishing returns from energy inputs. The example of maize (the most important grain crop grown in the United States, and ranking third in world production of food crops) illustrates the point: despite an increase in maize yields on United States farms from 34 bushels per acre in 1945 to 81 bushels per acre in 1970, the mean energy inputs increased from 0.9 million kcal to 2.9 million kcal. The total maize yield can be translated into energy equivalents so that in 1945 the maize yield was equivalent to 3.4 million kcal, and in 1970 to 8.2 million kcal. Hence, the yield in maize calories decreased from 3.7 kcal per fuel kilocalorie input in 1945 to a yield of about 2.8 kcal in 1970 (Pimentel *et al.*, 1973). Another way of viewing the implications of 'industrial' agriculture is that if all countries used as much energy to feed themselves as is currently practised in the UK, they would use forty per cent of present total world energy consumption (see Leach, 1976), an unlikely possibility and a warning against any complacency. Yet this is the sort of implication that must be dealt with by the market economists and technological optimists.

The Malthusian argument has greatest relevance in relation to those resources that have least potential for expansion, especially those resources that can be loosely defined as providing rural amenity. There has, for example, been a huge loss of wetlands in America. According to W. A. Rosenbaum (1973) there are now only 70 million acres of wetland in the United States, compared with 127 million acres which were once available. The loss of rural land in England and Wales to urban development will, according to estimates by R. H. Best (1976), have increased threefold from 1900 to the year 2000. At approximately one per cent growth in urban land per decade, some 14 per cent of the total agricultural land will have been lost by the end of the century. Furthermore, conflicts in the UK National Parks over mineral extractions, water resources development, and the impact of an increasing number of holiday-makers, all illustrate the problems of maintaining amenity for an increased population with higher living standards. In this respect, the arguments for a stationary state put forward by John Stuart Mill make greater sense than many more recent arguments. He argued that the loss of diversity in nature and of wilderness resulting from the need to produce more and more food was undesirable. He concluded:

If the earth must lose that great portion of its pleasantness which it owes to things that the unlimited increase of wealth and population would extirpate from it, for the mere purpose of enabling it to support a larger, but not a better or happier population, I sincerely hope, for the sake of posterity, that they will be content to be stationary, long before necessity compels them to it (1965:756).

A somewhat similar but less acceptable argument has recently been raised, with a good deal of favourable response, by F. Hirsch in *Social Limits to Growth* (1977). Hirsch makes a distinction between material goods such as food, which can be enjoyed irrespective of what other people are eating, and 'positional goods'. Positional goods can be enjoyed most if other people do not have access to them. The beautiful view from the front window is only enjoyed so long as there are not other houses in front enjoying the same view. The peaceful drive in the country only remains peaceful so long as there are not too many others searching for a peaceful drive. Now, according to Hirsch, social limits to growth exist because with increased growth competition moves increasingly from the material sector to the positional sector. As a consequence, the number of positional goods is fast decreasing in quantity and value.

The positional economy of 'what the few have today the many want tomorrow', according to Hirsch, is rapidly reaching its limits. This is an élitist view, because it is couched in terms of the interests of a minority. Nevertheless, it could, if it were true, explain why élite groups are less than willing to allow redistribution of wealth for it would imply that it is harder and more expensive for the élite to purchase the few remaining positional goods.

The similarity with the Malthusian position is not hard to see. It is advanced in such a way as to support policies that might maintain positional goods for the élite. It is also profoundly ideological in the sense of being an ascientific delusion. Like Malthus, little or no allowance is made for the creation of new 'positional' goods. The example of a peaceful ride in the motorcar is itself only possible given the invention of the car. New inventions are forever creating new positional goods whether they be motorboats, yachts, aeroplanes, hang-gliders, or whatever the latest plaything for the rich and leisured classes may be. Moreover, the potential for producing better ways of enjoying amenities for the great majority of people would not seem to be constrained by shortages of space or resources. There would be many ways of enriching the quality of life, access to privacy and sociability if greater effort were allowed to be put in this direction.

Other social limits to growth have also been put forward, such as the trend towards greater crime, violence, and blackmail, the greater danger of epidemics due to increased travel opportunities, the dangers of internecine warfare, the psychological remoteness of industrial society, the institutional chaos and complexity of wealth creating activity involving multinationals, multiple unions, finance houses and government (see Edison Electric Institute, 1976; Robertson, 1977/78). These problems and potential concerns are real enough, they certainly appear to be symptoms of a disease, but is the problem really related to economic growth itself or advanced capitalism and the monopoly power of big business? Surely none of these problems above need be a consequence of higher standards of living. Indeed there seems to be little hard empirical evidence that would support such an argument.

THE ECONOMIC TECHNOLOGICAL FIX POSITION

The argument from this position is essentially that the scarcity of resources is governed by market price factories which influence the search for new resources, substitution, recycling and conservation measures. For instance, Beckerman argues that 'the market mechanism has hitherto usually ensured that, sooner or later, either increasing demand for materials has always been matched by increasing supplies, or some other adjustment mechanism has operated' (1974:34–35).

As already noted, optimists such as Kahn point out that known reserves are more a reflection of mining companies' search policies than of total resources. North Sea oil is another case in point. Simulation studies at the Economic Geography Institute of Rotterdam in 1974 (Odell and Rosing, 1974), based in part upon previous appreciation of oil reserves over a period of time, predicted that total oil reserves in the North Sea would exceed currently declared known reserves by between four and seven times, and would be up to three times larger than BP's estimates of total reserves. What these estimates depend upon, however, is a favourable economic climate in which price guarantees assure profitable production. During a twelve-month period in 1975–76, the known North Sea oil reserves in the British sector increased from 1,000 million tonnes to 1,350 million tonnes. There were twenty-four oil discoveries, nearly as many as in the previous five years; but towards the end of this period the rate of discoveries was falling off, due to cost inflation and strained finance (*Guardian*, 30 April 1976). Production costs, oil prices, finance and available technology are therefore of crucial importance in assessing known and estimated reserves.

One of the weaknesses of the market mechanism is the long lead times necessary to develop resources to meet fluctuations in demand. In unplanned economies, these fluctuations lead to dramatic changes in price which cause havoc to Keynesian attempts to control growth, unemployment and inflation. With further growth, such fluctuations could increase in intensity. It is interesting to note that shortly after the horror resulting from the escalation of oil prices (beginning in 1973), both the United States and the British governments were anxious to maintain stable price levels to avoid inflation and to ensure that development of alternative energy sources would remain profitable.

The energy economist, M. Posner (1974), has argued that North Sea oil, as well as deep-mined coal or oil shales, may be only marginally profitable if the price of oil falls to $5 per barrel at 1974 prices. The crucial question in this context that economists have to face is principally political: namely, what will happen to the OPEC cartel if oil consumption decreases as a result of a fall in demand, conservation, and development of alternative supplies? Moreover, while the availability of both oil and other resources bears some relation to demand, the actual market price of natural resources appears to have little to do with their physical scarcity, but much to do with monopoly positions.

The liberal economic view, as S. R. Eyre (1978) points out, plays down the importance of resource availability as a factor in the potential wealth and growth of a nation. With the growth of nationalism and separatism which has been taking place since the early twentieth century, there is every indication that resource endowment will be more likely to play a crucial part in the wealth of nations. Eyre attributes the neglect of resource endowment by economists to Adam Smith's pervasive notion that the wealth of a nation is principally dependent upon the efficient use of labour.

Unfortunately, the distribution of resources in general is very uneven. Non-ferrous minerals important for industry tend to be concentrated in Southern Africa, South-East Asia and China, the USSR and the western part of the Americas (Roberts, 1978). For example, in the case of phosphorus some 80 per cent of the world's output is used in the manufacture of fertilizers and there is no obvious possibility of substitution. Moreover, 75 per cent of the production of phosphate rock is confined to three countries – the United States, the Soviet Union and Morocco. Given the large domestic consumption in the two super-powers, Morocco, with 34 per cent of the world trade, has much influence over supply (and ultimately over the price) of phosphate rock (*The Times*, 27 May 1975). This situation suggests that the availability of a crucial resource will be determined not just by economic and technical factors but by the politics of a few countries in a monopoly position.

Economists have tended to view pollution not as something that constrains economic growth, but as something that should be controlled to an 'optimum level', where any further benefits from control would be exceeded by additional costs. Although the market mechanism may be imperfect, the role of pollution control administrations should be, it is argued, to try and achieve this 'optimum level'. Technical progress will, if the demand exists, keep up with the problems of more efficient pollution control necessary within growing economies. Once again political factors may intervene, preventing the realisation of pollution control but, as with resource availability, physical limits to pollution control are not likely to be an important constraint.

THE MARXIST POLITICAL ECONOMY POSITION

This perspective, like the previous position, claims that resources and pollution control cannot be viewed apart from economic processes. However, unlike other perspectives, the questions of resource scarcity and pollution control are linked to the organization of capital, the modes of production, and the power bases within society. Marx's answer to Malthus was a rejection of the idea of an absolute law dictating that there will always be more people on land than can be maintained from the available means of subsistence unless checked by famine, war, pestilence or artificial controls. Marx (1970(c), 591–92) argued that every stage of economic development has its own law of population. It was the surplus population of unemployed workers that, in the capitalist system, led to poverty and the appearance of over-population. The creation of the surplus population was not a product of resource scarcity but of the capitalist mode of production. Capitalist accumulation decreased the proportion of variable capital to constant capital. The amount of labour is influenced by the amount of variable capital. Consequently, if the variable capital fails to rise with population growth due to capital accumulation, then a surplus population is created. In the words of Marx:

The fact that the means of production, and the productiveness of labour, increases more rapidly than the productive population, expresses itself, therefore, capitalistically in the inverse form that the labouring population always increases more rapidly than conditions under which capital can employ this increase for its own self-expansion (1970:604).

Even for those who are employed, low wages, influenced by a surplus population of unemployed, create inadequate demand (rather than need) for food and other products. There are no physical constraints on production, but the economic organization of society is responsible for the lack of demand among the poor. Engels rejected the 'limits' argument of Malthus as follows:

Too little is produced, that is the cause of the whole thing. But *why* is too little produced? Not because the limits of production – even today and with present-day means – are exhausted. No, but because the limits or production are determined not by the number of hungry bellies but by the number of *purses* able to buy and to pay. Bourgeois society does not and cannot wish to produce any more. The moneyless bellies, the labour which cannot be utilized *for profit* and therefore cannot buy, is left to the death rate (Meek, 1971:87).

The problem of effective demand for resources is of crucial importance in agriculture. There is, for instance, at present no *absolute* shortage of grains in the world, and yet there are acute *regional* shortages. According to Jean Mayer of Harvard University, the same amount of food consumed by 210 million Americans could adequately feed a population of 1.5 billion people at the Chinese level of diet (Power and Holenstien, 1976). N. Eberstadt (1976) has pointed out that the food production *per capita* rose by nine per cent in fifteen years after 1960, that there is more than enough food adequately to feed the world population, and yet millions of people still starve (see also Rothschild, 1976). In Africa barley, beans, cattle, peanuts and vegetables are exported despite the fact that malnutrition is worse in Africa than on any other continent (Lappe and Collins, 1977). Poverty is due to maldistribution of resources (both internationally and within nations), and not to the physical limits of producing the resources themselves. Indeed, given the situation of maldistribution of wealth, land and economic opportunity, the introduction of more productive agriculture (as in the case of the Green Revolution) can lead to a *worse* distribution of wealth and a lower effective demand for agricultural resources (see Chapter 5).

The organizational arguments may be taken further. One could argue, for instance, that capitalism depends upon the creation and management of new demand so as to maintain profits. We are therefore confronted daily by advertisements encouraging us either to buy more or to buy the latest product, and to scrap whatever is no longer considered to be modern. Scarcity, far from being a natural phenomenon or a state resulting from economic growth, is managed in such a way as to maintain a demand that exceeds supply and consequently results in a handsome profit. Only in such terms can one understand the waste resulting from the dumping of surplus milk by the Americans in the 1960s – or the cut-back in wheat acreages from 120 million to 81 million acres in the US, Australia, Argentina and Canada during 1968–70, the stock-piling of beef and butter mountains in the EEC which are sold off cheaply to the USSR, or the throwing away of vast quantities of French apples during the autumn of 1975. In the summer of 1977 the US Administration were again planning to reduce the growing surplus of world wheat by allowing millions of acres of productive farm land to become fallow. Despite the persistence of world hunger, the surplus of US grain was becoming unmanageable; its reduction would help to halt the fall in wheat prices, and so protect the American farmer (*Guardian*, 10 August 1977 and 1 September 1977; Rothschild, 1976). The importance of the profit motive is also crucial to understanding why consumer goods are designed to look more attractive rather than to be easy to recycle – and why they are made to be less durable than they could be, so that they are eventually scrapped and new goods purchased.

The question of whether or not resource scarcity and waste will be a problem in the future is therefore inextricably linked to further questions concerning what type of social relations will exist in the future. Contradictions leading to pollution and resource depletion are only one type of problem that capitalism faces. Alienation and wastage of labour could intensify these contradictions. In a socialist state innovations and mechanization which relieve the burden on man's labour would be greeted with joy and celebration. In a capitalist society, these developments threaten employment and are a source of potential Luddite reaction by workers. Advances in the micro-inducer industry, which in Britain alone 'threatens' to release several millions from the 'labour market' in the late twentieth century are consequently greeted with widespread alarm and despondency. Over-production and time-saving techniques can bring about undesirable social problems in a market economy; they may lead to depression and economic crisis: such are the distortions of capitalism.

The Marxist position, like the economic/technological fix position, has tended to ignore the importance of resource endowment in the development of wealth. While social relations of production and economic organization in general are obviously important there is, as Eyre (1978) has pointed out, a great geographical variation in resource endowments which certainly constrain the path towards a higher standard of living. There has always been a clash between Marxist and Malthusian theorists about the relationship between population growth and poverty. Nevertheless, for pragmatic reasons a population policy in countries of low resource endowment in relation to population size makes sense. To some extent China's policy on population has from time to time (especially between 1954 and 1958, 1962 and 1966 and since 1969) recognized this argument, even though China herself is reasonably well endowed with resources in comparison to other Asian countries such as India. Small family size and late marriage in China have, on the other hand, usually been encouraged for reasons of family health and prosperity.

Recently some Marxists have argued that scarcity of mineral reserves at a cheap price threaten advanced capitalist states. A. Gedicks (1977) claims that Marx recognized the importance of low cost resources in order for the process of capital accumulation to continue. Indeed, according to Marx the price of raw materials was more important than that of fixed capital because 'the value of the raw and auxiliary materials passes entirely into the value of the product in the manufacture of which they are consumed, while the elements of fixed capital transfer their value to the product only gradually in proportion to their wear and tear' (1967:108). Gedicks goes on to argue that scarcity of indigenous reserves will compel the United States to seek out stable supplies of cheap resources against the trend of growing nationalist tendencies.

The main example that Gedicks uses to support his thesis is that of American imperialism in Chile, the object of which was to protect supplies of cheap copper. Prior to the Allende Government in Chile, copper production was geared to the requirements of the American market. When these mines were nationalized, the US government began an economic and political campaign to undermine Allende's government. Eventually, with United States help, the Allende Government was overthrown and a military dictatorship established.

The threat of nationalism and loss of control over physical resources, albeit important, may not be quite as serious for the growth of capitalism as Gedicks implies. There may well be a shift of manufacturing to the less developed countries while the advanced countries shift increasingly towards becoming 'service' economies. K. Kumar (1979) argues that this trend is already taking place in Britain. Gone are the days when Britain was the major manufacturing exporter. In 1870 her exports claimed 40 per cent of the world trade in manufactures. In 1976 this figure had fallen to below 9 per cent. On the other hand, Britain is second only to the United States in the world trade of 'invisibles' (services).

Nevertheless, aside from questions as to whether or not the capitalist social order is about to break down, the Marxist account still offers the most plausible explanation of why there is still resource scarcity for large numbers of the population. Starvation and shortages of basic material requirements owe more to the influences of capitalist ownership and consequent imperialism and suppression of the working class, than to any real physical constraints on providing for those requirements. To this extent the pessimistic conclusions of the Malthusian standpoint are ill-founded and based upon ideological rather than scientific understanding. The economic/technical fix position is also ideological in the sense of being limited to supply and demand equations without considering the influence of capitalists in manipulating both in the interests of capital accumulation rather than of meeting human needs.

Predictions for the future

In a review of future studies, S. Cole, J. Gershany and I. Miles (1978) discovered no less than sixteen major reports on the predicament of man which were published between 1965 and 1977. Twelve of these have been published since 1970. This particular review assessed the reports in terms of three world views: conservative, reformist and radical. No attempt was made to evaluate the plausibility of the reports, but instead they were mapped according to their political views and their position in the Malthusian debate. Twelve possible directions were then contrasted by taking four profiles (high-growth egalitarian, high-growth inegaliterian, low-growth inegalitarian and low-growth egalitarian) and combining these with three world views (conservative, reformist and radical). While there may be some descriptive advantage in adopting this typological approach, it is necessary to make a more serious appraisal of these futuristic studies. This can be accomplished by evaluating the same three views that were considered in the limits to growth debate.

THE NEO-MALTHUSIAN POSITION

Some of the predictions have started from Malthusian assumptions about the limits to growth. R. L. Heilbroner's *An Inquiry into the Human Prospect* is a good example. He identifies three major problem areas which are externally generated and threaten 'the human prospect'. They are population, nuclear war, and the physical limits of the environment to the sustainment of growth. All of these problems he lays at the door of science and technology. The population problem is a consequence of 'a science-induced fall in death rates' (1975:56). The possibilities of nuclear war and environmental catastrophe are also linked to developments in science and technology. He argues that industrial developments induce similar social consequences, whether it be under capitalism or socialism.

Having decided that industrial growth will have to slow down because of the three limiting problems outlined above, Heilbroner then goes on to discuss the capacity of different political institutions to adjust. Acceptance of the concept of limits to growth produces a prediction for the future which he believes will probably require strong centralized political power. He doubts whether 'human nature' would allow for peaceful and organized changes in life-style.

E. J. Mishan (1977) falls into both the Malthusian and technological determinist trap. He argues that the predictions of Malthus and Ricardo were premature rather than wholly wrong. Recent economic and technological growth has threatened humanity because of consequences arising from improved transport and communications; rapid innovations; weapons technology; urban size and concentration. Once again Mishan attributes these dangers to economic and technological factors rather than to any underlying characteristics of the social order. Like Heilbroner, Mishan believes that the momentum of economic growth and technological development is only likely to be controled by a totalitarian state:

The growing fears today of violence, terrorism and urban disruption, the public's apprehension of the grave threats posed by the new technology and the intensification of group conflicts within our pluralistic societies – all of these untoward features, traceable (as indicated in the text) to the technological revolution of the past century, have weakened popular resistance to the assumption of wider powers of control by modern governments. As instinct for survival is impelling the Western democracies along the road to the totalitarian state (1977:265).

C. Taylor (1978) also accepts that population, resource scarcity and pollution threaten to limit growth, and as a consequence it will be necessary to move towards a Byzantium-type steady state. He too believes that this transition will probably come about under authoritarian regimes. The problem a capitalist society faces, he argues, is that inequalities are only bearable where there is economic growth. Stagnation would induce tension between privileged and less privileged groups. This could only be contained by more authoritarian regimes or even dictatorships which would either uphold the inequalities or do something about them. Taylor retains some optimism in that he hopes there would be a benevolent dictatorship which would see the sense of rationing and allocating resources to create universal standards and reduce tension.

The proposed new Byzantine state could probably occur most easily in 'small societies or societies that can be meaningfully decentralized'. Some semblance of a free society is rescued by Taylor for those living in the stable state would find some new stronger purpose in life. Taylor's stable decentralized society bears a close resemblance to *The Ecologist's A Blue print for Survival* (1972). One of the similarities is that both would rely on different technologies and recycling in order to avoid harmful environmental consequences.

These three predictions from Heilbroner, Mishan and Taylor bear close similarities. They can all be dismissed on the grounds of holding false premises derived from the Malthusian perspective and technological determinism.

Some of the radical views of the future which search for liberation from industrialization also suffer from misinterpretation of the nature of the crisis which would bring about this future. In the writings of I. Illich (1973), M. Bookchin (1971) and T. Roszak (1972) in America and E. F. Schumacher (1973), J. Robertson (1977/78) and a good many of the radical technology theorists in Britain, there is a common assumption that a crisis results from the independent development of science and technology. As K. Kumar comments, 'in this account the crisis is the inevitable product of the long-term tendency of industrialism towards the large-scale, greater centralization, a finer specialization and division of labour, and the replacement of human labour and human skill by a resource-consuming machine technology' (1979: 15).

THE ECONOMIC TECHNOLOGICAL FIX POSITION

The next series of predictions are those based upon premises derived from the economic/technological fix perspective. Futurologists such as Kahn (1976), D. Bell (1973) and P. F. Druker (1969) hold an essentially business-as-usual position. They are optimistic about the industrial future. The way the future is likely to differ from the present is considered in terms of the types of technologies that will be developed in order to sustain growth. The shift will be from conventional manufacturing to high technology such as nuclear fission and fusion. Widespread automation, further developments in transportation, aerospace, telecommunications, computerization and even the possibilities of space colonization will bring us into the hyper-industrial estate. The problem facing governments is how to make the transition as smooth as possible (see Robertson 1977/78).

Orwellian features of the hyper-industrial estate may in themselves be grounds for rejecting the likelihood of this prospect for the future occurring. Nevertheless, the likelihood of nuclear power becoming a major source of electricity supply is already with us. In many respects the hyper-industrial estate based upon liberal economic principles is a likely prospect because it is a projection of numerous tendencies that exist in the advanced capitalist nations today. The question that needs to be raised when assessing its plausibility is whether or not the contradictions of capitalism which today give rise to problems of pollution, resource scarcity and risks from Flixborough, Saveso and giant oil-spillage disasters can be overcome without both a change in social order and a change in the path of technological development. Given the record of capitalist countries in tackling these problems, and the tendency towards greater risks in industrial development, the prospects of this prediction occurring are grave indeed. Together with other contradictions of capitalism, such as poverty in the midst of plenty and high levels of unemployment, it is not unlikely that movements toward an alternative path of development will achieve some success.

H. Stretton (1976) has described three possible directions for the future based upon reformist policies. The first two directions involve a shift to the right. The first is that a reactionary class-ruled regime which adopts preservationist policies along strictly Malthusian lines will take control. Inequalities will increase and the state will become more authoritarian: the death penalty, strict population control policies and penal colonies may be some of the instruments of social control.

His second prediction suggests that political influences slightly to the right will bring about environmental reforms which mildly increase divisions and inequalities within society. Just as the better off have benefited most from environmental planning and pollution control in the past, so they continue to do so in the future: 'The democracies were thus gentler in the way they increased inequalities, but they did increase them. They did it negatively by their responses to shortages, involuntarily by their mechanisms of inflation, and positively by the way they distributed the costs and consequences of environmental reform' (1976:41).

Stretton's third prediction involves a political shift to the left; left-wing parties gain in strength from the 'cost-of-living troubles and rising inequalities . . . urban and environmental troubles, quality of life issues, local and community initiatives, business scandals and property prices and the problems of inflation (1976:97–98). The traditional Left and environmentalists, who were estranged from each other in the late 1960s and early 1970s, would find common ground in campaigning against environmental dangers to basic necessities. While private enterprise continues, its activities are increasingly governed by labour interests. Instead of the capitalist class controlling the state, the reverse process would gradually take place so that governments could claim that they:

> . . . now had better instruments of general economic policy. They had direct control of many environmentally sensitive resources and processes or production. They could use that control for environmental purposes: they could also use it, especially by pricing and allocative policies within the public sector, to influence the social distribution of many costs and benefits of environmental reform. There was a similar strengthening of government in national resource allocation and in the management of inflation . . . The rich could no longer say, 'Let us keep all we can spend and then a great deal more, or you'll get no growth.' Government could determine growth policy on its merits, and independently, inequality policy on *its* merits . . . For the first time in a capitalist history full of hopeful or fearful illusions on the subject, the overall pattern of inequalities could be substantially affected by democratic choice (1976:123–24).

Stretton is right to point out alternative paths of reform under capitalism. However, his predictions flirt with the possibilities of Malthusian constraints without assessing their likelihood. It is also doubtful whether the type of Leftist reforms which he envisages could take place while maintaining the capitalist economy intact. The history of labour reformist intervention to date does not suggest that political reforms alone will be sufficient to erode inequalities or the power of the capitalist ruling class (see Westergaard and Resler, 1976). Labour intervention, if successful, is more likely to transform capitalist economies into socialist economies. There is obviously a spectrum of possibilities between a *laissez-faire* economy and a socialist state where private ownership plays an insignificant role. However, the most important areas for change are not the state and policy-making institutions, but control over the forces of production.

It is only when product innovation, pollution control and resources utilization by firms are taken out of the control of management and entrepreneurs whose prime aim is to maximize profits that true progress can be made towards a healthier environment for all.

THE MARXIST POLITICAL ECONOMY POSITION

The last type of prediction stems from a Marxist viewpoint. It assumes that planning and technological choice and economic development will come under the control of the workers and the local community rather than the financial magnates of industry. Under both state and local control, economic development could be planned to improve environmental working and living conditions, and wastage would be reduced by avoiding unnecessary competition. Food, shelter, energy and mineral resources would be regarded as precious and not to be squandered as occurs today under the distortions of a market economy. Safety at work and a pollution-free environment would become of elevated importance and not mere externalities to be dealt with retrospectively. Individuals would become freer to travel with improved public transport, cycling and pedestrian conditions, and the wastage from half-empty cars would be avoided.

Today polluting industries, traffic hazards and other environmental disturbances are unevenly distributed so that the better off have prime access to higher quality environments. The rich and dominant class have been able to manipulate political institutions so that planning reinforces their narrow needs. In the socialist future political institutions and planning would serve a wider spectrum of interests. Industrial democracy and choice of products according to need rather than profit would ensure a more efficient use of resources. The struggle by the Lucas Aerospace shop stewards for their corporate plan would be remembered as a milestone in the creation of a new future where there was a real freedom of choice for the majority of people. People and politics would be in command rather than the demands of capital accumulation for its own sake.

Whether or not the socialist prediction would be constrained by the availability and price of physical resources would still be debateable, especially in countries with few resources. Exploration and development of physical resources would not, however, be determined by profit implications, and there would be less unnecessary exploitation for products which meet 'false needs'. The likelihood of this third prediction occurring is in doubt, but one can claim that its development would ensure a safer and more fulfilling future. Whether or not such changes are realized before the development of further major wars or before some major disaster from bio-chemical pollution or radiation remains to be seen.

Conclusions

In a typical liberal and pluralistic account, environmental problems arise at various stages during the process of industrialization. Consequent strains lead to the development of social movements. The state, pressure groups, and the public react to these problems and, depending upon the nature of the political system, there are varying degrees of consensus and conflict before acceptable solutions are found. In the democratic capitalist economies dominant social science and policy analysis implicitly deny that conflicts of material interest play a significant part in generating and resolving social and environmental problems. 'Scientific rationality' is, however, closely integrated with a system of capitalist production (see Gorz, 1976(b)). Hence cost–benefit analysis and technology assessment are legitimate and respected forms of policy analysis whereas the activities of workers' organizations aimed at transforming work organization and industrial production, such as by the Lucas Aerospace combine, is regarded as political rather than scientific.

If the policy outcome of cost–benefit analysis, behavioural studies, environmental impact assessment and technology assessment is shown to be politically biased – favouring middle-class owner-occupiers, for example – then this is often claimed to be due not to a political bias of the ideas governing policy analysis themselves but an abuse of these ideas. The development of ideas and theories governing policy and the understanding of social movements, pressure groups, the behaviour of firms and the growth of the state are assumed to be free from ideology. A sophisticated version of this view has been advanced in the sociology of science by S. Cotgrove. Influenced by the notion that ideas can be used as various types of social lever (see M. Douglas, 1972), Cotgrove suggests that 'styles of thought', both current and historical, 'can be harnessed to the promotion of a variety of alternative and competing values, including order as well as freedom' (1978:358).

This use/abuse model of scientific knowledge is supported in the main by historians and philosophers of science. Thus for K. R. Popper (1959) better theories replace inferior ones, and T. S. Kuhn (1962) believes that scientists look for better theories only when current theories run into trouble. In both cases the development of science is seen as following an independent and self-governing path. Neither of these influential theorists has been willing to grant any significance to the influence of external economic and social conditions on the nature and development of science.

Although there is a semblance of explanatory logic in pluralist, functionalist, behavioural and neo-classical theories, which dominate the social scientific analysis of environmental problems and policy, they can all be shown to be defective, in as much as they neglect material interests.

Systems of ideas, whether they be idealist or economic, which are divorced from the real material world serve to obscure the true basis of environmental and social problems. Those who support systems of thinking that are independent of the social organization of production and claim them to be ideologically neutral are profoundly misleading. The Marxist claims a distinction between ideology and science which is very different from that outlined above. Indeed much of what society accepts as scientific is regarded by him as ideology posing as science. He believes that the study of environmental problems and policy is dominated be defective explanations whose strength lies in the fact that they serve the objective interests of capital.

The view that science has increasingly been concerned with converting political issues into bogus technical ones and so legitimating policies of social control owes much to the work of the Frankfurt School of Philosophy. Recently Marxists have in general paid greater attention to Marx's theory of knowledge which stresses that knowledge about the world and how it can be changed is closely related to actual practice or the way scientific work is organised. In China 'experts' and scientists have been more accountable to the socialist commune and state, and there has not been the same differentiation of work and responsibility as in the West. In a capitalist society natural and social scientists are subject to the same debilitating forces of fragmentation and oppression as other workers. Science has consequently become part of the system of production and social control. According to H. and S. Rose (1976) some 75–95 per cent of scientific research in advanced industrial countries has either the political aim of social control or the economic aim of profit.

In the social sciences the production of knowledge is distorted by specialization and fragmentation of academic disciplines, and studies which play a functional role of supporting the *status quo* are particularly promoted within academic and policy institutions. The result is that the 'ruling ideas' are, as Marx asserted, the ideas of the 'ruling class'. The solution to environmental problems depends therefore not merely upon reforming the science and technologies available but transforming the social relations of production – production of policy, technology, and knowledge itself. Resistance to nuclear fast-breeder reactors, to dangerous industrial developments, to impersonal environmental planning, is not merely a matter of improving expertise and the scientific basis of decision-making. It is a matter of claiming the right for all to control what is produced and what is planned.

References

Abrams, M. February 1977: 'Who's left, what's right?' *Encounter* 48(2), 3–17.

Adams, J. 16 June 1977: 'The breakdown of transport planning.' *New Society* 40, 548–50.

Agarwal, A. 9 February 1978(a): 'Solar energy and the Third World.' *New Scientist* 77, 357–9.

Agarwal, A. 20 April 1978(b): 'Can industry grow without agriculture?' *New Scientist* 78, 143–4.

Albrecht, S. L. 1976: 'Legacy of the environmental movement.' *Environment and Behaviour* 8, 147–68.

Allison, L. 1975: *Environmental planning: a political and philosophical analysis.* London: Allen and Unwin.

Ambrose, P. 1975: *The property machine.* Harmondsworth: Penguin.

Anderson, R. J. and Crocker, T. D. 1971: 'Air pollution and residential property values.' *Urban Studies* 8, 171–80.

Anderson, R. W. 1974: 'Some issues in recreation economics.' In Culyer, A. J., editor, *Economic policies and social goals; aspects of public choice.* London: Martin Robertson, 219–38.

Apodaca, A. 1952: 'Corn and custom: the introduction of hybrid corn to Spanish American farmers in New Mexico.' In Spicer, E. H., editor, *Human problems in technological change.* New York: Russel Sage Foundation, 35–9.

Arendt, H. 1958: *The human condition.* Chicago: The University of Chicago Press.

Arnold, M. 1932: *Culture and anarchy* (1869). Cambridge: Cambridge University Press.

Ashby, E. 1976: 'Protection of the environment: the human dimension.' *Proceedings of the Royal Society of Medicine* 69, 721–30.

Assembly Committee on Local Government 1975: *The California Environmental Quality Act, an evaluation* Vol. 1, Sacramento, California.

Baran, P. A. and Sweezy, P. M. 1968: *Monopoly capital.* Harmondsworth: Penguin.

Barbour, I. G., editor, 1973: *Western man and environmental ethics: attitudes toward nature and technology.* Reading: Addison-Wesley.

Bardach, E. and Pugliaresi, L. 1977: 'The environmental impact statement vs. the real world.' *The Public Interest* 49, 22–38.

Barker, A. 1976: 'Local amenity societies – a survey and outline report.' In *The local amenity movement*. London: Civic Trust, 21–31.

Barkum, M. 1974: *Disaster and the Millennium*. New Haven: Yale University Press.

Barnett, H. J. and Morse, C. 1965: *Scarcity and growth: the economics of natural resource availability*. Baltimore: Johns Hopkins University Press.

Beardsley, W. G. 1972: 'The economic impact of recreational development: a synopsis.' In Doolittle, W., editor, *Outdoor recreation symposium* (Upper Darby, Pa., North East Forest and Range Experimental Station). Referred to in O'Riordan, 1976: 178.

Beaver, S. H. 1964: 'The Potteries, a study in the evolution of a cultural landscape.' *Transactions of the Institute of British Geographers* 34, 1–31.

Beaver Committee 1954: *Report of the Committee on Air Pollution*. Cmnd. 1322. London: HMSO.

Beckerman, W. 1974: *In defence of economic growth*. London: Cape.

Beckerman, W. 1975: *Pricing for pollution*. Hobbart Paper No. 66. London: Institute of Economic Affairs.

Bell, D. 1973: *The Coming of post-industrial society: a venture in social forecasting*. New York: Basic Books.

Berger, P. L. and Luckman, T. 1967: *The social construction of reality*. New York: Doubleday Anchor Books.

Best, R. H. 1976: 'The changing land use structure of Britain.' *Town and Country Planning* 44, 171–6.

Bhalla, A. S. 1975: 'Lessons from the case studies.' In Bhalla, A. S., editor, *Technology and employment in industry: a case study approach*. Geneva: International Labour Office, 309–24.

Bisset, R. July 1978: 'Environmental impact analysis.' *Royal Anthropological Institute News* 26, 1–4.

Black, J. H. 1970: *The dominion of man: the search for ecological responsibility*. Edinburgh: Edinburgh University Press.

Boddington, M. A. B. 1973: 'The evaluation of agriculture in land planning decisions.' *Journal of Agricultural Economics* 24, 37–50.

Bookchin, M. 1971(a): *Post-scarcity anarchism*. San Francisco: Ramparts Press.

Bookchin, M. 1971(b): 'Towards a liberatory technology.' In Benello, L. G. and Roussopoulos, D. R., editors, *The case for participatory democracy: some prospects for a radical society*. New York: Grossman, 95–139.

Bottomore, T. B. 1966: *Élites and society*. Harmondsworth: Penguin.

Bottomore, T. B. 1975: *Sociology as social criticism*. London: George Allen and Unwin.

Bottomore, T. B. and Rubel, M. 1963: *Karl Marx: selected writings in sociology and social philosophy*. Harmondsworth: Penguin.

Boulding, K. E. 1966: 'The economics of the coming Spaceship Earth.' In Jarrett, H., editor, *Environmental quality in a growing economy*. Baltimore: Resources for the Future, 3–14.

Bowman, J. S. 1975: 'The ecology movement.' *Journal of Environmental Studies* 8, 91–7.

Bowman, J. S. 1977: 'Public opinion and the environment: post-Earthday attitudes among college students.' *Environment and Behaviour* 9, 385–416.

Bracey, H. E. 1963: *Industry and the countryside: the impact of industry on the countryside.* London: Faber and Faber.

Braun, E. and Collingridge, D. 1977: *Technology and survival.* London: Butterworths.

Braverman, H. 1974: *Labour and monopoly capital.* New York: Monthly Review Press.

Breach, I. 1978: *Windscale fallout: a primer for the age of nuclear controversy.* Harmondsworth: Penguin.

Brenner, J. F. 1974: 'Nuisance law and the industrial revolution.' *The Journal of Legal Studies* 3, 403–33.

Brookes, E. 1976: 'On putting the environment in its place: a critique of EIA. In O'Riordan, T. and Hey, R. D., editors, *Environmental impact assessment.* Westmead, Farnborough: Saxon House, 167–77.

Brookes, S. K., Jordan, A. G., Kimber, R. H. and Richardson, J. J. 1976: 'The growth of the environment as a political issue in Britain.' *British Journal of Political Science* 6, 245–55.

Brookes, S. K. and Richardson, J. J. 1975: 'The environmental lobby in Britain.' *Parliamentary Affairs* 28, 312–28.

Brown, M., Fitzgerald, P., Goodenough, M., Hollenbach, D., Pector, J., Schwartz, D. and Swartz, J. May 1976: 'Nuclear power: who needs it?' *Science for the people* 8 (3), 4–12.

Buchanan Report 1963: *Traffic in towns.* London: HMSO.

Bugler, J. 1972: *Polluting Britain.* Harmondsworth: Penguin.

Bugler, J. 10 March 1978(a): 'The Windscale verdict.' *New Statesman* 95, 309–10.

Bugler, J. 27 July 1978(b): 'Windscale: a case study in public scrutiny.' *New Society* 45, 183–6.

Bulletin of the European Communities, 1976: *Environmental Programme 1977–1981.* Supplement 6/76.

Burchett, W. and Alley, R. 1976: *China: the quality of life.* Harmondsworth: Penguin.

Burrows, P. 1974: 'Pricing versus regulation for environmental protection.' In Culyer, A. J., editor, *Economic policies and social goals: aspects of public choice* (*York studies in economics*, No. 1). London: Martin Robertson, 273–83.

Buttel, F. H. 1975: 'The environmental movement: consensus, conflict and change.' *The Journal of Environmental Education* 7, 53–63.

Buttel, F. H. and Flinn, W. L. 1974: 'The structure and support for the environmental movement, 1968–1970.' *Rural Sociology* 39, 56–69.

Buttel, F. H. and Flinn, W. L. 1976: 'Environmental politics: the structuring of partisan and ideological cleavages in mass environmental attitudes. *The Sociological Quarterly* 17, 477–90.

Byers, W. M. 1970: *An economic impact study of Olympic and Mt Rainer National Parks, Washington.* Washington: National Park Service.

Cairns, W. 1978: 'The Flotta EIA study.' *Built Environment* 4, 129–33.

Calabresi, G. and Melamed, A. D. 1972: 'Property rules and inalienability – one view of the cathedral.' *Harvard Law Review* 85, 1,089–1,128.

Caldwell, M. 1977: *The wealth of some nations.* London: Zed.

California State Assembly Office of Research 1977: *Analysis of AB 2679* (77–892), issued on 11 January 1977. Sacramento, California.

Carson, R. 1962: *Silent spring.* London: Hamilton.

Castells, M. 1977: *The urban question: a Marxist approach.* London: Edward Arnold.

Catalano, R. and Reich, R. 1977: 'Local government law and the EIR: the California experience.' *The Urban Lawyer* 9, 195–206.

Catlow, J. and Thirlwall, C. G. 1976: *Environmental impact analysis.* Research Report 11. London: Department of the Environment.

Changing Directions. A Report from the Independent Commission on Transport 1974: London: Coronet.

Chapman, J. D. 1969: 'Interactions between man and his resources.' In National Academy of Sciences, editors, *Resources and man: a study and recommendations.* San Francisco: W. H. Freeman and Co., 31–42.

Chapman, P. 1975: *Fuel's paradise: energy options for Britain.* Harmondsworth: Penguin.

Cheng-Ko, W. May 1977: 'A chemical plant fights pollution.' *China Reconstructs* 26(5), 40–3.

Cheng-Ying, C. 20 January 1978: 'Power industry – the vanguard.' *Peking Review* 21(3), 16–20.

Chi-Chu, C. 19 August 1977: 'Farm mechanization in Wusih County' (111). *Peking Review* 20 (34), 33–7.

Chi-Chu, C. 28 November 1975: 'A clarion call to action.' *Peking Review* 48, 5–9.

Clark, B. 1976: 'Evaluating environmental impacts.' In O'Riordan, T. and Hey, R. D., editors, *Environmental impact assessment.* Westmead, Farnborough: Saxon House, 91–104.

Clark, B. D., Chapman, K., Bisset, R. and Wathern, P. 1978: 'Methods of environmental impact analysis.' *Built Environment* 4, 111–21.

Clarke, N. 1972: 'Technological dependency and underdevelopment.' *New Edinburgh Review,* 20, 11–15.

Clarke, R. May 1972: 'Soft technology: blueprint for a research community.' *Undercurrents* 2 (reprinted in Elliott and Elliott, 1976).

Clarke, R. 1973: 'The pressing need for alternative technology.' *Impact of Science on Society* 23, 257–71.

Clarke, R. 16 May 1974: 'The new Utopians.' *New Scientist* 62, 423.

Clawson, M. 1959: *Methods of measuring the demand for and the value of outdoor recreation.* Washington DC: Resources for the Future.

Cleaver, H. Jr. June 1972: 'The contradictions of the Green Revolution.' *Monthly Review* 24, 80–111.

Coase, R. 1960: 'The problem of social cost.' *The Journal of Law and Economics* 3, 1–44.

Cole, S., Gershuny, J. and Miles, I. 1978: 'Scenarios of world development.' *Futures* 10, 3–20.

Collins, C. C. 26 October 1972: 'Morningside: in the making.' *The Westsider* (New York), 1 and 10.

Commoner, B. 1966: *Science and survival*. London: Ballantine.

Commoner, B. 1972: 'The social use and misuse of technology.' In Benthall, J., editor, *Ecology, the shaping enquiry: a course given at the Institute of Contemporary Arts*. London: Longman, 335–62.

Commoner, B. 1973: 'Workplace burden.' *Environment* 15, 15–20.

Connelly, P. and Perlman, R. 1975: *The politics of scarcity in resource conflicts in international relations*. London: Oxford University Press.

Cooley, M. Winter 1977/78: 'Design, technology and production for social needs: an initiative by the Lucas Aerospace workers.' *New Universities Quarterly* 32, 37–49.

Cooper, C. 1973: 'Choice of technique: technological change as problems in political economy.' *International Social Science Journal* 25, 293–304.

Cooper, C., Kaplinsky, R., Bell, R. and Satyarakwit, W. 1975: 'Choice of techniques for can-making in Kenya, Tanzania and Thailand.' In Bhalla, A. S., editor, *Technology and employment in industry: a case study approach*. Geneva: International Labour Office, 85–121.

Cotgrove, S. 1975: 'Technology, rationality and domination.' *Social Studies of Science* 5, 55–78.

Cotgrove, S. 1976: 'Environmentalism and Utopia.' *The Sociological Review* 24, 23–42.

Cotgrove, S. 1978: 'Styles of thought: science, romanticism and modernization.' *British Journal of Sociology* 29, 358–71.

Council of the Organization for Economic Co-operation and Development 1974: *Recommendation of the Council on the analysis of the environmental consequences of significant public and private projects*. Paris: OECD.

Council on Environmental Quality 1973: *Environmental quality: fourth annual report*. Washington DC: Government Printing Office.

Council on Environmental Quality 1974: *Environmental quality: fifth annual report*. Washington DC: Government Printing Office.

Council on Environmental Quality 1975: *Environmental quality: sixth annual report*. Washington DC: Government Printing Office.

Council on Tribunals, *Annual Report* 1974–75.

Crenson, M. A. 1971: *The un-politics of air pollution: a study of non-decision-making in the cities*. London: Johns Hopkins University Press.

Cross, N. 1978: *Methods guide*. Open University Control of Technology Course T361, Unit 8. Milton Keynes: Open University.

Dahl, R. A. 1961: *Who governs? Democracy and power in an American city*. New Haven: Yale University Press.

Dalrymple, D. 1974(a): *The Green Revolution, past and prospects*. Washington DC: USAID.

Dalrymple, D. 1974(b): *Development and spread of high yield varieties of wheat and rice in less developed nations*. Washington DC: US Department of Agriculture.

Dartmoor Preservation Association 1967: *The Meldon story.* Yelverton, Devon: Dartmoor Preservation Association.

Dasgupta, B. 1977: 'India's Green Revolution.' *Economic and political Weekly* 12, 241–60.

Dasgupta, B. 1978: 'The environment debate: some issues and trends.' *Economic and Political Weekly* 13, 385–400.

De Weese III, C. L. 1976: 'Computer context analysis of printed media: a limited feasibility study.' *Public Opinion Quarterly* 40, 92–104.

Dean, G. 18 May 1972: 'China's technological development.' *New Scientist* 54, 371–73.

Dennis, N. 1972: *Public participation and planners' blight.* London: Faber and Faber.

Department of the Environment (Highways Economic and Modelling Analysis Division) 1973: *COBA – a method of economic appraisal of highway schemes* Technical Memorandum No. H5/73.

Deutsch, S. and Van Houten, D. 1974: 'Environmental sociology and the American working class.' *Humboldt Journal of Social Relations* 2, 22–6.

Dickey, J. W., Glancy, D. M. and Jennelle, E. M. 1973: *Technology assessment: its application to solid waste management programmes of urban governments.* Massachusetts: Lexington Books.

Dickson, D. 1974: *Alternative technology and the politics of technical change.* Glasgow: Fontana.

Dijksterhuis, E. J. 1961: *The mechanization of the world picture.* London: Oxford University Press.

Dillman, D. A. and Christenson, J. A. 1972: 'The public value for pollution control.' In Burch, W. R. Jr., Cheek, N. H. Jr., and Taylor, L., editors, *Social behaviour, natural resources and the environment.* New York: Harper and Row, 237–56.

Dillman, D. A. and Christenson, J. A., 1974: 'Toward the assessment of public values.' *Public Opinion Quarterly* 38, 206–21.

Disney, R. 1977: 'Economics of "Gobar-Gas" versus fertilizer; a critique of intermediate technology.' *Development and Change* 8, 77–102.

Disney, R. and Aragaw, H. 1977: 'The choice of technology in the production of fertilizer: a case study of ammonia and urea.' *World Development* 5, 853–66.

Dobry, G. 1974: 'Review of the development control system.' (interim report January 1974, final report February 1975) London: HMSO.

Document: The State of the Environment in 1976 – Report of the Executive Director of the United Nations Environment Programme (UNEP) 1976: *Earth Law* 2, 172–88.

Dolbey, S. J. 1969: 'The politics of Manchester's water supply, 1961–67.' Ph.D. thesis, University of Manchester.

Douglas, M. 1972: 'Environment at risk.' In Benthall, J., editor, *Ecology, the shaping enquiry: a course given at the Institute of Contemporary Arts.* London: Longman, 129–45.

Downs, A. 1957: *An economic theory of democracy.* New York: Harper and Row.

Downs, A. 1972: 'Up and down with ecology – the "issue–attention cycle".' *The public interest* 28, 38–50.

Downs, R. M. and Stea, D. 1977: *Maps in minds: reflections on cognitive mapping*. New York: Harper and Row.

Dror, Y. 1967: 'Policy analysts: a new professional role in government service.' *Public Administration Review* 27, 197–203.

Drucker, P. F. 1969: *The age of discontinuity*. New York: Harper and Row.

Du Boff, R. B. 1974: 'Economic ideology and the environment.' In Van Raay, H. G. T. and Lugo, A. E., editors, *Man and environment Ltd*. The Hague: Rotterdam University Press, 201–20.

Dunlap, R. E. 1973: 'Legislative voting on environmental issues: an analysis of the impact on party membership.' Doctorate dissertation, University of Oregon.

Dunlap, R. E. and Van Liere, K. D. 1977: 'Further evidence of declining public concern with environmental problems: a research note.' *Western Sociological Review* 8, 108–12.

Durkheim, E. 1950: *Rules of sociological method*. Eighth edition, Glenco, Illinois: The Free Press.

Easlea, B. 1973: *Liberation and the aims of science: an essay on obstacles to the building of a beautiful world*. London: Chatto and Windus.

Easton, S. 1976: 'Explaining ideology.' *Sociological Analysis and Theory* 6, 187–204.

Eberstadt, N. 19 February 1976: 'Myths of the food crisis.' *The New York Review of Books* 23, 32–7.

Edison Electric Institute 1976: *Economic growth in the future: the growth debate in national and global perspective*. New York: McGraw-Hill Book Company.

Editors of *The Ecologist*, 1972: *A blueprint for survival*. Harmondsworth: Penguin.

Edwards, M. 1977: *The ideological function of cost–benefit analysis in planning*. Discussion Paper No. 25. London: University College.

Ehrlich, P. R. 1972: *The population bomb* (first published 1968). London: Pan/Ballantine.

Ehrlich, P. R. and Ehrlich, A. H. 1970: *Population, resources, environment: issues in human ecology*. San Francisco: W. H. Freeman and Co.

Elkington, J. 12 May 1977: 'Cushioning the impact.' *New Scientist* 74, 334–6.

Elkington, J. 1 June 1978: 'Fuelling the EIA flame.' *New Scientist* 78, 583–5.

Elliott, D. 1977: *The Lucas Aerospace workers' campaign*. Young Fabian pamphlet No. 46. London: Fabian Society.

Elliott, D. and Elliott, R. 1976: *The control of technology*. London: Wykeham.

Elliott, D. and Emerson, T. 1976: 'The democratization of decision-making.' In Barratt Brown, M., Emerson, T., and Stoneman, C., editors, *Resources and the environment: a socialist perspective*. Nottingham: Spokesman Books, 113–29.

Ellul, J. 1964: *The technological society*. New York: Knopf.

Elson, R. M. 1964: *Guardians of tradition: American textbooks of the nineteenth century*. Lincoln: University of Nebraska Press.

Engels, F. 1950: 'Socialism: Utopian and scientific' (first published 1892). In Marx, K. and Engels, F. *Selected Works*, Volume 2. London: 116–55.

Engels, F. 1964: *Outlines of a critique of political economy* (first published 1844). New York: International Publishers.

England, R. and Bluestone, B. 1973: 'Ecology and social conflict.' In Daly, H., editor, *Toward a steady state economy.* San Francisco: W. H. Freeman and Co., 190–214.

Enzensberger, H. M. 1974: 'A critique of political ecology.' *New Left Review* 84, 3–31.

Erskine, H. 1972: 'The polls: pollution and its costs.' *Public Opinion Quarterly* 36, 120–35.

Everett, M. 1977: 'Benefit–cost analysis for labour-intensive transportation systems.' *Transportation* 6, 57–70.

Eversley, D. E. C. 1976: 'Some social and economic implications of environmental impact assessment.' In O'Riordan, T. and Hey, R. D., editors, *Environmental impact assessment.* Westmead, Farnborough: Saxon House, 126–41.

Lord Eversley. 1910: *Commons, forests and footpaths.* London: Cassell.

Expenditure Committee on 'Public Expenditure of Transport' 1974: House of Commons Paper No. 269.

Eyre, S. R. 1978: *The real wealth of nations.* London: Edward Arnold.

Fanning, O. 1975: *Man and his environment: citizen action.* New York: Harper and Row.

Farvar, M. and Milton, J. P. 1972: *The careless technology: ecology and international development.* Garden City, New York: Natural History Press.

Feder, E. 3 April 1976: 'McNamara's little Green Revolution: World Bank scheme for self-liquidation of Third World peasantry.' *Economic and Political Weekly* 11, 532–41.

Fenton, J. 20 January 1978: 'Power to the corridor.' *New Statesman* 95, 66.

Ferris, J. 1972: *Participation in urban planning: the Barnsbury case.* Occasional papers on social administration, No. 48, London: G. Bell.

Finer, S. E. 1969: *Anonymous empire: a study of the lobby in Great Britain* (first published 1958). London: Pall Mall.

Fischer, D. W. 1974: 'Environmental impact assessment as an instrument of public policy for controlling economic growth.' *International Journal of Environmental Studies* 6, 233–42.

Fischoff, B. 1977: 'Cost–benefit analysis and the art of motorcycle maintenance.' *Policy Sciences* 8, 177–202.

Fleming, D. 1972: 'Roots of the new conservation movement.' *Perspectives in American History* 6, 7–91.

Flood, M. and Grove-White, R. 1976: *Nuclear prospects: a comment on the individual, the state and nuclear power.* London: Friends of the Earth Ltd. in association with The Council for the Protection of Rural England and The National Council for Civil Liberties.

Flowerdew, R. and Cooke, R. 1975: *Environmental impact assessment: a brief survey of procedure in the USA and the State of California.* Resource Management Seminar, working paper no. 3. London: University College.

Foley, G. 1976: *The energy question.* Harmondsworth: Penguin.

Forester, T. 28 April 1977: 'Do the British sincerely want to be rich?' *New Society* 40, 158–61.

Foster, M. J. 1976: 'Taxation as an instrument of pollution control' (part 2). *Environmental Policy and Law* 2, 133–6.

Foulkes, K. M. 1970: 'The background and terms of the Clear Air Act, 1956.' M.Sc. thesis, Sussex University.

Frankel, M. Spring 1974: 'The Alkali Inspectorate: the control of industrial air pollution.' *Social Audit* 1 (4) Supplement, 1–48.

Franks Report 1957: *Report of the Committee on administrative tribunals and inquiries*. Cmnd. 218. London: HMSO.

Frederickson, H. G. and Magnas, H. 1972: 'Comparing attitudes towards water pollution in Syracuse.' In Thompson, D. L., editor, *Politics, policy and natural resources*. New York: The Free Press, 264–80.

Freeman, L. 1977: 'Trade effluents: the charges and the consequences.' *Water* 17, 13–16.

Friesema, H. P. and Culhane, P. J. 1976: 'Social impacts, politics and the environmental impact statement.' *Natural Resources Journal* 16, 339–56.

Funkhouser, R. 1973: 'The issues of the sixties: an exploratory study in the dynamics of public opinion.' *Public Opinion Quarterly* 37, 62–75.

Garman, C. and Alper, K. September/October 1976: 'Alternative technology: not a revolutionary strategy.' *Science for the people* 8(5), 14–17.

Gedicks, A. 1977: 'Raw materials: the Achilles heel of American imperialism?' *The insurgent sociologist* 7, 3–13.

Gerrand, A. 1975: 'American alternatives.' *Architectural Design* 45, 18–22.

Gibbons, M. and Voyer, R. 24 May 1973: 'Technology assessment: bias-free analysis.' *New Scientist* 58, 466–69.

Glacken, C. J. 1970: 'Man against nature: an outmoded concept.' In Helfrich, H. W. Jr., editor, *The environmental crisis: man's struggle to live with himself*. New Haven: Yale University Press, 127–42.

Glass Manufacturers Federation 1975: *The glass container industry and the environmental debate*. London: Glass Manufacturers Federation.

Goldsmith, E. 1977: 'De-industrializing society.' *The Ecologist* 7, 128–43.

Golub, R. and Townsend, J. 1977: 'Malthus, multinationals and the Club of Rome.' *Social studies of science* 7, 201–22.

Goodey, B. 1971: *City scene: an exploration into the image of central Birmingham as seen by area residents*. Research memorandum No. 10. Birmingham: Centre for Urban and Regional Studies.

Goodman, R. 1972: *After the planners*. Harmondsworth: Penguin.

Gorz, A. 1976(a): 'Technology, technicians and class struggle.' In Gorz, A., editor, *The division of labour: the labour process and class struggle in modern capitalism*. Hassocks, Sussex: Harvester Press.

Gorz, A. 1976(b): 'On the class character of science and scientists.' In Rose, H. and Rose, S., editors, *The political economy of science. Ideology of/in the natural sciences*. London: Macmillan, 59–71.

Gosling, D. and Montefiore, H., editors, *Nuclear crisis: a question of breeding.* Dorchester: Prism Press.

Gould, P. and White, R. 1974: *Mental Maps.* Harmondsworth: Penguin.

Gray, J. 1978(a): 'Mao and the Chinese rural economy,' *World Development* 6, 567–81.

Gray, J. 22 June 1978(b): 'China: another great leap forward?' *New Society* 44, 657–59.

Greenberg, M. R. and Hordon, R. M. 1974: 'Environmental impact statements: some annoying questions.' *Journal of the American Institute of Planners* 40, 164–75.

Gregory, R. 1971: *The price of amenity.* London: Macmillan.

Gregory, R. 1974: 'The Minister's Line: or, the M4 comes to Berkshire.' In Kimber, R. and Richardson, J. J., editors, *Campaigning for the environment.* London: Routledge and Kegan Paul, 103–35.

Greis, P. T. 1973: 'The environmental impact statement: a small step instead of a giant leap.' *Urban Lawyer* 5, 264–303.

Grove-White, R. 1975: 'The framework of law: some observations.' In Smith, P. J., editor, *The politics of physical resources.* Harmondsworth: Penguin, 1–21.

Grove-White, R. Winter 1977: 'Executive out of control.' *CPRE Bulletin* 5, 4–5.

Grove-White, R. 1978: 'The judge and his judgement.' *Vole* 5, 6.

Habermas, J. 1971: *Towards a rational society.* London: Heineman.

Hall, I. M. 1976: *Community action versus pollution: a study of a residents' group in a Welsh urban area.* University of Wales, Social Science Monographs No. 2. Cardiff: University of Wales.

Hall, P. G., Gracey, H., Drewett, R. and Thomas, R. 1974: *The containment of urban England.* London: Allen and Unwin.

Hamer, M. 1974: *Wheels within wheels: a study of the road lobby.* London: Friends of the Earth.

Hanlon, J. 26 May 1977: 'India: back to the villages. Does AT walk on plastic sandals?' *New Scientist* 74, 467–9.

Hardin, C. M. 1974: 'Observations on environmental politics.' In Nagel, S. S., editor, *Environmental Politics.* London: Praeger, 177–94.

Hardin, G. 1972: *Exploring new ethics for survival.* New York: The Viking Press.

Harper, P. 1973: 'In search of allies for soft technologies.' *Impact of Science on Society* 23, 287–305.

Harper, P. 1976: 'Economics of autonomy.' In Boyle, G., Harper, P. and the editors of *Undercurrents*, editors, *Radical technology.* London: Wildwood House, 156–62.

Harper, P., Boyle, G. and the editors of *Undercurrents*, editors, 1976: *Radical technology.* London: Wildwood House.

Harry, J. 1974: 'Causes of contemporary environmentalism.' *Humboldt Journal of Social Relations* 2, 3–7.

Harvey, D. 1971: 'Social processes, spatial form and redistribution of real income in an urban system.' In Chisholm, M., Frey, A. E. and Haggart, P., editors, *Regional Forecasting.* Proceedings of the twenty-second symposium of the

Colston Research Society held in the University of Bristol, 6–10 April 1970. London: Butterworths, 267–300.

Harvey, D. W. 1972: *Society, the city and the space-economy of urbanism*, Resource Paper Number 18. Washington DC: Association of American Geographers.

Hayami, Y. and Ruttan, V. 1971: *Agricultural development: an international perspective*, Baltimore: Johns Hopkins University Press.

Hays, S. P. 1959: *Conservation and the gospel of efficiency: the progressive conservation movement*. Cambridge, Massachusetts: Harvard University Press.

Healy, R. G. 1976: *Land use and the States*. Baltimore: Johns Hopkins University Press.

Heckroth, C. W. December 1976: 'Will 1977 be the year for water?' *Water and Wastes* 13, 26–31.

Hedges, B. 1972: *Attaching money values to environmental disturbance*. London: Social and Community Planning Research Centre for Sample Surveys.

Heilbroner, R. L. 1975: *An inquiry into the human prospect*. London: Calder and Boyars.

Heyneman, D. October 1971: 'Why we must prevent foreign aid from becoming an ecological nightmare.' *Science Forum* 4, 3–9.

Hill, N. E. 1977: *California advances the state of the art*. ASCE Fall Convention and Exhibit, reprint 3062. San Francisco.

Hirsch, F. 1977: *Social limits to growth*. London: Routledge and Kegan Paul.

Hoda, M. M. 1973: 'Development in a two-way street toward survival.' *Impact of Science on Society* 23, 273–85.

Hoda, M. M. 1976: 'India's experience and the Gandhian tradition.' In Jéquier, N. *Appropriate technology: problems and promises*. Paris: OECD, 144–55.

Holt, R. T. 1977: 'Technology assessment and technology inducement mechanism.' *American Journal of Political Science* 21, 283–301.

Hornback, K. E. 1974: 'The role of age in the environmental movement's attentive public, 1968–1972.' Doctorate dissertation, Michigan State University.

Hsirn, F. 16 June 1973: 'Economic development and environmental protection. *People's Daily* (translated by G. C. Dean, Science Policy Research Unit, Sussex Univ., Brighton).

Illich, I. D. 1973: *Tools for conviviality*. London: Calder and Boyars.

Illich, I. D. 1974: *Energy and equity*. London: Calder and Boyars.

Ingold, T. 1976: *The Skolt Lapps today*. Cambridge: Cambridge University Press.

Inhaber, H. 18 May 1978: 'Is solar power more dangerous than nuclear?' *New Scientist* 78, 444–6.

Jackson, A. February 1975: 'Agonizing reappraisal for the environmental quality act.' *California Journal*, 59–61.

Jéquier, N. 1976: *Appropriate technology: problems and promises*. Paris: OECD.

Jevons, W. S. 1965: *The coal question: an inquiry concerning the progress of the nation and the probable exhaustion of our coal mines* (first published 1865). Third edition, editor, Flux, A. W. New York: Kelley.

Juergensmeyer, J. C. 1971: 'Common law remedies and protection of the environment.' *U.B.C. Law Review* 6, 215–36.

Kahn, H., Brown, W. and Martel, L. 1976: *The next 200 years – a scenario for America and the world*. New York: Morrow.

Kapp, K. W. 1974(a): '"Recycling" in contemporary China.' *Kyklos* 27, 286–303.

Kapp, K. W. 1974(b): *Environmental policies and development planning in contemporary China and other essays*. The Hague: Mouton.

Kates, R. W. 1962: *Hazard and choice perception in flood plain management*. Department of Geography Research Paper No. 78. Chicago: University of Chicago.

Kelley, D. R., Stunkel, K. R. and Wescott, R. R. 1975: 'The politics of environment.' In Milbraith, L. W. and Inscho, F. R., editors, *The politics of environmental policy*. London: Sage, 115–34.

Kelley, D. R., Stunkel, K. R. and Wescott, R. R. 1976: *The economic superpowers and the environment*. San Francisco: W. H. Freeman and Co.

Kimber, R. and Richardson, J. J., editors, 1974(a): *Campaigning for the environment*. London: Routledge and Kegan Paul.

Kimber, R., Richardson, J. J. 1974(b): 'The Roskillers: Cublington fights the airport.' In Kimber, R. and Richardson, J. J., editors, *Campaigning for the environment*. London: Routledge and Kegan Paul, 165–211.

Kingston, J. 1976: 'It's been said before and where did that get us?' In Harper, P., Boyle, G. and the editors of *Undercurrents*, editors, *Radical technology*. London: Wildwood House, 238–48.

Kneese, A. V. and Schultze, C. L. 1975: *Pollution, prices and public policy*. Washington DC: The Brookings Institution.

Knetsch, J. C. 1963: 'Outdoor recreation demands and benefits.' *Land Economics* 39, 387–96.

Kropotkin, P. 1974: *Fields, factories and workshops tomorrow* (first published 1888–90). London: George Allen and Unwin.

Kuhn, T. S. 1962: *The structure of scientific revolutions*. Chicago: University of Chicago Press.

Kumar, K. 1979: 'Thoughts on the present discontents in Britain: a review and a proposal.' To be published in *Theory and Society*.

Ladd, F. 1967: 'A note on "the world across the street".' *Harvard Graduate School of Education Association Bulletin* 12, 47–48.

Langdon, S. 1975: 'Multinational corporation. Taste, transfer and underdevelopment: a case study from Kenya.' *Review of African Political Economy* 2, 12–35.

Lappe, F. M. and Collins, J. 1977: *Food first: beyond the myth of scarcity*. New York: Houghton Mifflin Co.

Leach, G. 1976: *Energy and food production*. Guildford, Surrey: IPC Science and Technology Press.

Lee, N. and Wood, C. 1978: 'EIA – A European perspective.' *Built Environment* 4, 101–10.

Leiss, W. 1974: *The domination of nature*. Boston, Massachusetts: Beacon Press.

The Leitch Committee 1978: *Report of the advisory committee on trunk road assessment*. London: HMSO.

Lock, D. 1976: 'Implications for interest groups: the need for planning aid.' In O'Riordan, T. and Hey, R. D., editors, *Environmental impact assessment*. Westmead, Farnborough: Saxon House, 191–201.

Lovins, A. B. 1975: 'Introduction: non-nuclear futures.' In Lovins, A. B. and Price, J. H., editors, *Non-nuclear futures: the case for an ethical energy strategy*. New York: Friends of the Earth International, XVII–XXXII.

Lovins, A. B. 1976: 'Energy strategy: the road not taken.' *Foreign Affairs* 55, 65–96.

Lovins, A. B. 1977: '*Soft energy paths: toward a durable peace.*' Harmondsworth: Penguin.

Lowe, P. D. 1975(a): 'Science and government: the case of pollution.' *Public Administration* 54, 287–98.

Lowe, P. D. 1975(b): 'The environmental lobby: a survey.' *Built Environment Quarterly* 1, 73–6.

Lowe, P. D. 1977: 'Amenity and equity: a review of local environmental pressure groups in Britain.' *Environment and Planning*, 9, 35–58.

Lowe, P. and Worboys, M. 1978: 'Ecology and the end of ideology.' *Antipode* 10, 12–21.

Lucas, R. C. 1972: 'Wilderness perception and use – the example of the boundary waters canoe area.' In Thompson, D. L., editor, *Politics, Policy and natural resources*. New York: The Free Press, 308–23.

Lukes, S. 1974: *Power: a radical view*. London: Macmillan.

Lukes, S. 1977: *Essays in social theory*. London: Macmillan.

Lynch, K. 1964: *The image of the city*. Cambridge, Mass.: MIT Press.

McCarthy, J. D. and Zald, M. N. 1977: 'Resource mobilization and social movements.' *American Journal of Sociology* 82, 1,212–41.

McCarthy, M. 1976: 'The politics of influence – an analysis of the methodology of an environmental pressure group.' M.A. thesis, University of Keele.

McCormac, H. 1830: *On the best means of improving the moral and physical condition of the Working Classes, being an address delivered on the opening of the first monthly scientific meetings of the Belfast Mechanics Institute*. London: Longman.

McDermont, J. 1972: 'Technology: the opiate of the intellectuals.' *The New York Review of Books* (31 July 1969). Reprinted in Teich, A. H., editor, *Technology and Man's Future*. New York: St Martin's Press, 151–78.

McEvoy, III J. 1972: 'The American concern with environment.' In Burch, W. R. Jr., Cheek, N. H. Jr., and Taylor, L., editors, *Natural resources and the environment*. New York: Harper and Row, 214–35.

McHale, J. 1971: *The ecological context*. London: Studio Vista.

McLoughlin, J. 1976: *The law and practice relating to pollution control in the UK*. London: Graham and Trotman.

MacRae, J. 1977: 'What price water quality in government spending?' *Municipal Engineering* 154, 441–3.

Maddox, J. 1975: *Beyond the energy crisis*. London: Hutchinson.

Magida, A. J. 1976: 'Environment report/movement undaunted by economic, energy crises.' *National Journal* 17, 61–8.

Majone, G. 1976(a): 'Standard setting and the theory of institutional choice: the case of pollution control.' *Policy and Politics* 4, 35–51.

Majone, G. 1976(b): 'Choice among policy instruments for pollution control.' *Policy Analysis* 2, 589–613.

Mallory, W. 1926: *China, land of famine.* New York: American Geographical Society.

Malthus, T. R. 1970: *An essay on the principle of population* (first published 1798). Harmondsworth: Penguin.

Mandel, W. M. 1972: 'The soviet ecology movement.' *Science and Society* 36, 385–416.

Mansfield, N. W. 1969: 'Recreation trip generation.' *Journal of Transport Economics and Policy* 3, 1–13.

Marcuse, H. 1964: *One-dimensional man.* London: Routledge and Kegan Paul.

Marglin, S. A. 1976: 'What do bosses do?' In Gorz, A., editor, *The division of labour: the labour process and class-struggle in modern capitalism.* Hassocks, Sussex: Harvester Press.

Margolis, H. 1977: 'The politics of auto emissions.' *The Public Interest* 49, 3–21.

Marquand, J. 2 October 1976: 'An economist's view of water pollution charges as regulatory instruments.' *Chemistry and Industry* 19, 835–39.

Marsh, G. P. 1967: *Man and nature* (or more descriptively entitled in later editions, *The earth as modified by human action*) (first published 1864). Cambridge, Massachusetts: Harvard University Press.

Martin, B. May/April 1978: 'Soft energy, hard politics.' *Undercurrents* 27, 10–13.

Martinson, C. B. and Wilkening, E. A. 1975: 'A scale to measure awareness of environmental problems: structure and correlates.' Paper presented at the 1975 annual meeting of the Mid-West Sociological Society.

Marwick, A. 1970: *Britain in the century of total war; war, peace and social change 1900–1967.* Harmondsworth: Penguin.

Marx, K. 1967: *Capital,* Volume 3 (first published 1894). New York: International Publications.

Marx, K. 1970(a): *Preface to a critique of political economy* (first published 1859). Moscow: Progress Publishers, 19–23.

Marx, K. 1970(b): *The German ideology* (first published 1932). London: Lawrence and Wishart.

Marx, K. 1970(c): *Capital,* Volume 1 (first published 1867). Moscow: Progress Publishers.

Maslow, A. H. 1943: 'A theory of human motivation.' *Psychological Review* 50, 370–96.

Matthews, W. H. 1975: 'Objective and subjective judgements in environmental impact analysis.' *Environmental Conservation* 2, 121–31.

Mauss, A. L. 1971: 'On being strangled by the stars and stripes: the New Left, the Old Left, and the national history of American radical movements.' *Journal of Social Issues* 27, 185–202.

Mauss, A. L. 1975: *Social problems as social movements.* New York: J. B. Lippincott.

Meadows, D. H., Meadows, D. L., Randers, J. and Behrens III W. W. 1972: *The Limits to Growth*. New York: University Books.

Meek, R. L. 1971: *Marx and Engels on the population bomb*. Berkeley, California: Ramparts Press.

Meyers, S. 1976: 'US experience with national environmental impact assessment.' In O'Riordan, T. and Hey, R. D., editors, *Environmental impact assessment*. Westmead, Farnborough: Saxon House, 45–55.

Milgram, S. and Jodelet, D. 3 November 1977: 'The way Parisians see Paris.' *New Society* 42, 234–7.

Miliband, R. 1973: *The state in capitalist society*. London: Quartet Books.

Miliband, R. 1977: *Marxism and politics*. Oxford: Oxford University Press.

Mill, J. S. 1965: *Principles of political economy* (first published 1848). London: Routledge and Kegan Paul.

Ministry of Transport (Highways Economics Unit) 1967: *The economic appraisal of Inter-Urban road schemes*. Technical Memorandum No. T5/67. London.

Misham, E. J. 1970: 'What is wrong with Roskill?' *Journal of Transport Economics and Policy* 4, 221–34.

Mishan, E. J. 1977: *The economic growth debate: an assessment*. London: George Allen and Unwin.

Mitchell, R. C. 1978: *The nuclear debate*. Washington DC: Resources for the Future.

Mitchell, R. C. and Davies III, J. C. 1978: *The United States environmental movement and its political context: an overview*. Discussion Paper D-32. Washington DC: Resources for the Future.

Moloney, J. C. and Stovonsky, L. 1971: 'The pollution issue: A survey of editorial judgements.' In Roos, L. L., editor, *The politics of ecosuicide*. New York: Holt, Rinehart and Winston.

Molotch, H. 1971: 'Santa Barbara: oil in the velvet playground.' In Meek, R. L. and Straayer, J. A., editors, *The politics of neglect: the environmental crisis*. Boston: Houghton Mifflin Co., 183–96.

Moncrief, L. W. 1970: 'The cultural basis of our environmental crisis.' *Science* 170, 508–12.

Moodie, G. C. 1970: *Opinions, publics and pressure groups*. London: George Allen and Unwin.

Morris, W. 1891: *News from nowhere*. London: Reeves & Turner.

Muller, M. 8 June 1978: 'Cigarettes kill the poor and black, too.' *New Scientist* 78, 679–81.

Munton, D. and Brady, L. 1970: *American public opinion and environmental pollution*. Technical report, Ohio State University, Behavioural Sciences Laboratory, Department of Political Science.

Mutch, W. E. S. 1977: 'The expansion of Turnhouse, Edinburgh Airport.' In Sewell, W. R. and Coppock, J. T., editors, *Public participation in planning*. London: Wiley, 43–58.

Nash, R. 1967: *Wilderness and the American mind*. New Haven: Yale University Press.

Nasr, S. H. 1968: *The encounter of man and nature: the spiritual crisis of modern man*. London: George Allen and Unwin.

National Commission on Supplies and Shortages 1976: *Government and the Nation's resources.* Washington DC: United States Government Printing Office.

National Executive Committee of the Labour Party 1978: *Reform of the House of Commons* (reported in *The Times,* 3 April 1978).

Nelkin, D. 1975: 'The political impact of technical expertise.' *Social studies of Science* 5, 35–54.

Nelkin, D. 1977(a): 'Scientists and professional responsibility: the experience of American ecologists.' *Social studies of science* 7, 75–95.

Nelkin, D. 1977(b): *Technological decisions and democracy: European experiments in public participation.* London: Sage.

Neuhaus, R. 1971: *In defense of people.* New York: Macmillan.

Newsom, G. and Sherratt, J. G. 1972: *Water pollution.* Altringham, Cheshire: J. Sherratt.

Newton, T. 1972: *Cost–benefit analysis in administration.* London: George Allen and Unwin.

Nicholson, M. 25 November 1976: 'The ecological breakthrough.' *New Scientist* 72, 460–3.

Nordhaus, W. D. 1974: 'Resources as a constraint on growth.' *American Economic Review* 64, 22–6.

Nowotny, H. 1976: *Social aspects of the nuclear power controversy.* Research Memoranda, IAEA/IASA Vienna.

Noyes, J. H. 1966: *Strange cults and Utopias of nineteenth-century America* (first edition in 1870 was entitled *History of American socialism*). New York: Dover Publications.

Nuaneri, V. C. 1970: 'Equity in cost–benefit analysis, a case study of the Third London Airport.' *Journal of Transport Economics and Policy* 4, 235–54.

Odell, P. R. and Rosing, K. E. 1974: 'Weighing up the North Sea wealth.' *The Geographical Magazine* 47, 150–55.

OECD. 1973: *Pollution charges: an assessment.* Paris: OECD.

OECD. 1976: *Economic measurement of environmental damage.* Paris: OECD.

Ogus, A. J. and Richardson, G. M. 1977: 'Economics and the environment: a study of private nuisance.' *Cambridge Law Journal* 36, 284–325.

O'Riordan, T. 1976(a): *Environmentalism.* London: Pion.

O'Riordan, T. 1976(b): 'The role of environmental issues in Canadian–American policy-making and administration.' In Watson, J. M. and O'Riordan, T., editors, *The American environment: perceptions and policies.* London: Wiley, 277–327.

Orleans, L. A. 1975/76: 'China's environomics: backing into ecological leadership.' *Environmental policy and law* 1, 189–93.

Orleans, L. A. 1976: 'China's environomics: backing into ecological leadership.' *Environmental policy and law* 2, 28–31.

Orleans, L. A. and Sultmeier, R. P. 1970: 'The Mao ethic and environmental quality.' *Science* 170, 1,173–76.

Owen, R. 1970: *A new view of society, 1813–1814, and Report to the County of Lanark* (1821). Harmondsworth: Penguin.

Pack, H. 1974: 'The employment – output trade-off in LDCs – a microeconomic approach.' *Oxford Economic Papers* 26, 388–404.

Page, W. 1973: 'The non-renewable resource sub-system.' In Cole, H. S. D., Freeman, C., Jahoda, M. and Pavitt, K. L. R., editors, *Thinking about the future: a critique of the limits to growth.* London: Chatto and Windus, 33–42.

Pahl, R. 1971: *Whose city?* London: Longman.

Paine, S. 1976: 'Development with growth: a quarter century of socialist transformation in China.' *Economic and Political Weekly* 11, 1,349–82.

Paine, S. 1978: 'Some reflections on the presence of 'rural' or of 'urban bias' in China's development policies 1949–1976.' *World Development* 6, 693–707.

Palmer, I. 1972: *How revolutionary is the Green Revolution?* London: VCOAD.

Parenti, M. 1970: 'Power and pluralism: a view from the bottom.' In Surkin, M. and Wolfe, A., editors, *An end to political science.* New York: Basic Books, 111–43.

Parker, The Hon. Mr. Justice. 1978: *The Windscale Inquiry Report.* London: HMSO.

Parry, J. 1975: 'Intermediate technology building.' *Appropriate Technology* 2(3), 6–8.

Parsons, H. L. 1977: *Marx and Engels on ecology.* Westport, Connecticut: Greenwood Press.

Passmore, J. 1974: *Man's responsibility for nature: ecological problems and western traditions.* London: Duckworth.

Pavitt, K. and Worboys, M. 1977: *Science, technology and the modern industrial state.* London: Butterworths.

Pearce, D. W. 1976: *Environmental economics.* London: Longman.

Pearse, A. 1977: 'Technology and peasant production: reflections on a global study.' *Development and Change* 8, 125–59.

Pehrson, E. W. 1945: 'The mineral position in the United States and the outlook for the future.' *Mining and Metallurgy Journal* 26, 204–14.

Pelto, P. 1973: *The snowmobile revolution.* California: Cummings.

Perkins, D. 1978: 'Meeting basic needs in the People's Republic of China.' *World Development* 6, 561–6.

Peskin, H. M. 1975: 'Accounting for the environment.' *Social Indicators Research* 2, 191–210.

Peters, G. H. 1970: 'Land use studies in Britain: a review of the literature with special reference to application of cost–benefit analysis.' *Journal of Agricultural Economics* 21, 171–214.

Pickford, J. 1977: 'Appropriate technology for Third World water supply and sanitation.' *Environmental Pollution Management* 7, 50–1.

Pimentel, D., Hurd, L. E., Bellotti, A. C., Forster, M. J., Oka, I. N., Sholes, O. D., and Whitman, R. J. 2 November 1973: 'Food production and the energy crisis.' *Science* 182, 443–9.

Plamenatz, J. 1970: *Ideology.* London: Macmillan.

Plowden, S. 1970: *The cost of noise.* London: Metra Consulting Group.

Polanyi, M. 1964: *Personal knowledge.* New York: Harper and Row.

Policy for Roads: England. 1978: Cmnd. 7132. London: Department of Transport.

Polsby, N. 1963: *Community power and political theory.* New Haven: Yale University Press.

242   *References*

Popper, K. R. 1959: *The logic of scientific discovery*. London: Hutchinson.

Posner, M. 1974: 'Energy at the centre of the stage.' *The Three Banks Review* 104, 3–27.

Posner, R. A. 1972(a): *Economic analysis of the law*. Boston: Little, Brown and Co.

Posner, R. A. 1972(b): 'A theory of negligence.' *The Journal of Legal Studies* 1, 29–96.

Posner, R. A. 1975: 'The economic approach to law.' *Texas Law Review* 53, 757–82.

Poulantzas, N. 1973: *Political power and social classes*. London: New Left Books.

Power, J. and Holenstein, A. 1976: *World of hunger – a strategy for survival*. London: Temple Smith.

Project Appraisal for Development Control Team at Aberdeen University 1976: *Assessment of major industrial applications – a manual*. Research Report No. 13. London: Department of the Environment.

Quarmby, D. A. 1967: 'Choice of travel mode for the journey to work: some findings.' *Journal of Transport Economics and Policy* 1, 273–314.

Quigg, P. W., editor, 1974: *World directory of environmental education program*. New York: Bouler.

Rapoport, A. 1969(a): 'The *pueblo* and the *hogan*.' In Oliver, P., editor, *Shelter and Society*. London: The Crescent Press, 66–79.

Rapoport, A. 1969(b): *House form and culture*. Englewood Cliffs, New Jersey: Prentice Hall.

Reddy, A. K. N. 1975: 'Alternative technology: a viewpoint from India.' *Social Studies of Science* 5, 331–42.

Reich, C. 1971: *The Greening of America*. Harmondsworth: Penguin.

Reich, M. and Huddle, E. G. 1973: 'Pollution and social response.' *Area Development in Japan* 7, 34–47.

Report on the Review of Highway Inquiry Procedures 1978: Cmnd. 7133. Department of Transport and Department of the Environment.

Ricardo, D. 1962: *Principles of political economy and taxation*. London: Dent.

Rieser, R. 1973: 'The territorial illusion and behavioural sink: critical notes on behavioural geography.' *Antipode* 5, 52–7.

Ringrose-Voase, C. J. 1970: *CPRE branch survey*. London: CPRE.

Riskin, C. 1978(a): 'Political conflict and rural industrialization in China.' *World Development* 6, 681–92.

Riskin, C. 1978(b): 'China's rural industries: self-reliant systems or independent kingdoms?' *The China Quarterly* 73, 77–98.

Roberts, F. 6 April 1978: 'And now – a resources shortage?' *New Scientist* 78, 16–17.

Robertson, J. 1977/78: 'Towards post-industrial liberation and reconstruction.' *New Universities Quarterly* 32, 6–23.

Rose, A. 1967: *The power structure*. New York: Oxford University Press.

Rose, H. and Rose, S. 1976: 'The incorporation of science.' In Rose, H. and Rose, S., editors, *The political economy of science: ideology in the natural sciences*. London: Macmillan, 14–31.

Rosenbaum, W. A. 1973: *The politics of environmental concern.* New York: Praeger.

Roszak, T. 1968: *The making of a counter-culture: reflections on the technocratic society and its youthful opposition.* London: Faber and Faber.

Roszak, T. 1972: *Where the wasteland ends.* London: Faber and Faber.

The Rotheram Study 1973: London: Department of the Environment.

Rothman, H. 1972: *Murderous providence: a study of pollution in industrial societies.* London: Hart-Davis.

Rothschild, E. 1976: 'Food politics.' *Foreign Affairs* 54, 285–307.

Royal Commission on Environmental Pollution 1971: *First report.* Cmnd. 4585. London: HMSO.

Royse, D. C. 1969: 'Social inferences via environmental cues.' Ph.D. dissertation. Harvard University, Cambridge, Massachusetts.

Sandbach, F. R. 1977(a): 'Have rivers now reached the age of consent?' *Municipal Engineering* 154, 430–4.

Sandbach, F. R. 1977(b): 'Farewell to the god of plague – the control of schistosomiasis in China.' *Social Science and Medicine* 11, 27–33.

Sandbach, F. R. 1978(a): 'A further look at the environment as a political issue.' *International Journal of Environmental Studies* 12, 99–110.

Sandbach, F. R. 1978(b): 'The rise and fall of the limits to growth debate.' *Social Studies of Science* 8, 495–520.

Saunders, P. J. W. 1976: *The estimation of pollution damage.* Manchester: Manchester University Press.

Schnaiberg, A. 1973: 'Politics, participation and pollution: the "environmental movement".' In Walton, J. and Carns, D. E., editors, *Cities in change: studies on the urban condition.* Boston: Allyn and Bacon, 605–27.

Schnaiberg, A. 1975: 'Social syntheses of the societal – environmental dialectic: the rate of distributional impacts.' *Social Science Quarterly* 56, 5–20.

Schnell, O. 1973: 'China's way with waste.' *The Ecologist* 3, 56–9.

Schon, D. A. 1971: *Beyond the stable state.* London: Temple Smith.

Schumacher, E. F. 1973: *Small is beautiful: a study of economics as if people mattered.* London: Bland and Briggs.

Schumacher, E. F. 1974: 'Urban impasse.' *Architectural Design* 44, 548–50.

Schumacher, E. F. 1976: 'Patterns of human settlement.' *Ambio* 5, 91–7.

Schumacher, E. F. and McRobie, G. 1969: 'Intermediate technology and its administrative implications.' *Journal of Administration Overseas* 8, 89–96.

Searle, G. 1975: 'Copper in Snowdonia National Park.' In Smith, P. J., editor, *The politics of physical resources.* Harmondsworth: Penguin, 66–112.

Seddon, G. 1972: 'The rhetoric and ethics of the environmental protest movement.' *Meanjin Quarterly* 31, 427–38.

Self, P. 1970: 'Nonsense on stilts: the futility of Roskill.' *Political Quarterly* 41, 249–60.

Self, P. 1975: *Econocrats and the policy process, the politics and philosophy of cost–benefit analysis.* London: Macmillan.

Sellers, L. and Jones, D. W. Jr. 1973: 'Environment and the mass media.' *The Journal of Environmental Education* 5, 51–7.

244   References

Sharman, F. A. May 1977: 'John Tyme and highway inquiries: an interim report.' *Journal of Planning and Environment Law*, 293–8.

Sharp, C. and Jennings, T. 1976: *Transport and the environment.* Leicester: Leicester University Press.

Sharp, L. 1952: 'Steel axes for stone-age Australians.' In Spicer, E. H., editor, *Human problems in technological change.* New York: Russel Sage Foundation, 69–90.

Shenfield, A. 11 August 1977: 'Energy and doomsayers.' *The Daily Telegraph*, 16.

Sigurdson, J. 1972: 'China: re-cycling that pays.' *Läkartidningen* 69, 2,837–41.

Sigurdson, J. 1973: 'The suitability of technology in contemporary China.' *Impact of Science on Society* 23, 237–60.

Sigurdson, J. 1976: 'Development of rural areas in India and China.' *Ambio* 5, 98–107.

Sigurdson, J. 1978: 'Rural industrialization; a comparison of development planning in China and India.' *World Development* 6, 667–80.

Sills, D. L. 1975: 'The environmental movement and its critics.' *Human Ecology* 3, 1–41.

Simmie, J. M. 1974: *Citizens in conflict.* London: Hutchinson.

Simmons, H. G. 1973: 'Systems dynamics and technocracy.' In Cole, H. S. D., Freeman, C., Jahoda, M. and Pavitt, K. L. R., editors, *Thinking about the future: a critique of the limits to growth.* London: Chatto and Windus, 192–208.

Sinclair, T. C. 1973: 'Environmentalism.' In Cole, H. S. D., Freeman, C., Jahoda, M. and Pavitt, K. L. R., editors, *Thinking about the future: A critique of the limits to growth.* London: Chatto and Windus, 80–9.

Singer, H. 1977: *Technologies for basic needs.* Geneva: International Labour Office.

Smil, V. 1977: 'Energy solution in China.' *Environment* 19, 27–31.

Smith, R. J. 1971: 'The evaluation of recreation benefits: the Clawson method in practice.' *Urban Studies* 8, 89–102.

Smith, R. J. and Kavanagh, N. J. 1969: 'The measurement of benefits of trout fishing: preliminary results of a study of Grafham Water, Great Ouse Water Authority, Huntingdonshire.' *Journal of Leisure Research* 4, 316–22.

Solesbury, W. 1976: 'The environmental agenda.' *Public Administration* 64, 379–97.

Springer, J. F. and Constantini, E. 1974: 'Public opinion and the environment – an issue in search of a home.' In Nagel, S. S., editor, *Environmental politics.* London: Praeger, 195–224.

State of California Office of Planning and Research 1976: *The California Environmental Quality Act: a review.* Sacramento, California.

Steck, H. J. 1975: 'Private influence on environmental policy: the case of the National Industrial Pollution Control Council.' *Environmental Law* 5, 241–81.

Stern, G. April–May 1977: 'Motorway madness – a cure?' *Undercurrents* 21, 35–7.

Stewart, F. 1977: *Technology and underdevelopment.* London: Macmillan.

Stoel, T. B. and Scherr, S. J. 1978: 'Experience with EIA in the United States.' *Built Environment* 4, 94–100.

Storey, D. J. 1976: 'The economics of water pollution control: an application of Posner's law?' *British Journal of Law and Society* 3, 76–84.

Storey, D. J. 1977: 'A socio-economic approach to water pollution law enforcement in the United Kingdom.' *International Journal of Social Economics* 4, 207–24.

Storey, D. J. and Elliott, D. J. May 1977: 'An effluent charging scheme for the River Tees.' *Chemistry and Industry*, 335–8.

Stretton, H. 1976: *Capitalism, socialism and the environment*. Cambridge: Cambridge University Press.

Sullivan, J. B. and Montgomery, P. A. 1972: 'Surveying highway impact.' *Environment* 14, 12–20.

Taylor, C. 1978: 'The politics of the steady state.' *New Universities Quarterly* 32, 157–84.

Taylor, N. 1973: *The village in the city*. London: Maurice Temple Smith.

Thoreau, H. D. 1960: *Walden and 'civil disobedience'* (1854). New York: Signet Classic.

Thorrold, A. O. 1975(a): 'What can UK environmentalists learn from the operation of the law in the USA?' In *The Provision and financing of legal services for the environmental movement*, the edited proceedings of a conference held at the ICA, The Mall, SW1 on 6 December 1974. London: Lawyers Ecology Group, 8–17.

Thorrold, A. O. 1975(b): *Application of the environmental impact statement in the United Kingdom*. The European Environmental Bureau seminar on the environmental impact statement at Louvain, Belgium.

Todd, J. 1976: 'Pioneering for the twenty-first century: a new alchemist's perspective.' *The Ecologist* 6, 252–7.

Transport Policy. 1976: Consultation Document, Vol. 2. London: HMSO.

Transport Policy. 1977: Cmnd. 6836. London: Department of Transport.

Tuan, Yi-Fu 1970: 'Our treatment of the environment in ideal and actuality.' *American Scientist* 58, 244–9.

Tuan, Yi-Fu 1974: *Topophilia: a study of environmental perception, attitudes and values*. Englewood Cliffs, New Jersey: Prentice Hall.

Tyme, J. 6 November 1975: 'M-way inquiries: a corruption of government?' *New Scientist* 68, 320–2.

Tyme, J. 1978: *Motorways versus democracy*. London: Macmillan.

Uhlig, S. J. and Bhat, B. A. 1977: 'Capital goods manufacture and the choice of technique in the maize-milling industry.' *World Development* 5, 803–11.

Ure, A. 1967: *The philosophy of manufactures* (first published 1835) London: Cass.

Van der Schalie, H. November 1974: 'Aswam Dam revisited.' *Environment* 16, 18–26.

246   *References*

Wade, N. 20 December 1974(a): 'Green Revolution (1): a just technology, often unjust in use.' *Science* 186, 1,095–6.

Wade, N. 27 December 1974(b): 'Green Revolution (2): problems of adapting a Western technology.' *Science* 186, 1,186–92.

Wallace, A. 1925: *The wonderful century: the age of new ideas in science and invention* (first published 1903). New revised edition. London: George Allen and Unwin.

Wandesforde-Smith, G. 1977: 'Projects, policies and environmental impact assessment: a look inside California's black box.' *Environmental Policy and Law* 3, 167–75.

Ward, B. and Dubos, R. 1972: *Only one earth: the care and maintenance of a small planet.* Harmondsworth: Penguin.

Wates, N. 1976: *The battle for Tolmers Square.* London: Routledge and Kegan Paul.

Wathern, P. 1976: 'The role of impact statements in environmental planning in Britain.' *International Journal of Environmental Studies* 9, 165–8.

Westergaard, J. and Resler, H. 1976: *Class in a capitalist society.* Harmondsworth: Penguin.

Wheelwright, E. L. and McFarlane, B. 1973: *The Chinese road to socialism.* Harmondsworth: Penguin.

Whitby, M. C., Robins, D. L. J., Tansey, A. W. and Willis, K. G. 1974: *Rural Resource Development.* London: Methuen.

White, D. 31 March 1977: 'Nuclear power: a special *New Society* survey.' *New Society* 39, 647–50.

White, L. 1967: 'The historical roots of our ecological crisis.' *Science* 155, 1,203–7.

White, L. J. 1976(a): 'Effluent charges as a faster means of achieving pollution abatement.' *Public Policy* 24, 111–25.

White, L. J. 1976(b): 'American automotive emissions control policy: a review of the reviews.' *Journal of Environmental Economics and Management* 2, 231–46.

Wiedenmeyer, N. 1976: 'The polls: do people worry about the future?' *Public Opinion Quarterly* 40, 382–91.

Wildarsky, A. 1969: 'Rescuing policy analysis from PPBS.' *Public Administration Review* 29, 189–202.

Williams, A. 1972: 'Cost–benefit analysis: bastard science and/or insidious poison in the body politic?' *Journal of Public Economics* 1, 199–225.

Williams, S. F. 1978: 'Running out: the problem of exhaustable resources.' *The Journal of Legal Studies* 7, 165–99.

Wilson, J. 1973: *Introduction to social movements.* New York: Basic Books.

Winner, L. 1977: *Autonomous technology: technics-out-of-control as a theme in political thought.* London: MIT Press.

Woodcock, L. December 1971: 'Labour and the politics of environment.' *Sierra Club Bulletin*, 11–16.

World Bank 1973: *Environmental, health and human ecological considerations in economic development projects.* Washington DC: World Bank.

Wynne, B. 3 August 1978: 'Nuclear debate at the crossroads.' *New Scientist* 78, 349–51.

Young, K. 1977: 'Environmental management in local politics.' In Kavangah, D. and Rose, R., editors, *New trends in British politics*. London: Sage, 141–65.

Additional journals and papers

China Reconstructs, 21 June 1972.
China Reconstructs, 22 February 1973.
Civic Trust News, July/August 1977.
CPRE Bulletin, 1973: 8 (7/8), 1–3.
Environment, November 1973.
Environmental Periodicals Bibliography 1976, 5.
Express and News, 17 September 1975.
Guardian, 24 September 1975.
Guardian, 30 April 1976.
Guardian, 28 June 1977.
Guardian, 10 August 1977.
Guardian, 1 September 1977.
Guardian, 10 December 1977.
Guardian, 30 October 1978.
House of Commons debate on Nuclear Power, 2 December 1977. 940 (No. 22) Cols 883–981. Quote from Abse, L. Col. 903.
Journal of Planning and Environmental Law, November 1977.
The Listener, 14 November 1974: 625.
House of Lords debate on Highway (inquiries procedure) rules, 2 July 1976, Col. 986.
New Scientist, 29 June 1978: 77,891.
Peking Review, 23 June 1972: 'China's ten cardinal principles on amending "Declaration on Human Environment".' 25, 9–11.
Peking Review, 30 June 1978, No. 26.
Peking Review, 14 July 1978, No. 28.
People's Daily, 16 June 1973.
The Times, 7 November 1973.
The Times, 27 May 1975.
The Times, 27 May 1976.
The Times, 29 July 1976.
The Times, 24 August 1976.
The Times, 31 January 1977.
The Times, 11 January 1978.
The Times, 27 November 1978.
The Times Higher Education Supplement, 24 June 1977: 'The constrained freedoms of the British Press.'
Undercurrents, 1977, 25, 2.
Undercurrents, October–November 1977, 24.

Court cases

Att. Gen. v. *Birmingham* (1958) 4 K & J, 539–40.

Borough of Westville v. *Whitney Home Builders* (1956) 122A, (2d), 244–5. (Quoted from Juergensmeyer, 1971.)

Brocket v. *Luton Corporation* (1948) W.N., 352.

Friends of Mamouth v. *Board of Supervisors of Mono County* 8 Cal. 3d 1, 500P 2d 1360, 104 Cal. Rptr. 16/1972.

Lockwood v. *Brentwood Park Investments Ltd.* (1967) 64 D.L.R., (2d), 212. (Referred to in Elder, 1973.)

Mann v. *Willey* (1900) N.Y.S., 590. (Referred to in Juergensmeyer, 1971.)

Pride of Derby v. *British Celanese Ltd.* (1953) Ch. 181.

St Helen's Smelting Co. v. *Tipping* (1865) 11 H.L.C., 642.

Scenic Hudson Preservation Conference v. *Federal Power Commission* (1965) 354 F. 2d, 615.

Shelfer v. *City of London Electric Lighting Co.* (1895) 1 Ch., 322.

Spur Industries v. *Del E. Webb Development* (1972) 494 P. zd, 700.

Sturges v. *Bridgman* (1879) 11 Ch. D., 852.

Sub. Nom. Black v. *Canadian Copper Co.* (1917) O.W.N. 243 (H.C.). (Quoted from McLaren, 1972.)

John Young v. *Bankier Distillery Co.* (1893) A.C., 698.

Subject Index

Author Index